MORE THAN THE EYES

More Than The Eyes
Art, Food & The Senses

Ellen Mara De Wachter

atelier éditions | d·a·p

I Eat

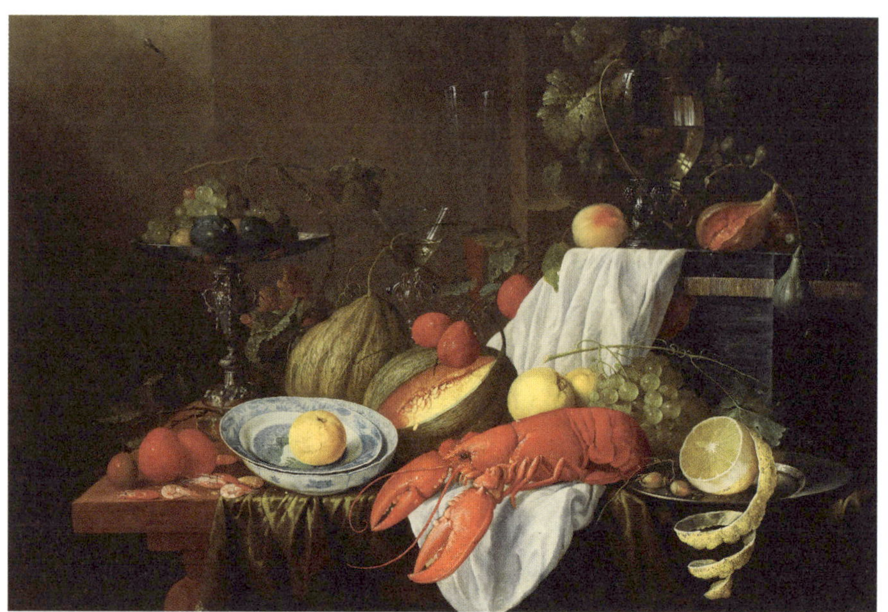

Therefore

I Am

Jan Davidsz. de Heem, *Still Life with a Lobster, Fruit and Blue and White "Kraak" Dishes*, c.1650. Oil on canvas.

Food is a radical tool. If you want to bring up difficult issues, involve food. If you want to know what's going on in a culture, look at what is happening with food. Food is an arena in which the dialogues between the individual and community play out with intensity.

Artists have long created images of food to convey messages connected to values and morals, cherishing it as a subject that enables them to tell the stories they want to tell, or were commissioned to tell. There is a rich history of representations of food in still-life painting, in particular in the subgenre of 17th century Dutch *vanitas* and *memento mori* works. Their seductive displays of meat, fruit, and flowers teeter on the edge of decay, and are loaded with the symbolism of evanescent earthly pleasures. Depictions of food and objects including skulls, musical instruments, and hourglasses convey impermanence, and while *vanitas* paintings signaled the wealth and luxurious standards of those who commissioned them, they also served a social function, reminding admirers of the futility of sensuality in the face of the ultimate certainty of death, and prompting them to act in accordance with the moral codes of the time. The still life was associated with the feminine realm of the home and often hung in the kitchen, evidence of the genre's lowly status when compared with the grand history paintings or stately portraits displayed in formal dining rooms or salons. From the 16th to the 19th centuries, genre scenes representing markets, banquets, and kitchens situated food at the heart of social and economic life, instructing viewers in the clear delineations of class and gender roles. More generally, in representations of food the sensual was cast in opposition to the spiritual or rational.

This book looks at food's presence in contemporary art from a different angle. Rather than pictures of food, the subject is food itself, a material used by artists from the 1960s to the present day in performances, sculptures, and installations, and at the intersection of art and daily life. By working with food, these artists are able to produce a range of unexpected sensory experiences. They use food to celebrate the sensual aspects of life, from the pleasurable to the offensive. They bring a radical, emotional, and bodily understanding to a field that is often restricted to the purely visual and conceptual. The result is a powerful challenge to our understanding of what art can be, and how we can experience the world beyond the gallery.

Food directly supports organic life, making it perhaps the single most important resource. In addition to its role in sustaining our bodies, it plays a central part in all cultures: it is the vital stuff around which personal, family, and social rituals are performed. Its production anchors us to the land and connects us to the fluctuations of weather and seasons. Food is key to identity, both individual and collective. When we migrate, we carry our recipes with us, adapting traditional dishes to new circumstances and ingredients. Through cooking, sharing, and eating, food becomes something with which every one of us shares a fierce intimacy. We think about food, we desire it and plan for its enjoyment; sometimes we try to control our relationship with it. Whatever we do, food becomes us.

Food and its mechanisms are also expressions of power and, often, injustice. Take the everyday activity of cooking, for example. In the kitchen, gender intersects with class and privilege, ethnicity, and immigration status, age, and experience. In spite of several waves of female liberation, it is still the case that the burden of home cooking tends to be borne by women and the privilege of commercial cooking is largely held by men. Women tend to cook in private, men in public. This brings with it a particular distribution of power. Or consider the physical labor involved in producing food—something that is routinely ignored in favor of concerns such as organic status, environmental impact, or food miles. Often the people who pick and produce our food are treated as invisible. But at the same time, the food we eat is one of the most obvious ways in which social identity is reproduced and made public, for example in the desire among wealthy classes to be seen consuming "fine" foods, superfoods, or medicinal food, or the prevalence of "junk" foods in lower-income communities for whom fresh and varied ingredients, not to mention the time to source and prepare them, are unaffordable. The kitchen and the field, like the artist's studio and other workspaces, operate as microcosms of society.

The stories we hear about the food we eat, as well as the silences surrounding certain aspects of food production, contribute to shaping our worldview—a worldview that will necessarily be limited to the narratives to which we are exposed. Through these narratives we are conditioned to respond to esthetic experiences, including eating, in ways that can replicate and strengthen existing social, economic, and racial hierarchies. This book approaches the topics of food, art, and the senses from the perspectives of European and North American culture and history, which are of course limited and partial. It is also true that unfair advantages underpin the very possibility of considering these themes. To discuss food's relevance to art implies the availability of both, something that isn't guaranteed to all.

In 2001, the chef and author Anthony Bourdain, who acknowledged his privilege as a cis white man from the Global North, wrote about his encounter with a group of vegans in California. Bourdain, a noted meat-lover, anticipated a clash of cultures, sensing there would be friction during the meal, but what struck him most about the meeting had little to do with the food being served. Instead, what upset him was the ignorance his hosts betrayed about the plight of people around the world, and how it was crystalized around the question of food:

It was difficult for me to be polite (though I was outnumbered). I'd recently returned from Cambodia, where a chicken can be the difference between life and death … Just being able to talk about this issue in reasonably grammatical language is a privilege, subsidized in a yin/yang sort of a way, somewhere, by somebody taking it in the neck. Being able to read these words, no matter how stupid, offensive, or wrongheaded, is a privilege, your reading skills the end product of a level of education most of the world will never enjoy. Our whole lives—our homes, the shoes we wear, the cars we drive, the food we eat—all built on a mountain of skulls.[1]

Yet food, thanks to the way it can bypass entrenched ideas and directly engage a multitude of physical senses, can help erode the enclosures around certain types of thinking. It can slacken the restraints on the way we experience and reproduce the world, as art does.

We routinely think of food and art as having different cultural roles. In many cases, art proudly wears its aspiration to transcendence. It is deemed to be a kind of nourishment for the soul, separated off from other forms of material and creative production. On the other hand, it is often judged to be mundane, considered a fleeting physical pleasure or seen as trafficking in the corrupt currency of gluttony. Artworks such as the marble statues of antiquity and the Renaissance, or classical symphonies, are elevated as eternal, sublime, and the product of unaccountable genius; food is kept low, to be cooked, eaten, excreted. It is relegated to the realm of direct and fleeting bodily experience. But if we look carefully, food has so much to tell us about the way the world operates, and about our understanding of ourselves and each other. Maybe you were brought up to think that book learning afforded proper knowledge, while food was just for fun. The reality is that the food in our shopping baskets, in our cupboards, and on our plates contains vast realms of information, which artists can help us metabolize, through new experiences, into knowledge. The foods with which they work are dense with the realities of the world around us.

In the decades between the early 1960s and the turn of the millennium, a number of artists in America and Europe turned to food as an artistic medium through which they could uniquely express their ideas. Using food, they developed new ways of enlivening and affecting their own sensations and experiences of art, and those of others.

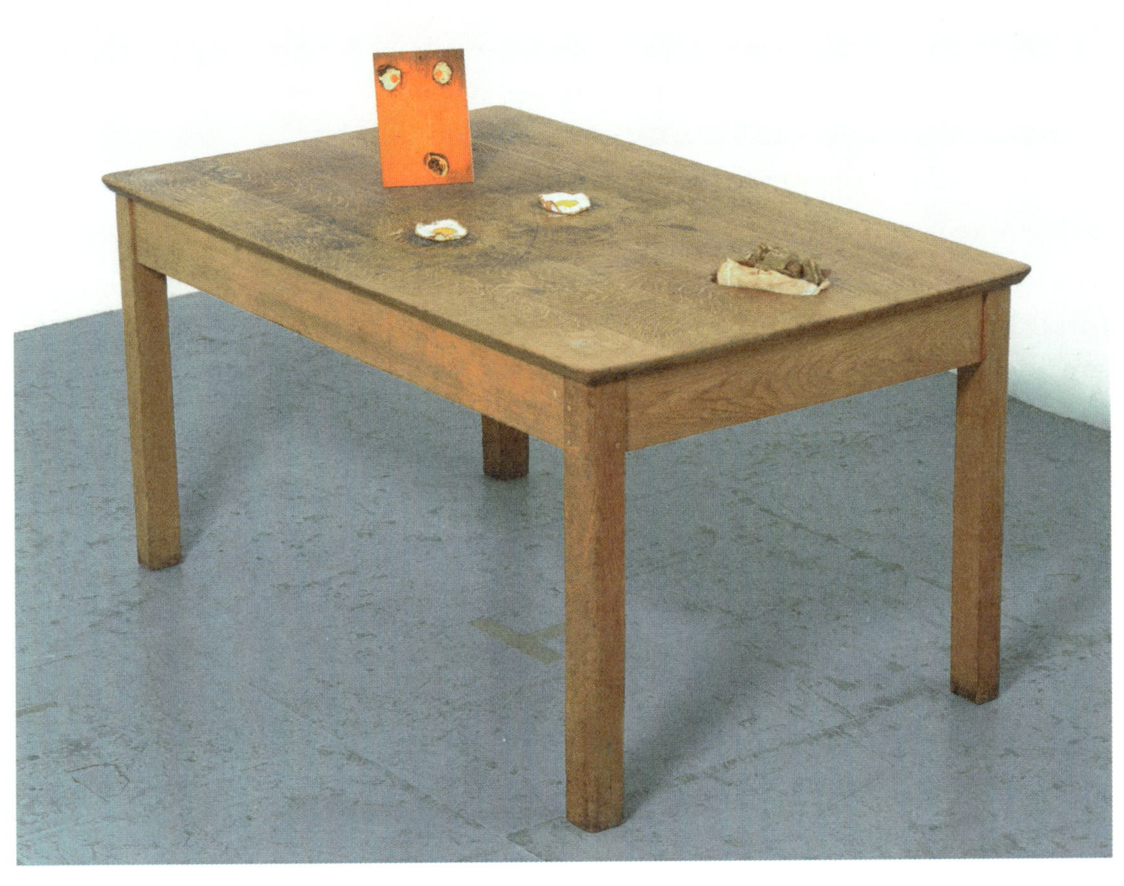

Sarah Lucas, *Two Fried Eggs and a Kebab*, 1992.
Table, fried eggs, kebab, and photograph.

These are conceptual artists, powerfully motivated by ideas. But by using food they also chose a physically stimulating material to express their ideas, engaging the bodily senses of touch, smell, hearing, taste, and deeply felt gut responses. When confronted with their works, it becomes clear that these artists helped to bring about a more fully embodied experience, and understanding, of art. They help us glimpse the reality that our ideas don't exist just in our heads, as abstract puffs, but that they reside in our bodies, tissues, and cells, as well as in our shared material world. By triggering complex sensory responses, these works have profound implications for how we might begin to appreciate art in a culture that is often restricted to the visual. In bringing together food and art, they link questions around the politics of the human body with those of food production and distribution; they highlight problems around artistic and financial values, and explore art and food as simultaneous experiences. Ultimately, they hint at the possibility of using our whole bodies and all our senses to live a more fleshly life.

Going beyond mere representations of food, the artists in this book have created art that uses actual food, expressing themselves in ways that would be impossible through any other material. They use food to stun, titillate, amuse, shock, and signal identity in unusual ways. Some of them offer food for people to taste, smell, and eat, others unlock in food the capacity to catalyze emotions including fear, rage, and grief. In these works, food functions as a tool for connection, provocation, ritual, and play. It stimulates and interrogates the senses, especially those deeper senses that are not usually touched by so-called "fine art": the visceral, animal, instinctual senses that our language is not primed to articulate.

This book focuses on the thought-provoking art involving food that was made during the second half of the last century. In this period, artists handled and sculpted food, they put it on and in their bodies, they cultivated it and served it and stitched it—all in the name of art. It was a time when working with food was unheard of in many circles, which gave the material a potent experimental charge. These experiments confronted and seduced audiences, producing a range of reactions and behaviors. They nourished the culture of their time, and subsequent generations of artists have fed from them, for example by teasing out questions around how food stands for and influences geopolitics, which Agnes Denes explored in 1982 with *Wheatfield: A Confrontation*; or by exposing the paradox of how value is assigned to art as a commodity, as Felix Gonzalez-Torres did with his candy works (1990–6); or simply as part of a lineage of artists who share an inclination to feed the people around them, like the trio behind FOOD, the artist-run restaurant established in 1971 by Tina Girouard, Carol Goodden, and Gordon Matta-Clark. Some of these works have proved to be foundational moments for contemporary art, yet the use of food as a material in art remains a relatively unmapped area.

There are two other factors that make this 40-year timeframe so relevant to exploring artists' use of food as a material. The first has to do with unprecedented global developments in the production and consumption of food during that period, and the second with the way art was made and discussed at the time. Since many of the artists in this book were living and working in the US or Europe, they benefited from a sustained period of post-war growth and an abundance of new, cheap, and often processed foods. The establishment of international supply chains, the rapid development of industrial-scale food production, and the exploitation of farming practices around the globe meant that food was available for them to eat, to give away, and to experiment with. In some ways, food during that time became less sacred than it had ever been; in other ways, more.

At the same time, the art world was in a phase of loosening up. The gradual liberation from object-based forms of art such as painting and sculpture gave way to expanded and exploded notions of what art could be. Fluxus, the experimental performance group initiated in the early 1960s and devoted to abolishing the boundary between life and art, used the format of the event-score, which offered instructions for creating art to anyone who wanted to use them. Alison Knowles's event-scores for *Make a Salad* (1962) and *The Identical Lunch* (1969) instruct people to do those things. They are artworks that lead to the creation of meals to be eaten. Such works complicated the supposedly straightforward relationship between the ideal of the artwork as a permanent object, and the viewer as a subject observing the art from a distance. As Knowles said of *Make a Salad*, these radical works were definitely "not born in museums." [2]

Art made from food challenges the traditional temporality of art, in particular its aspiration to be eternal. In the works discussed in this book, foods with a long shelf-life, for example dried beans, chewing gum, and hard candy, expose culture's aspirations to permanence. On the other hand, more volatile ingredients such as fresh fruit or raw fish and meat tap into the viewer's organic experiences and fluctuating sensations of pleasure or disgust, and are vulnerable to disease, rot, and decay. When it came to using a substance that could both constitute the work and be ingested, artists set up the possibility for onlookers and artworks to become fused.

As well as crossing boundaries between artist and viewer, gallery and home, these artists used food to explore their bodies and identities. Performing in their own work, artists such as Carolee Schneemann, Hannah Wilke, and Adrian Piper occupied both the position of maker and that of object. By combining food and their own bodies in their work, they eschewed a sanitized version of themselves, instead offering the glorious mess and chaos of life. They re-enchanted their bodies, wielding their power with foods and the attendant strong and sweet smells, dry and slippery textures, firm and soft flesh or meat.

Since their original creation, time has added layers of meaning to these works. Artworks, like foods, reflect the politics, mores, fashions, and tastes of their time. When raw chickens, fish, and hot dogs were tossed over the semi-naked bodies of performers in the Paris premiere of Carolee Schneemann's 1964 kinetic theater piece *Meat Joy*, the use of meat as an artistic material held a symbolic charge that was different from that in Jørgen Leth's film *66 Scenes from America* (1982) when in Manhattan, Andy Warhol punctiliously unwrapped and ate a Burger King hamburger, or ten years later in London when Sarah Lucas laid out two fried eggs and balanced a split pitta bread stuffed with gyros meat in the slit she had carved into a wooden table.

Many of the artists whose stories you will read chose to make work in an ephemeral way, knowing that art involving food exceeded the existing parameters of museums and art history. Their work was immediate and transient, sensory, and shared. It occurred in the moment and could not be fully captured or summarized in images. The intersection of art and food is an unruly topic, and these works fall between the cracks of genre divisions: not clearly just sculpture, photography, performance, a meal, a treat, a sensory assault, they are all of these and more. They live on in the stories told about them, and in the new ways in which we can relate them to personal experience, ideas, and global events. But the sensual and ephemeral nature of such works also presents a particular challenge to writing about them: words will never fully capture or convey sensory experience, the cross-modal symphonies of smell, taste, touch, temperature, texture, size, viscosity, resistance, melting point, salivary lubrication; the experience of walking into a room redolent with a meal, in anticipation of a food performance; the ineffable nuances in any multi-sensory moment. But thanks to the power of the imagination, descriptions can trigger physical responses in our bodies. When we imagine smelling, touching, or eating these ephemeral works, many of which are now long gone, we plumb the depths of our integrated, fleshly knowledge, relying on our bodies and personal experience with food to guide us. We each have a lifetime of sensory practice with food on which to draw in constructing our internal impression of a work. I invite you to use yours.

Coming

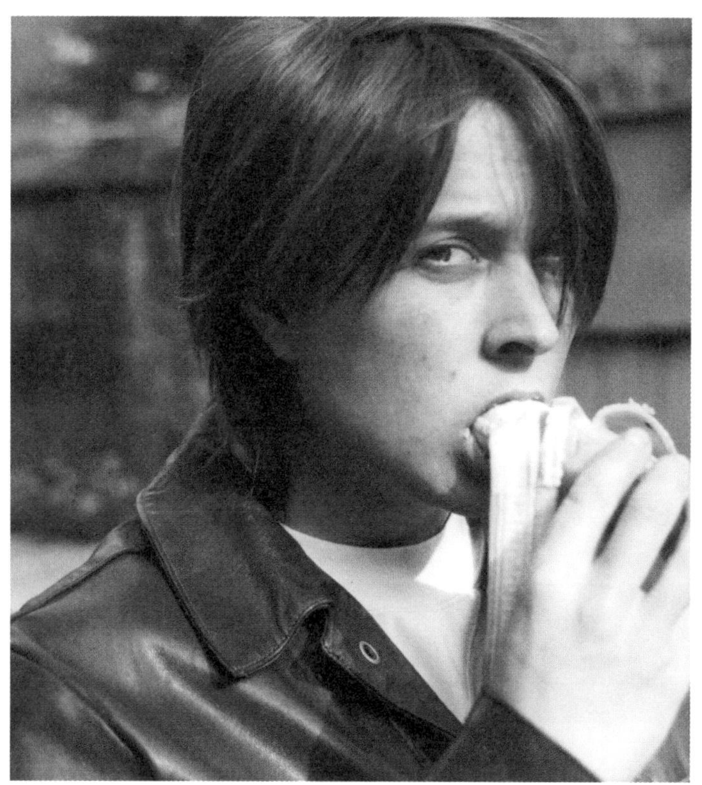

to Our

Senses

Sarah Lucas, *Eating a Banana*, 1990.
Black and white photograph.

Pause for a moment and consider the last meal you had. Can you still taste it? Perhaps there is an aroma lingering in your mouth, or a puckering of the tongue from too much salt or sour. Maybe there is numbness, brought on by excessive heat; or phlegm in the throat, a by-product of something tart and sweet. Can you feel the food as it travels through your gut? Are you bloated, acidic, full; are you empty? Maybe you are content.

Eating is a sensory experience. We take food into our mouths, preferably with alacrity, occasionally with disgust or trouble; we taste, swallow, and incorporate it. This intimate relationship with food means that using it to make art can be deeply subversive. Art made with food has the potential to upset historical conventions that apply to traditional forms of art-making, such as marble sculpture and oil painting, disrupting embedded cultural narratives and suggesting a whole new set of criteria for appreciating art and life. In short, the presence of food in art can reveal the limitations of existing ways of experiencing art and life, and open up new ways of coming to our senses.

In day-to-day life, our experience of the world is often subsumed under a single sense, which can limit its lavish multi-sensory potential.

In contemporary industrialized societies, it is the sense of sight that dominates much of our experience and is valued over other bodily senses. Most people deem sensory information acquired through the eyes to be more reliable—and more important—than the impressions we get from our ears, nose, mouth, skin, or gut. Sight is taken for granted as the primary mode of encounter with artworks, the other senses treated as secondary. By putting food at the center of their practice, the artists in this book quicken a range of sensations beyond visual perception, helping us access and liberate aspects of our experience that have been pushed out by sight. Because the use of food in art can also upend the traditional hierarchy of the senses, the works in this book invite a radical interrogation of the systems and structures of power that depend on such a limited engagement with the world.

The ascendancy of sight is the product of historical influences that disinvested knowledge of its multi-sensorial qualities and elevated vision along with its associated faculty of intellect over hearing, smell, taste, touch, and a range of visceral and erotic senses located in the skin, gut, and pelvis. Vision has long been associated with rational thought and the intellect, but this was not always so. While some might accept it as a law of nature that humans possess five physical senses, the number and attributes of the senses are social constructs dependent on the dominant cosmology of their time. For Aristotle, the five senses enabled humans to perceive external reality, affecting both the body and the soul. Within the body, the senses supported vital functions, while in the soul they fueled the imagination and thought, in order to generate knowledge. This view of the senses as the root of our understanding of the world was held until the Middle Ages. During this time, the senses were deemed capable of transmitting as well as receiving information, and speech was considered a natural faculty that sometimes counted as a sixth physical sense.

But, as culture changes, so do paradigms of sensory perception and expression. With the unfolding of the Enlightenment in Europe, a worldview anchored in multiple bodily senses gave way to one dominated by sight, shifting the hierarchy of the senses into its present arrangement. An important contributing factor for this shift was the growth of print media and literacy after Gutenberg's invention of the printing press in the 15th century. This facilitated the mass-production and circulation of books, bolstering the status of vision as the privileged sense through which humans access knowledge. A person's physical appearance also became more important thanks to the prevalence of portrait painting as a means for disseminating images of those in power, and to the increased production of mirrors. Technological advances meant windows and lighting were cheaper and better, making interiors more clearly visible and diminishing the importance of touch as a way of orienting oneself in the dark. On a more scientific—and philosophical—level, the development of telescopes and microscopes made visible realms that had previously been invisible to the naked eye.

In post-Enlightenment Europe, sight was characterized in opposition to the "proximity senses" of taste, touch, and smell, which require close contact with the stimulating material. Vision, a detached sense that operates at a distance from the object of interest, opened up a space within which reason was supposed to operate, allowing for objectivity. In science, mechanical models of the universe that could be explained with pictures and diagrams took over from a more sensual understanding of the cosmos. Visually observable phenomena also had the perceived benefit of being measurable and quantifiable, while smells and sounds were considered less so, which downgraded their scientific status.

The elevation of sight and reason above other senses caused the top of the head to divorce itself from the rest of the body. Much is lost in this artificial separation, such as the ability to act based on both abstract thought and gut feeling, or to trust somatic experience even when it doesn't tally with thoughts and expectations. Returning to a more full-bodied relationship with our world can enhance our lives, both as individuals and collectively. New research in neuroscience supports the drive to broaden our sensory references: scientists have recently mapped between 23 and 33 senses of human perception, including senses of space, balance, respiration, and hunger. These are often connected with interoception, the sense of what is going on inside the body, as are a number of other senses experienced in the body and mind, such as the senses of belonging, justice, and injustice, disgust, sexual arousal, and safety. Furthermore, recent research has demonstrated that all sensory experiences are cross-modal.[3] This means that the act of tasting does not just consist of stimulating the sense of taste, but also includes smell, sound, texture, temperature, comfort, and other senses that have yet to be mapped and named. There is also now a better understanding of neurodivergence and the ways in which people can process sensory input in very different ways, resulting in a broad spectrum of experience. When an artist works with food, stimulating and evoking senses such as taste, smell, desire, and disgust, they are also inviting connections across varied feelings and experiences that might include memory, emotion, bodily feeling, belonging, and alienation.

A brief look at the history of the senses reveals the way multiple senses operated in the field of culture before sight took over. Early museums of the late 17th and 18th centuries,[i] which established the practice of looking at something for edification and enjoyment, were precursors to the gallery spaces we know today. They contained artifacts from all over the known world, and were considered microcosms within which one could gain an understanding of the laws of the universe as they were understood at the time, and admire exemplars of human creativity and achievement. Perhaps surprisingly, they were also places in which people were encouraged to encounter an art object or artifact through the full gamut of the senses, to satisfy individual and tactile

i The Ashmolean Museum in Oxford was founded in 1683.

curiosity, as well as scientific interest and the desire for a spiritual connection with ancestors and other cultures.

Still, sense historian Constance Classen has noted that visitors to early museums frequently reported having "seen" exhibits, even when they explicitly described having used other senses such as touch, smell, and taste—for example, when eating samples of plants or other specimens. Classen came to realize that what was attributed to sight in common parlance often encompassed knowledge acquired through the other senses, and "seeing" operated as a shorthand for the more "full-bodied approach"[4] that was then the norm.

Early museology was close to science, or what was then known as natural philosophy. Both were guided by a method of empirical research using evidence from multiple senses. In pre-Enlightenment times, handling, sampling, and smelling were integral to the inspection of an object, whereas sight was deemed the least serious mode of engagement: "gazing" was what children did when presented with pretty pictures. In the second half of the 17th century, Robert Hooke, the curator of the Royal Society's repository, a major tourist attraction at the time, advocated handling collection objects and making "diligent study" of them by noting qualities such as "Sonorousness or Dulness. Smell or Taste, or Cold ... Gravity, or Levity. Coarseness, or Fineness. Fastness, or Looseness. Stiffness, or Pliableness. Roughness, or Brittleness. Claminess, or Slipperiness."[5] Today, this might seem invasive and detrimental to the object, but at the time curators routinely tasted specimens as part of a full enquiry. Some even devoted themselves to the classification of sensory properties such as the echoes of caves and the odors of fossils, areas of particular interest for Robert Plot, the first Keeper of the Ashmolean Museum.

Between the 17th and 19th centuries, museums were places where "the mythical and the magical often mingled with the natural and the historical,"[6] and the senses were key to gaining embodied understanding of what was on show. Hands-on appraisal was encouraged because, as Classen notes, "the curious character of a museum piece may have resided in a quality imperceptible to the eye,"[7] for example its weight, texture, or temperature. Like many privileges, touching museum holdings was reserved for the upper classes and scholars, who were usually male, and sensory experiences and data gathered

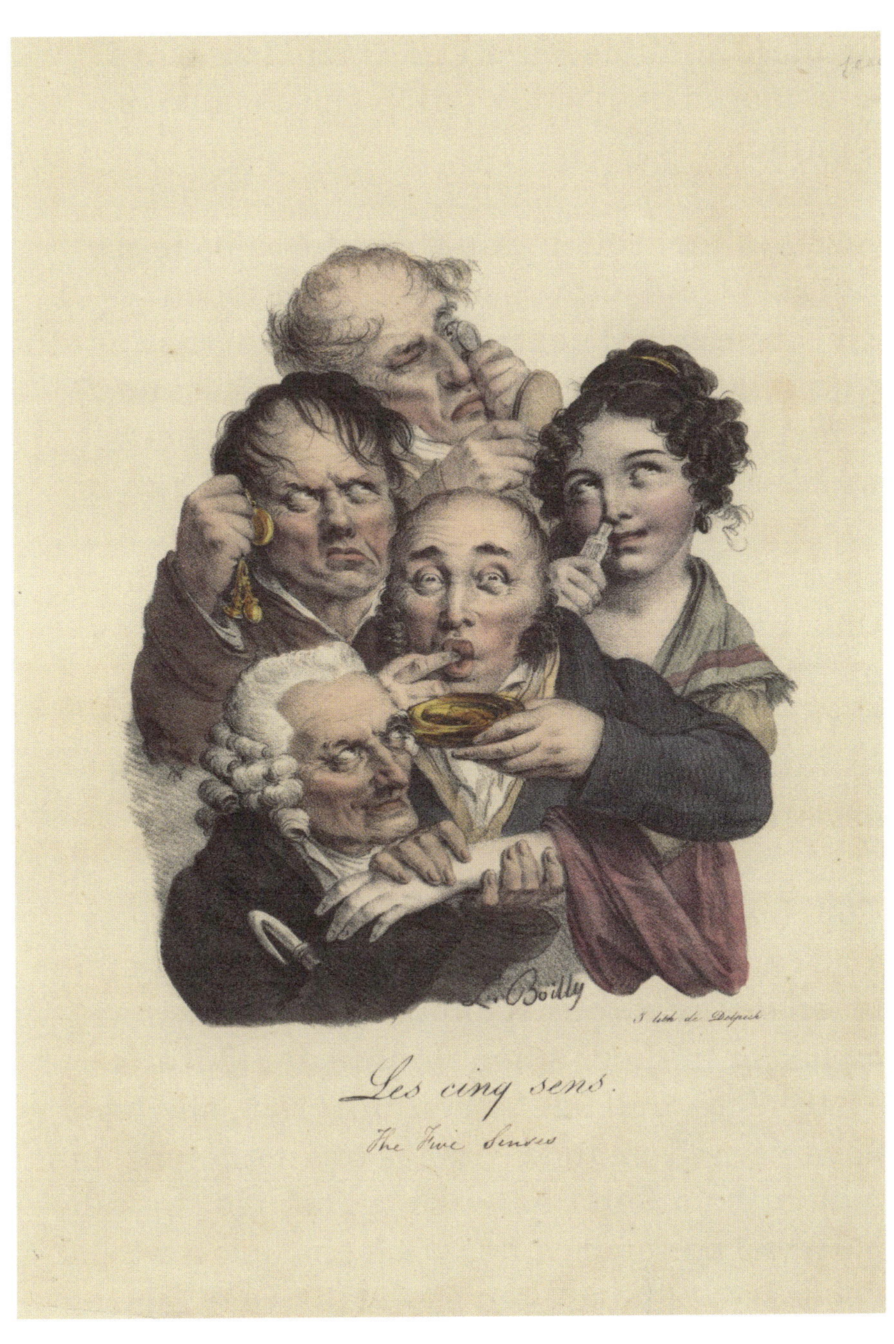

Louis-Léopold Boilly, *The Five Senses*, 1823.
Illustration from the series *Recueil des Grimaces*,
published by Delpech, Paris.

by male connoisseurs and scientists were considered of greater value than those of common visitors.

At the time, touch was thought to be more reliable than sight because it provided direct physical certainty and it verified what sight had registered from a distance. Since the Middle Ages, the sense of touch was associated with the laying on of hands, the healing touch of saints and priests, and the practices of handling or kissing relics. On a more mundane level, touch was a way of affirming social bonds and community, through practices such as eating from a common pot, sharing baths and beds, and dancing while holding hands.

Touch also provided a way of accessing the abstract properties of an object, for example by enabling a connection with its original owner or maker. When Sophie de La Roche visited the British Museum in 1786, she used her fingers to rub the ashes of an ancient urn mourning a female figure, a gesture that she believed connected her with the spirit of the deceased: "I felt it gently, with great feeling… I pressed the grain of dust between my fingers tenderly, just as her best friend might once have grasped her hand."[8] As Classen notes, such sensorial engagement with an artifact carried "the seeming ability of touch to annihilate time and space."[9] Touching was also a way to express intimacy with works of art. It was not unusual for collectors, such as the Roman Ippolito Vitelleschi, to embrace and even kiss the statues in their collections.

Taking a sample of an object was another way of interacting with artworks, a practice that allowed educated gentlemen to have direct access to the properties of an object, though it wasn't always sanctioned. The German traveler Zacharias Conrad von Uffenbach, who chronicled his visit to London in 1710, wrote of his desire to "scrape off a little" of "the famous stone of the Patriarch Jacob" in the Chapel of St Edward the Confessor in Westminster Abbey. He was forbidden to do that, but he was allowed to touch and weigh several objects, including a sword on display.

Likewise, tasting fragments of an object was deemed a way of physically internalizing or even ingesting the magical, medicinal, or religious properties of particular artifacts. This practice was supported by the belief that the "rare and wondrous qualities that made an object a likely museum piece might also make it strong medicine."[10] Precious objects that made their way into cabinets of curiosity or museums were potential "sources of vital energy"[11] that could be transferred into the eater. They included animals, plants, and mummy flesh, as well as samples of stone axes and fossils, taken in powdered form. If such artifacts were potential food, eating them was "the ultimate act of ownership."[12]

The sense of hearing remained quite ethereal and removed from early museums, especially since it was associated with sanctity and events such as being called by the words of God or hearing the music of the angels. Smell, however, pervaded the sensory environment of early museums, not least as it wafted from the displays of shells, skins, and the remains of animals whose flesh had been eaten on the ships that transported them from their place of origin. Visitors were often allowed to picnic in the presence of the collections, which contributed to the olfactory intensity of a museum visit, as this rather snooty description of the early National Gallery in London, founded in 1824, makes clear: "Not only were the pictures crowded on the walls, but the clothing of visitors (who often were merely sheltering from the rain), their consumption of food, the general smell and the influx of smoky air, all contributed to make a zoo of the Gallery."[13]

As museums became more popular and visitor numbers increased, concerns grew over the preservation and conservation of artifacts. Once sight became the primary means of understanding the world, there was no longer the same scientific justification for touching objects in museums. At the same time, social divisions based on class and gender further restricted a democratic and multi-sensorial engagement. By the mid-1800s, museums began discouraging the public from touching collections, deeming it an uneducated practice. Working people —or the "lower" classes—and women were believed to have an uneducated form of touch, appropriate for manual labor but too crude for museums, where their rough handling was judged likely to sow disorder and damage collections. Around that time, the destruction of cultural monuments in a string of revolutions across the European continent prompted a fear that the working classes would also want to destroy prized objects in collections as a political gesture. This led to further circumspection when it came to welcoming them into the museums, and the introduction of strict rules prohibiting touch. All of this increasingly made the museum a space of exclusion, in which science, and "high" forms of art such as painting and sculpture, bolstered the vision-centric sensory model upheld by the upper classes.

The era of the early museums coincided with the rise of colonialism, which saw the first encounters between Europeans and the inhabitants of Africa and the Americas. European interests in controlling resources and people led to incalculable atrocities, which were rationalized with theories of natural history that associated newly encountered populations with lowly sensuality and animal instincts rather than intellect. The 19th-century German natural historian Lorenz Oken proposed a hierarchy of population groups classed according to the senses, which was devised entirely according to the Western imagination's classifications and stereotypes of race, rather than any intrinsic human qualities. Lorenz's spurious schema crowned the European "Eye Man" and labeled the Asian "Ear Man," the Native American "Nose Man," the Australian "Tongue Man," and the African "Skin Man." As the neurobiologist Steven Rose has written, "questions about a person's race are meaningful only in a racist society," and in Lorenz's attribution of specific senses to different populations we see how integral theories of the senses were to the Western foundations for racism.

Charles Darwin's theory of evolution further "justified" the European hierarchy of senses. Darwin argued that human development was progressive, beginning with barbarians and culminating in civilized man (by which he meant Western man), who used his sight and reason to apprehend and oversee the world—literally, to look down on it. Darwin justified his account of the ascent of man and his senses with reference to the evolution of animals into humans, noting the way animals transitioned from all fours to standing upright, lifting their noses off the ground and into the air, and their eyes to scan the horizon. However, so-called "primitive" people, like animals, were characterized as relying primarily on their senses of smell and touch, whose main receptive organs are below the eyes.

Categories of gender and class were also contrived according to presumed sensory characteristics. The cultural historian Jim Drobnik has written that in the 19th century the proximity senses of smell, taste, and touch were considered "primitive, infantile, and animalistic, even neurotic and perverse."[14] These senses were central to activities carried out in the home, particularly in the kitchen and the nursery—typically the province of women, who cooked, sewed, and reared children for the benefit of society.

The working classes were also characterized in terms of the supposedly morally inferior senses. Their physical labor, confined living conditions, and rituals and festivals celebrated through the pleasures of music, dance, food, and physical contact were associated with sensual vices and bodily sin. In contrast, the privileged classes, and men in particular, were encouraged to use their "higher" senses of reason and sight to supervise: to study, travel, and rule over others.

The dominance of the visible was turbocharged in the 20th century with the arrival of cinema, television, and ultra-sophisticated advertising and marketing techniques allied to the rise of capitalist growth. Social media has further intensified vision-power and contracted the realm of the senses, with just the tips of the fingers needed to navigate the whole world through a screen. Even virtual reality, touted as a gateway to fully immersive experiences, intrinsically privileges sight above any other sense in the body.

The cultural and financial capital invested in sight's dominion over the other senses has informed the design of spaces for art, where works are installed on immaculate walls washed with bright white light for optimal viewing, and people are reduced to "viewers." The architectural paradigm is the sterile white cube, with its stark laboratory-grade furnishings and etiquette of silence. These features encourage an internalized experience in which intellectual responses to art are encouraged, but the multi-sensorial is not. Such an environment highlights what has been lost with the advent of modernity: the sense of enchantment that comes with embracing and belonging to a sensuous world; the aliveness of matter experienced through a prism of sensations.

The denigration of smell, taste, and touch —the senses most closely related to food— means they can be thought of as "othered" senses. These senses have been, and sometimes still are, associated with groups, objects, and materials considered of lower cultural value. But from their peripheral position they provide an opportunity: they offer an alternative means for accessing and experiencing culture that understands the way the senses have been carved up and ranked, and eschews both the absolute primacy of vision over other senses and the brittle mind–body dualism inherited from Enlightenment Europe.

Today, we are finally beginning to relinquish the artificial division of body, mind, and spirit. In our experiences of the world, of art and food, our sensory impressions and our thoughts are not separate. There is no clear dividing line indicating where sight separates from sound, or where taste, smell, and touch end and the thinking mind begins: they are all entwined, sometimes gorgeously, sometimes terrifyingly, but always in ways that reward close scrutiny.

Our thoughts are influenced by the body's state at any given moment, and our tissues are built largely as a result of what we eat, and don't eat. We recognize that food is central to how our bodies operate, and therefore inseparable from how we think, behave, and create our world. I think, therefore I am? Not likely. Instead: I eat, therefore I am. For too long the roles of vision and the intellect have been overvalued as the functions through which we construct the world. This has not only severely limited our capacity to engage fully with our surroundings and each other, but has caused untold damage to whole communities and ecosystems. It's time for a deeper, truer, more sensory kind of knowledge to guide us, articulated via the mouth, throat, stomach, intestines, rectum, in the stages of food passing through the body. Our gut is how we survive, and how we perceive the world. It is in large part responsible for the functioning of the brain, for perception, feeling, and inner knowledge. We need to linger on our sensory experiences, because they hold the answer to many of the big questions. By using food to sensualize the art encounter, the artists in this book help us feel our way forward with a more embodied approach. In doing so they begin to unravel some of the most deeply embedded delusions of human history. To acknowledge and investigate the full gamut of sensory experiences, from delicious to disturbing, thrilling to soothing, familiar to strange, can reveal new truths about a world we thought we knew well enough from what we saw of it.

ADRIAN PIPER

Power is Bad for the Lining of the Stomach

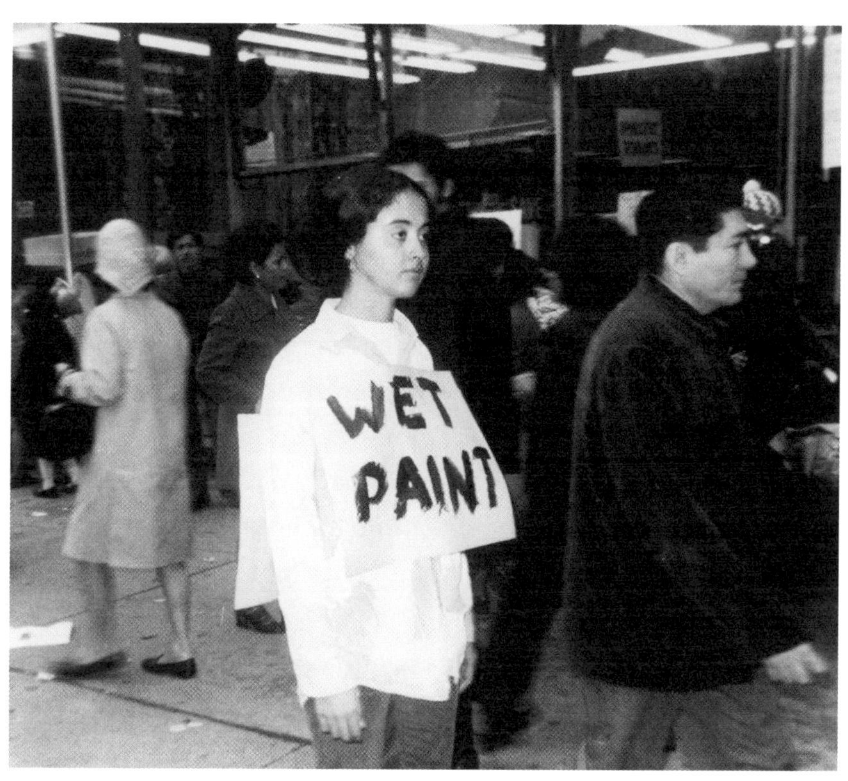

Adrian Piper, *Catalysis III*, 1970. Documentation of the performance. Three silver gelatin prints (reprinted *c.*1998).

OVER THREE DAYS, from 11 to 13 October 1968, American conceptual artist Adrian Piper served David Rosner, her then boyfriend, a meal as part of an action that she would later title *Meat into Meat*. She documented the work in a series of eight color snapshots, which she glued to black pages and inserted into a ring binder alongside a typed narrative about the event, presented as picture captions.

In the first photograph, taken on Friday 11 October, a pound of supermarket ground hamburger meat packaged in cellophane and labeled with a white sticker sits on a wooden kitchen table. It is an inert mound of pink stuff. A pair of images dated Saturday 12 October show a grid of four raw hamburger patties, first set out on a white plate, then crowded into a pan positioned on a gas stove awaiting a flame. On Sunday 13 October, four snapshots document Rosner repeatedly lifting his fork to his mouth as he eats the cooked hamburgers. He wears a white button-down shirt with sleeves rolled up as if in readiness for the hard work of eating, and sports a red tie and a blond beard. The quartet of images, shot between 10.50 and 10.56 a.m., form a sequence depicting Rosner with four, three, two, and then a single hamburger on the plate. A final shot shows the empty plate with just a fork for company. Originally titled *Five Unrelated Time Pieces*, the work chronicles the meeting of four hamburgers and one boyfriend, and how five became one.

The offering of four pink meat patties on a plate didn't unfold as straightforwardly as the pictures might suggest. While Rosner, who had helped Piper make her work but offered a running commentary about "what did it mean and it was silly to do it,"[1] was wolfing down the hamburgers, Piper began her own observations, pointing out the irony of being, as Rosner was, "on the one hand a committed Marxist and on the other hand to be consuming enough meat to feed a small third-world country for a month."[2] These explicitly political concerns are reflected in the extended title she gave to a subsequent version of the photographs, which are labeled as *Found Private Confrontational Performance [See Five Unrelated Time Pieces] A. Piper, D. Rosner, 1lb. Hamburger. Topic: Marxism vs. Vegetarianism*.[3]

As the times registered in the captions indicate, Rosner ate the four hamburgers in the space of six minutes—a gut-busting speed—"defiantly continuing to stuff himself with the meat past the point of satiation."[4] In the process, he became "increasingly antagonistic,"[5] a mood that is palpable in a ninth photo, which shows Rosner leaning back in his chair, holding a quart of milk and something that looks like bread, and glaring at the camera. There's a suggestion in his expression that something or someone has gone too far. The question is: was it Piper, Rosner, or both of them? And what mark was it that they overstepped during this fraught meal?

In 1968, Piper moved into a loft on Hester Street in Manhattan's Lower East Side, a space that combined the activities of both home and work. *Meat into Meat* transformed materials from their raw state into a consumable output—something both art and cooking do—and it transposed food into the realm of conceptual time-based art, breaking down the process into carefully annotated stages, and translating the acts of preparing, cooking, serving, and eating into the language of photography, a discipline associated with seriality and documentation.

Meat into Meat sets in motion a banal, excessive, and unappealing form of transformation: the conversion of meat as dead flesh into meat as living flesh. We watch the man eating too much meat, and for a moment we might sense how he feels: like a hamburger, the symbol of modern American prosperity, freedom, and careless pleasure, but also an emblem of industrial farming, obesity, and capitalist exploitation. The work fleshed out Piper's concerns at the time, turning Rosner into "an art object of my informed art consciousness."[6]

The friction between Piper and Rosner around the morality of meat was ongoing. Her diatribe was in part a response to Rosner's derogatory remarks concerning issues she felt strongly about but he dismissed, including her "incipient feminism … interest in yoga, meditation, vegetarianism, and the kind of spiritual morality described at great length in the Bhagavad Gita and the Upanishads"[7]—texts she had been studying since her mid-teens, which discussed, among other things, karma, renunciation, and the interconnectedness of all things. Piper's disapproval of Rosner is even visible in the angle from which the images are shot: the camera is higher than the table and looks down on him and his rapidly vanishing plate of burgers. As though channeling Piper's incandescent rage, the flash blows out the colors and the focus is blurry. Rosner later said he was surprised Piper made him the burgers because they didn't eat meat in their shared apartment. According to Piper, he "was generally dismissive and contemptuous of her work as 'art.'"[8] In this case, he took part willingly but "disliked being objectified by being photographed,"[9] even though, as Piper pointed out, "he felt differently about the nude portrait drawings of him I had done."[10] With *Meat into Meat*, Piper had originally thought she was "performing an abstract metaphysical investigation into the nature of space and time,"[11] but she later realized that "the subtext was [her] relationship with David."[12] Beneath the work's dark humor is a sadistic undertone, in which antagonistic dynamics are at play through cooking, offering, and eating food.

Domestic life often coalesces around food and discussions about whose responsibility or privilege it is to decide what is eaten, where and when it will be consumed, as well as who will provide it and who will prepare it. But aside from practical, social, and political considerations, food has abstract physical and mental ramifications, for instance in the mechanisms by which the human body transforms food into energy and the way it fuels thought and creativity. At the other end of the spectrum, abstaining from food can also be used as a means to trigger spiritual experiences and affirm one's faith, and fasts are practiced in all major world religions. Piper abstained from eating for her work *Food for the Spirit* (1971), a private performance for which she isolated herself in her loft, fasted, and practiced yoga while writing a paper on the German Enlightenment philosopher Immanuel Kant, documenting it with photographs and text that she later made public. With *Meat into Meat* and *Food for the Spirit*, Piper explored the effects of both the presence and the absence of food—in the first case within the relationship between two people, and in the second for an individual's creativity and spirituality.

Adrian Piper was born in 1948, in Washington Heights, New York City. An only child whose grandmother taught her to draw from the age of three, she began attending classes at the Art Students League of New York while she was still in high school. In 1967, she first saw the work of the American conceptual artist Sol LeWitt in an exhibition at Dwan Gallery, New York. LeWitt's experiments with seriality, progressions, and variations resonated with Piper. She saw in his work a "rigor of system and the playfulness of idiosyncrasy,"[13] qualities that would also infuse her own output. When LeWitt's show received a poor review from renowned art historian Rosalind Krauss writing in *Artforum*, Piper sent him a letter of consolation, to which he replied.[14] As a result, Piper, who had recently turned 20, and LeWitt, who was then 40, struck up a friendship, and from 1968 to 1974 she lived upstairs from LeWitt in her Hester Street loft, and joined a circle of conceptual artists working in New York that included Carl Andre, Robert Smithson, Hans Haacke, and Hanne Darboven.[15]

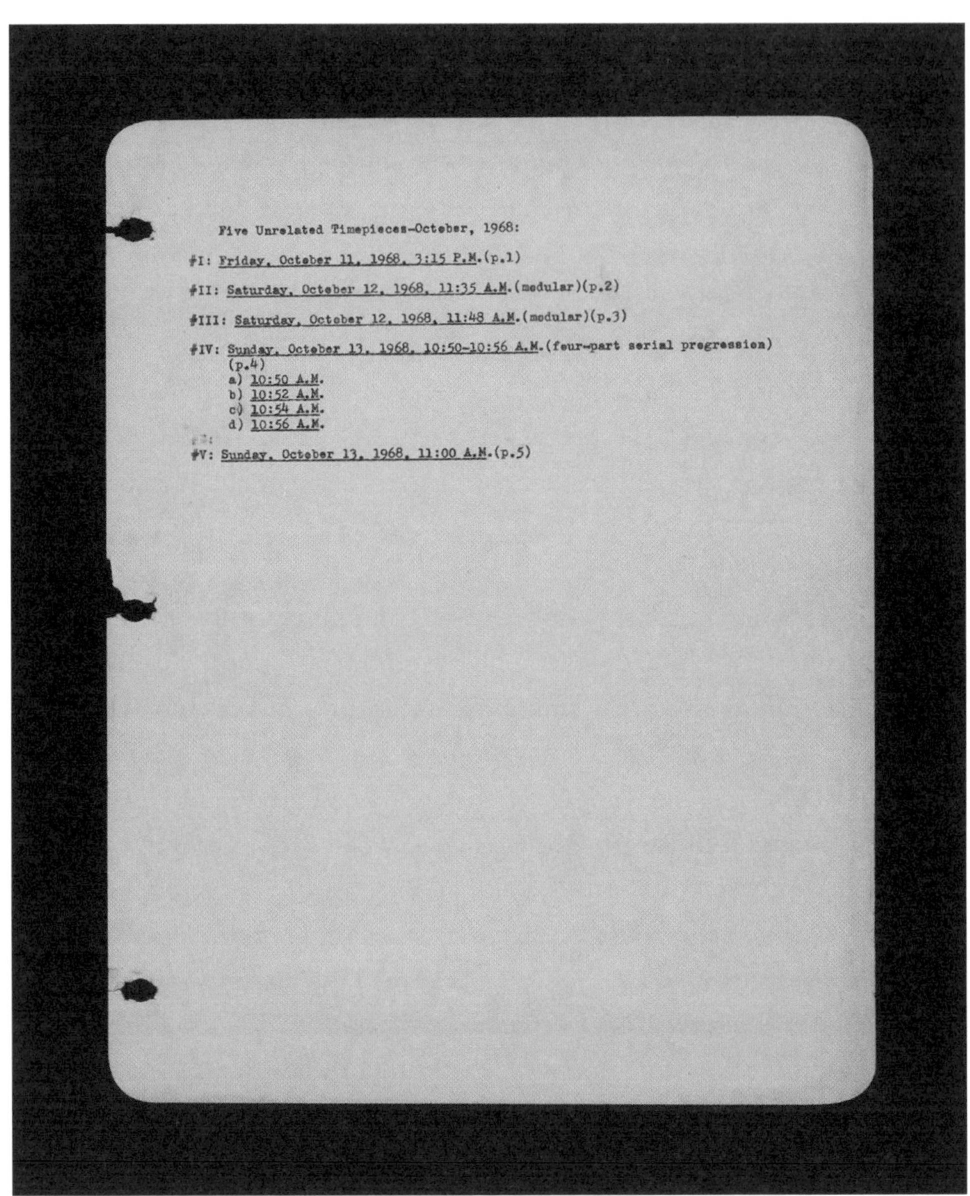

Five Unrelated Timepieces-October, 1968:

#I: Friday, October 11, 1968, 3:15 P.M.(p.1)

#II: Saturday, October 12, 1968, 11:35 A.M.(modular)(p.2)

#III: Saturday, October 12, 1968, 11:48 A.M.(modular)(p.3)

#IV: Sunday, October 13, 1968, 10:50-10:56 A.M.(four-part serial progression)
(p.4)
a) 10:50 A.M.
b) 10:52 A.M.
c) 10:54 A.M.
d) 10:56 A.M.

#V: Sunday, October 13, 1968, 11:00 A.M.(p.5)

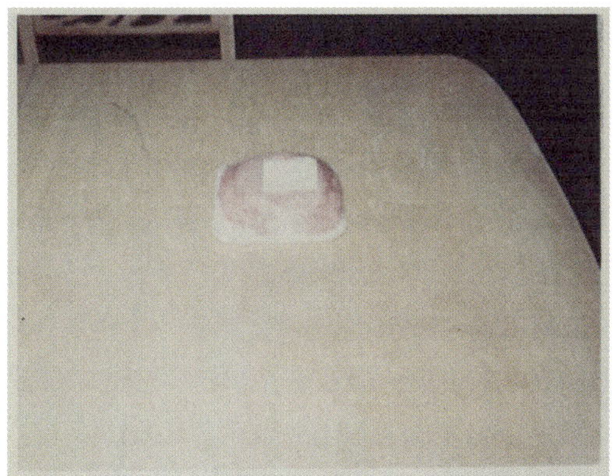
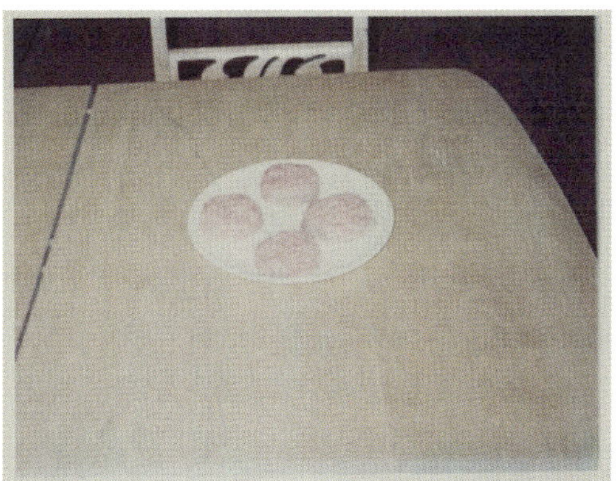
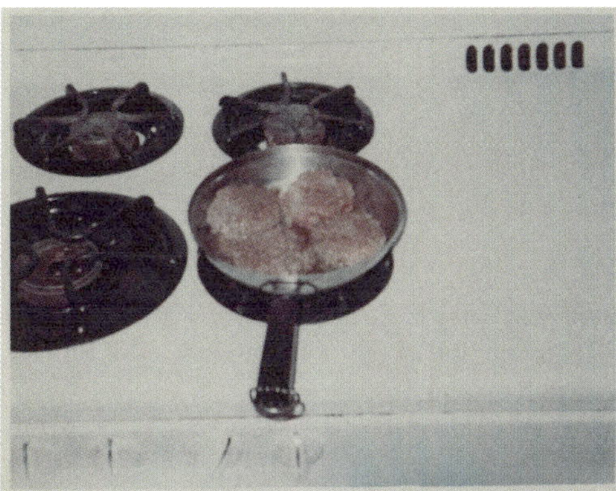
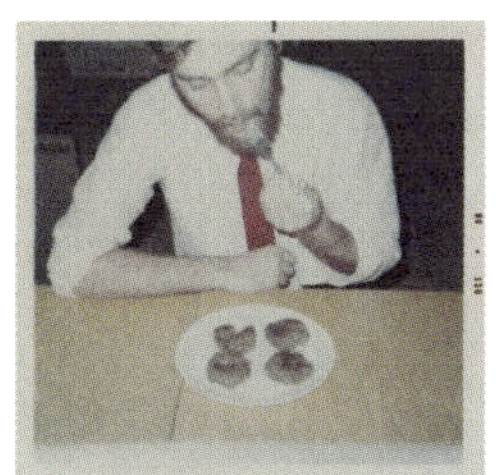
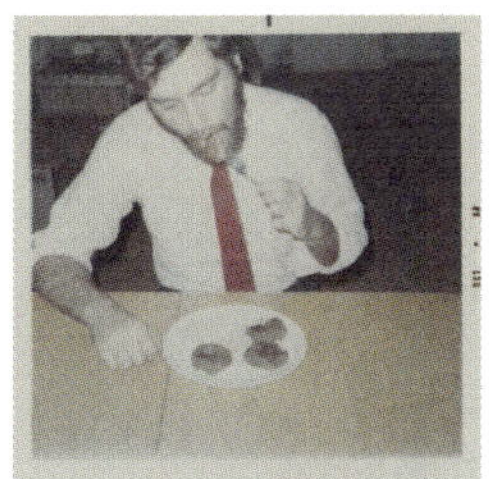
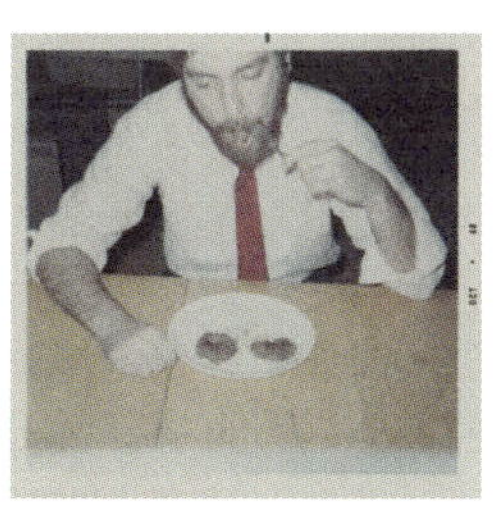
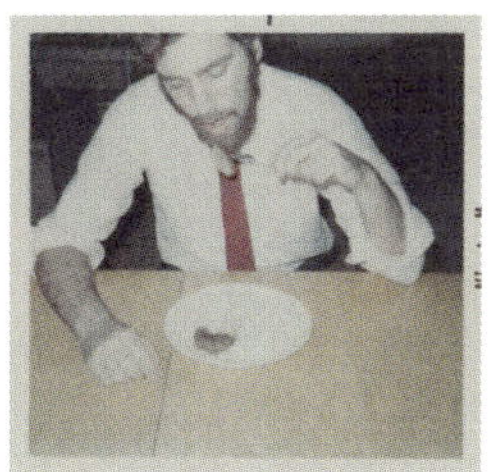
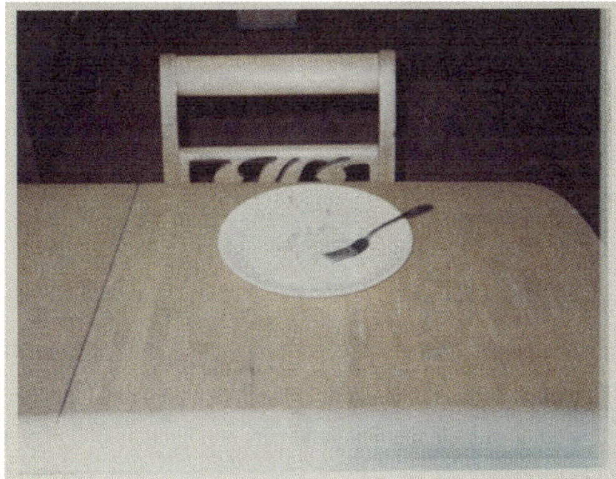

Adrian Piper, *Five Unrelated Time Pieces (Meat into Meat)* (detail), 1968. Six pages. One typescript page and eight color photographs mounted on black paper.

Piper has been a lifelong scholar of both Western and Eastern philosophy, committed since she was in her late teens to mastering texts originating in both traditions, from the writings of Immanuel Kant to the Yoga Sutras. In 1965, she began practicing yoga, around the time she first read the Beat poets Allen Ginsberg, Jack Kerouac, and William S. Burroughs, worked as a discotheque dancer at the Ginza and Entre Nous nightclubs, and experimented with psychedelics, first taking LSD after reading Ginsberg's *Howl*. She repeated the experience a handful of times over six months, which influenced her early psychedelic self-portraits—optically intense pictures with high-contrast zigzag and radiating patterns. Piper's decision to channel her spirit of inquiry into academic philosophy was unusual in the world of conceptual artists working in New York in the 1960s and 1970s, and she has remained an outlier in her dual activities as a professional philosopher and artist. In the early 1980s, she earned a PhD in philosophy from Harvard University and went on to teach at Wellesley College, where she created a philosophy of yoga course and chaired the Black Task Force.

In 2015, Piper was awarded the Golden Lion for the best artist at the Venice Biennale, but her relationship to the art world and its markets has never been straightforward. Since early on, she has called out the detrimental effects of art commerce on the body–mind–spirit complex, writing about how the dynamics of public interactions, politics, and economic status lodge in the body, perhaps nowhere more tersely than in her 1973 text "A Political Statement":[16]

Power is bad for the lining of the stomach. Financial success causes overweight and heart trouble. Art-world parties are bad for the liver. Galleries cause headaches and blood-sugar attacks. Dealers cause dislocation of the jaw. Critical reviews cause digestive upsets and emphysema. Competition between fellow artists for any of the above is a known carcinogen.[17]

While Piper's language pastiches health warnings about the toxic effects of junk food and alcohol on the body, her wry denunciation leaves out any mention of the pleasures both the art world and junk food can provide.

Early in her career, many friends, colleagues, and critics expressed their surprise on discovering that Piper was African American. Her light skin tone led some people to challenge her when she affirmed "I'm black," as she did in her 1988 video *Cornered*.[18] People who hadn't met her also often assumed she was a man because of her name. She worked these assumptions around her race and gender into several pieces that vary in tone from controversial to joyous, notably her drawing *Self-Portrait Exaggerating My Negroid Features* (1981) and *Funk Lessons* (1982–4), a series of audience-participatory performances and a video in which she teaches groups composed mostly of white people how to listen to and dance to funk music. In September 2012, to mark her 64th birthday, Piper targeted the absurdity of racial categorization, following the twisted logic of race to its absurd conclusion in a work titled *Thwarted Projects, Dashed Hopes, A Moment of Embarrassment*. This self-portrait bears an announcement of her decision to "retire from being black" and to change her "racial and nationality designations," declaring that she would henceforth be "neither black nor white but rather 6.25% grey, honoring [her] 1/16th African heritage."[19]

These works relating to Piper's identity are laced with an edgy and absurd sense of humor, which also infuses a series of actions she conducted over the course of two years, in 1970 and 1971. What she later titled the *Catalysis* series unfolded on the streets and in the public spaces of New York City. Some of the actions were documented in photographs, while others reach us solely by way of Piper's descriptions in writing and interviews, but they are some of her best-known works, including the first in the series, for which she used food to striking effect, to explore the boundaries of identity and accepted behavior. For *Catalysis I*, Piper made a concoction of different foodstuffs, including vinegar, raw egg, milk, and cod-liver oil. She soaked a set of clothes in the mixture for one week, during which time it became increasingly fetid, and left the outfit to dry before wearing it while riding the New York City subway during evening rush hour. She wore the same ensemble on a Saturday night while browsing in the Marboro bookstore, a popular place that sold remaindered books. She later explained that she did all this because she had decided to "smell all over the place."[20]

In scientific language, the term "catalysis" refers to the acceleration of a chemical reaction by a catalyst; for example, iron is the catalyst that helps transform nitrogen and hydrogen into ammonia. *Catalysis I* was the first in a series of actions with which Piper sought to catalyze reactions by deliberately taking up space in various and awkward ways, with unwieldy accessories, eccentric movements, or, in this case, a powerful smell. In its use of unsavory foodstuffs, *Catalysis I* evokes the childlike behavior of reveling in extreme sensory stimulation: making a mush of all the gross things available and then handling it and handing it around.

For *Catalysis III*, she coated her clothing in white paint and visited Macy's to shop for sunglasses and gloves while wearing a "Wet Paint" sign around her neck. For *Catalysis IV*, she dressed in a conservative style, wearing jeans, a white t-shirt, and a simple jacket, and stuffed a bath towel into the sides of her mouth so that her cheeks bulged and the rest of the towel trailed down her front while she rode the bus and subway and took the elevator up and down the Empire State Building. For *Catalysis VI*, she tied Mickey Mouse helium balloons to her ears, nose, two front teeth and strands of her hair then walked through Central Park and the lobby of the Plaza Hotel, and rode the subway during the morning rush hour.

When she undertook her *Catalysis* actions, Piper proceeded by stealth, choosing not to perform in designated art spaces or to declare her actions art. She believed that the reassurance that comes with knowing that one is witnessing an art performance "makes everything all right,"[21] stymying the creative and explosive potential of the situation. Performing in public was an ideal way for her to disrupt people's received wisdom about what art could and should be, since most people would have had no frame of reference for what they were seeing, hearing, and smelling.

With each of the *Catalysis* works, Piper confronted her fellow New Yorkers with anomalies within the urban environment. One imagines that such situations must have catalyzed a range of responses, from the instinctual retreat of people shocked by a revolting smell, to the intellectual reflection of those trying to make sense for themselves of what they are experiencing. As the art historian John P. Bowles has written, "*Catalysis* provided Piper with a model for investigating socially determined boundaries of acceptable behavior and, more importantly, for making the viewers of her work aware of their own expectations and prejudices."[22] Piper recognized that "like everyone else, I am a paradigm of this society. The society's treatment of me shows me what I am, and in the products of my labor I reveal the nature of the society."[23]

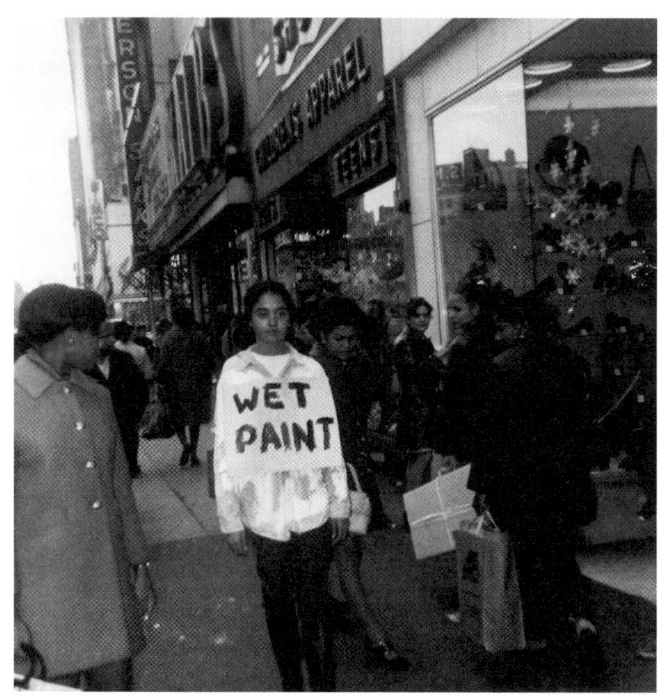

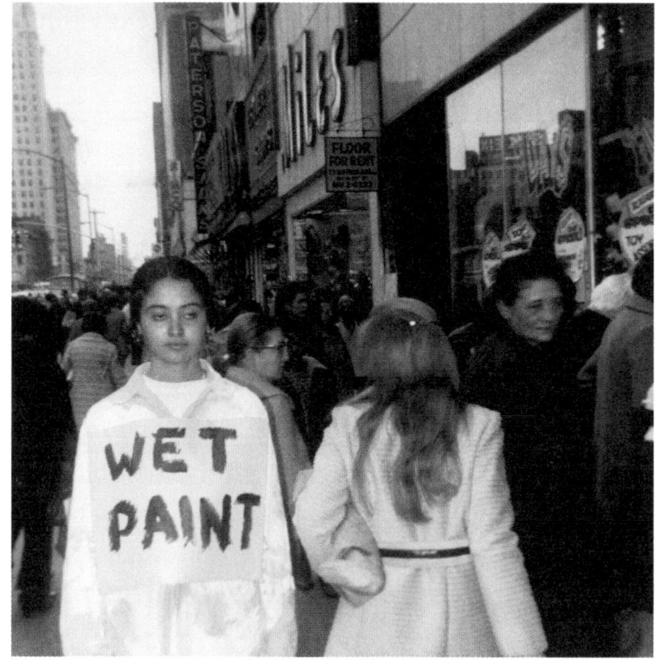

Adrian Piper, *Catalysis III*, 1970. Documentation of the performance. Three silver gelatin prints (reprinted c.1998).

While the *Catalysis* works can be seen as fun, confrontational, or absurd, what was really at stake for Piper was how they affected unsuspecting people. She later wrote: "I define the work as the viewer's reaction to it: to me the strongest, most complex, and most esthetically interesting catalysis is the one that occurs in uncategorized, undefined and non-pragmatic human confrontation."[24]

As she had done with the hamburgers that she prepared and fed to Rosner for *Meat into Meat*, with *Catalysis I* Piper used food, specifically the fumes and traces of food past its best, as a confrontational device. Her fug transgressed the limits of the other, invading the space of innocent bystanders, settling in their noses, and colonizing their respiratory systems. "I intrude myself upon other people's realities," she told art critic Lucy Lippard the following year.[25] Although we don't have accounts from those who witnessed *Catalysis I*, Piper's sensory intrusion must have caused them to reconsider their impressions of the seemingly ordinary young woman in front of them, or to change their mind about the salubriousness of a city that would allow someone like her to carry on in such a condition.

We call bad smells "offensive," as if they have defaulted on their moral responsibilities. Historically, smell, like the other bodily senses, was enmeshed in a system of virtue. During the Renaissance, sanctity was associated with fragrance while sin was linked to stench. In the 18th and 19th centuries, scientific links were made between stench and disease transmission, and both bad smell and bad health were imputed to the working classes and the poor. Later, rather than having a particular scientific or medical significance, stench was related to the experience of disgust, but its role in propping up social hierarchies still applies today.

Piper had intended the rotten food mixture to imitate the smell of a homeless person, so that those encountering her would be confused by a young woman who did not smell the way she looked.[26] But it was not just her smell that would have been perceived as offensive because it contravened acceptable behavior; the fact that she chose to stink, on purpose, compounded the wrong. Although her movements might have been interpreted as passive—she was mostly standing still in subway cars and bookshop aisles—Piper actively presented herself as the object of other people's judgment. The mismatch between her appearance and her deathly smell scrambled the codes of good behavior.

Piper's intentional misuse of food provided her with both an assault weapon and a shield with which to insert herself into the collective sensorium. If there is an aggressive tone to her action, it is expressed as a violence to the sensory world of another. But the work can also be seen as pranks: like a stink bomb let off surreptitiously, it triggered an intense sensation, a thrill for the body and a fox for the mind trying to figure out the origins of the unpleasant smell. To unexpectedly and abruptly dial up the senses, provoking involuntary responses, is a gag. But at whose expense is the joke made? And is the payoff shared or solitary?

In a bid to maintain her composure and identity during the *Catalysis* series, Piper pretended people weren't there, something that was not always easy. Occasionally, they behaved in ways she could not ignore, which also highlighted how vulnerable she had made herself, such as when a group of businessmen on the subway stared at her in a way that made her feel "like they really wanted to fuck"[27] her. The sexual potency of *Catalysis I* was an aspect of the work Piper had not considered, but a friend explained that by presenting herself in public in such a state, "it seemed that [she] didn't have any respect for [her] body, so why should anybody else?"[28]

Food has long been associated with feminine sensuality and sex, whether through its strong connection to women's domestic labor, or the stereotyping of women as a passive, consumable gender. Piper considered her deliberate reek to be a form of "voluntary self-objectification."[29] Her stench was "an act of political defiance, a gesture of brazen shamelessness, a celebration of self that absolutely crushes and makes ridiculous any attempt at devaluation or disapproval."[30]

By using food as a central part of the highly unusual scenarios of *Meat into Meat* and *Catalysis I*, Piper showed how food can operate as a means of keeping people apart, just as much as it can bring them together. Decades later, in contemplating Piper's actions, I imagine the rank liquid, its dry effusions, and the ill aura that must have surrounded her as she manifested her stench in subway cars crowded with people and in aisles stacked with literature. Did the work, in confronting the living with the evidence of putrid foods, hold a charge comparable to that of the earliest *memento mori* paintings in which exquisitely rendered fruits and foods appear to succumb to pests, rot, and decay? Apart from its strangeness, the ersatz corpse juice in which Piper clothed herself before imposing it on New Yorkers going about their business reminds us that in time we too will liquefy after our death.

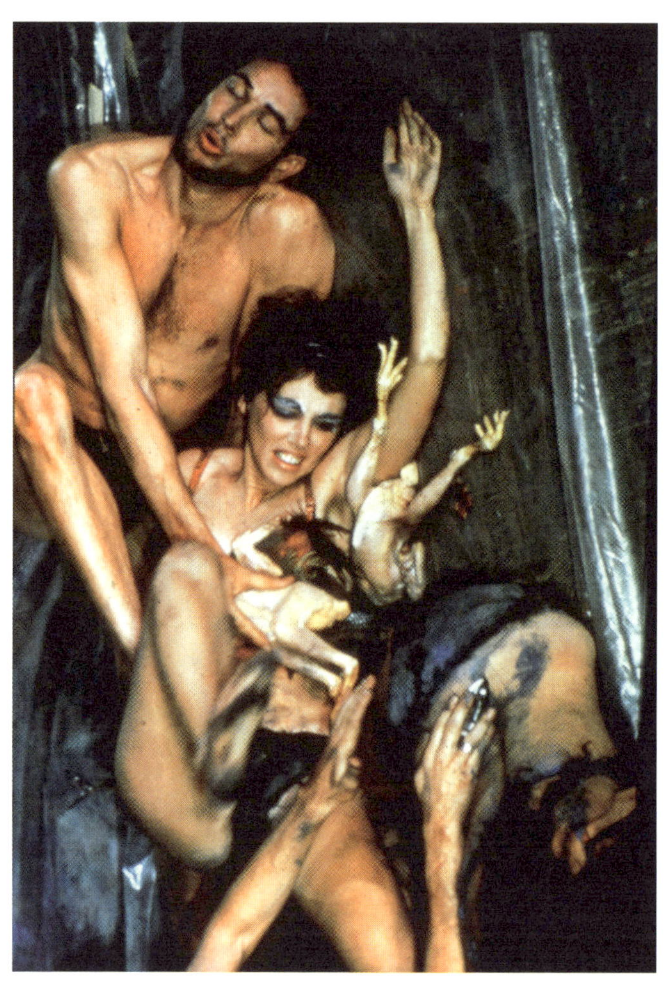

Carolee Schneemann, *Meat Joy*, 1964. Documentation of the performance held at the Judson Dance Theater, Judson Memorial Church, New York.

CAROLEE SCHNEEMANN

Go Feed Yourself!

AMERICAN ARTIST CAROLEE SCHNEEMANN'S 1964 performance *Meat Joy* used similar ingredients to Piper's *Meat into Meat*, but to extremely different ends. Here, meat—in the form of raw animal carcasses, hot dogs, and fish—was scattered around a performance area in a work about pleasure, play, and shared sensuality. Alongside the live bodies of the performers, *Meat Joy* used—as props, paint, and sculptural matter—dead animals that might have ended up as food.

Schneemann was 25 years old when she created *Meat Joy*. When Jean-Jacques Lebel, the organizer of the 1964 Festival de la Libre Expression (Festival of Free Expression) at the American Cultural Center in Paris, invited her to take part, she wrote to him explaining her wish to create a work relating to French butcher shops, the French writer Antonin Artaud, and the American Beat poet Michael McClure. McClure, who considered humans "bags of meat," wrote about the "beastliness of mankind" in his "Meat Science Essays," which celebrated the "shared biological connection among all human and non-human creatures."[1] Artaud, meanwhile, advocated undiluted spectacle, writing that "a real theatrical experience shakes the calm of the senses, liberates the compressed unconscious and drives towards a kind of potential revolt."[2]

As a final layer of reference, *Meat Joy* was also informed by dream material that Schneemann collected in her diaries over a period of four years, including her accounts of the process of orientation through the senses that she went through as she woke from sleep. In her proposal to Lebel, Schneemann detailed the sensory aspects of the piece she was conceiving: the smell and feel of the meat, the meeting of women and men, and the relationships that might form between bodies and individuals along with "a mass of meat slices."[3] What she was proposing was a radical and provocative use of food and performers that crossed boundaries between species.

Schneemann's arrival in Paris to realize the piece did not go smoothly. She didn't speak any French and was penniless apart from some money from Martinique that her father had given her, having mistaken it for French currency. According to Schneemann, Lebel had not believed she would make it all the way to Paris, but he bought her a plane ticket and when she arrived he put her up in the hotel La Louisiane on the rue de Seine, where she immediately got to work, hanging her microphone out of the window to record "all the cries of the fish vendors."[4]

Schneemann created a detailed score for *Meat Joy* featuring four men and five women, a series of movements and tableaux, lighting and sound cues, and a narrative text. At 12 pages, it specified action intended to last between 60 and 80 minutes, precisely choreographed around striking formal elements guiding performers, lighting, and sound through geometric and linear movements that would "cut through the overall circular structures of *Meat Joy*."[5]

The first performance took place on 29 May 1964 (further performances were held later that year at London's Dennison Hall at the Vauxhall Meeting House and at the Judson Dance Theater in New York). It began with the sounds of street vendors hawking meat, chickens, and fish that Schneemann had recorded from her hotel window, mixed with audio of her learning French. As the audience filtered in, the performers sat around a table eating and drinking, chatting, smoking, and applying makeup. The names of the characters in *Meat Joy* refer to their position within the space that Schneemann had devised for the performance: there are two Lateral Men, two Lateral Women, one Central Man, one Central Woman (played by Schneemann in the Paris performance), one Independent Man, one Independent Woman, and one Serving Maid. They are dressed in work clothes or street clothes, with the Independent Woman donning a kimono, the outfits selected to reflect a range of social identities. For these roles, Schneemann cast participants from among her friends and people she found on the street or in cafés, never asking a performer to do anything she wouldn't do herself.

Schneemann envisaged the work as "a sensitized situation in which the participants practice relational spontaneity."[6] It involves a number of formal elements that Schneemann had conceived, including an "undressing walk," in which Central Man and Central Woman take turns to undress each other using only one hand; "body packages," for which the Lateral Men wrap the women in paper and rope; a "leg mixture," which involves Lateral Men and Women lying down with their bottoms touching and their legs dancing together; a "love-paint-exchange" between the Central Man and Woman, who shake their bodies together and then paint each other with liquid paint and brushes; "the Intractable Rosette," where the men attempt to fashion the women into a shape in which they can move together as a unit; and finally "The Tree," for which the women stand facing each other in a circle with their arms reaching up and their legs tied together.

Throughout the piece, the performers execute playful and athletic movements, including body rolls, jumping, pulling, and skidding. Comedy and excitement coexist with absurdity, but also with brusque and aggressive actions that Schneemann had developed based on "how cats feint and play and jostle and give advantage and take advantage."[7] The choreography of the performance built on her early 1960s "movement image," which she created with dancers from the Judson Dance Theater, including Yvonne Rainer, Lucinda Childs, and Trisha Brown, coming together in a proto-feminist experimental group. These performances led Schneemann to devise an approach she called "kinetic theater," which was an evolution of the multi-sensory free expression of happenings, and combined movement, improvisation, bodily contact, sculpture, and film.

Aside from the physical encounters generated by Schneemann's stage directions, a number of social encounters also take place in *Meat Joy*. At one point, the Independent Woman retrieves some objects hidden among the audience, including a mattress, a tea set, pillows, books, cakes, and oranges. As she drinks her tea and eats her snacks, Independent Man joins her, which leads to them bouncing oranges on their bellies and between their two bodies.

When the Serving Maid hands out plastic sheeting, the audience gets the first hint of a shift in the action. To a soundtrack of The Supremes' "Where Did Our Love Go?" a hit that year, the Serving Maid "slowly, extravagantly" distributed fish, chicken, and hot dogs over the performers. Given its title, the appearance of meat in *Meat Joy* should hardly have come as a surprise. But although Schneemann was committed to rehearsing with her performers, she kept some elements of the final rendition secret, including the involvement of meat. She later recalled that the fish, chickens, and hot dogs introduced during the performance, as well as the paint, "came as a visceral shock"[8] to her cast. They rose to the occasion, interacting with the meat, exploring, playing, and responding with enthusiasm. The sensory dynamism of the moment is captured in Schneemann's description of the performers' "slips, flops, flips, jumps, throwing and catching, drawing, falling, running, slapping, exchanging, stroking. Tenderly, then wildly. All are finally inundated with fish, chickens, hot dogs."[9]

The animal carcasses and meat functioned both as props and as prostheses, extending the performers' bodies, forming bridges between them and, through their seeping blood and mucus, providing a shared substance on their surfaces. It is easy to imagine the smell adhering to the skin of the performers, bonding with their sweat into a slick and odorous cellular cocktail. Schneemann's stage directions emphasized the tactile qualities of the meat—"wet fish, heavy chickens, bouncing hot dogs."[10] They also guided the performers' physical responses, both voluntary and involuntary—"twitching, pulling back, hands reaching, touching, groans, giggles."

Schneemann wanted the audience for *Meat Joy* to be as close to the performance as possible, so they could experience the sensory aspects of the work first hand: to smell the raw meat and fish, and risk being splattered with paint or touched by performers. The Korean American video artist Nam June Paik gave a succinct summary of his experience as an audience member: "I remember the smell of fish."[11] Schneemann envisaged the audience, which sat on the floor, as an "energy complement" to the piece, "encircling, resonating"[12] what was happening in the performance area.

There is a common misconception about *Meat Joy* that it was a messy, bloody rumpus throughout. In reality, the action was highly organized, planned, and rehearsed, with space and time allocated for improvisational elements and spontaneous responses to the audiences' reactions. Schneemann designed the lighting to range from washes of light across the performance area to bursts of "sudden strong illumination on energy clusters," and she accorded the lighting technicians freedom to respond to shifts in energy among the performers and the audience. As a respite, four blackouts provided "blank[s] in which perception [was] halted and the imagery settle[d] in the mind."[13]

Meat Joy was a multi-sensorial experiment that recruited food to enliven all the senses. To enable a critique of the boundaries commonly imposed on the human body's naturalness and expressiveness, it used sight and sound; movement and touch; sensory qualities such as firmness and softness, wetness, slipperiness, and weight and pressure; contact; and revulsion.

Schneemann envisioned the piece as "sensual, comic, joyous, repellent," a work in which "layered elements mesh and gain intensity" in order to explore the erotic potential of excessive and ecstatic experiences that were routinely suppressed: ways of going through the body to get beyond it. This exploration made the work radical and revolutionary for the time. Reflecting on *Meat Joy* some 50 years after it was performed, Schneemann noted that her "early erotic enactments were too disturbing for collectors or institutions to support."[14]

Carolee Schneemann was born on 12 October 1939, in Fox Chase, Pennsylvania. She studied philosophy and poetry at Bard College in upstate New York, and then painting at the University of Illinois. Painting was a constant in her life and she brought a painterly sensibility to all her work, including her photography, video, and performance. From early on, a major influence was the work of Paul Cézanne. She shared Cézanne's ambition for painting to portray perception and sensation as they were directly experienced in the world, rather than reproducing an idea of what was in the world. Upon first encountering his work, Schneemann assumed Cézanne was a woman because his name included "Anne." She enshrined her confusion over his gender in her 1976 artist's book *Cézanne, She Was a Great Painter*, which featured her writings and childhood drawings.

Schneemann's early works focused on painting constructions with boxed elements, which aimed to liberate the image from the flat surface of the canvas. As she developed her performance practice, she conceived of her work as "a painter who has left the canvas to activate actual space and live time."[15] When she arrived in New York in the early 1960s on leave from Bard to study at Columbia, the Abstract Expressionist movement of the 1940s and 1950s was in crisis. Its lodestone,

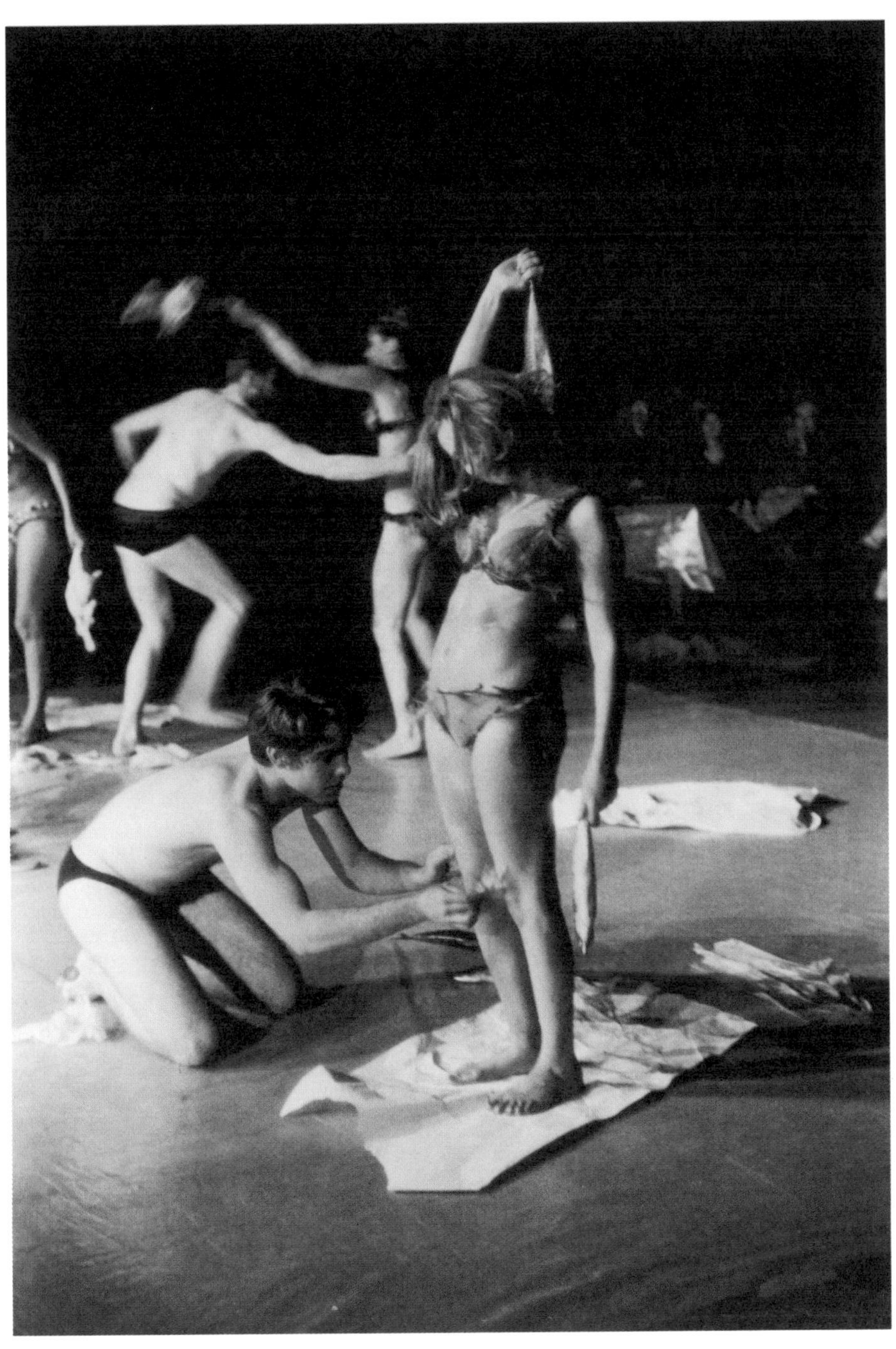

Carolee Schneemann, *Meat Joy*, 1964. Documentation of the performance held at the Judson Dance Theater, Judson Memorial Church, New York.

Jackson Pollock, had died in a car crash in 1956, an event to which Schneemann alluded when she scathingly described seeing her heroes "drunk, fighting, fucking, jumping through windows (sometimes in my loft), crashing their cars, performing all the infantile heroics that diverted castration fantasies into symbolic inviolability."[16]

As part of the downtown New York scene in the 1960s, Schneemann appeared in Claes Oldenburg's happenings *Store Days* (1961) and *Waves and Washes* (1966). For *Store Days* she was put in a spangled dress and positioned at the edge of a fireplace with a knife, and asked to stab a wall for several hours while other performers improvised with furniture, art materials, and each other around her. The whole thing "was like wandering into a live, visceral dream of bodies and materials."[17] Live experimental performance was a risky business, both physically and commercially, and Schneemann later noted that many of the male artists involved in happenings and events by the experimental performance group Fluxus went back to sculpture and painting, which she saw as a regression from live art back to objects, which could be sold and were a surer way of guaranteeing financial success.

As a student, Schneemann had read Simone de Beauvoir's feminist classic *The Second Sex* (1949), which helped her realize that as a woman working across the boundaries of artistic media and genres she posed a threat to the established order of male art history. She felt that women were the truly brave artists, and more likely than men to continue with performance, saying that "among the women from my first years in New York, Yoko Ono, Alison Knowles, Charlotte Moorman, Marta Minujin, Yayoi Kusama, and I persist in making an admixture of objects, installations, and actions."[18]

In her life and art, Schneemann displayed a distinct lack of squeamishness around the naked human body, and animals (alive or dead), and contact between the two. She attributed her appreciation of the physicality of human and animal flesh to her upbringing, in particular the influence of her father, a doctor who "always provided a motive to let me see what was going on with the body."[19] She also attributed her steadiness in the face of potentially gruesome material to her work as a chicken farmer when she was a young woman in Pennsylvania, and described in intimate detail how she would clean just-slaughtered animals, claiming it was "an entrancing experience. I had my own chopping block and my own little axe, and then I steamed them, plucked them, eviscerated them, and I loved to go inside and get the warm head, the little tiny eggs, the liver, and the gizzard."[20]

In contrast to her appreciation of the animal body, Schneemann felt that as a woman her body was perceived through the prejudices of society: "My sexuality was idealized, fetishized, but the organic experience of my own body was referred to as defiling, stinking, contaminating."[21] The problem, according to Schneemann, was rooted in society's polarization of the sexes and its sanitization of the physical aspects of life, which she believed had a knock-on effect when it came to people's ability to experience pleasure. With her art, she called for culture "to have its physicality reproportioned" by re-engaging the senses and attuning to enjoyment. This would move things away from the split between "stereotypic and prurient pornography concerning the feminine, and … macho-militarism overshadowing masculinity." A fervent advocate of enlivening the sensuous parts of life, she placed intellectual, sensual, and sexual experience on the same plane, shunning binaries of body and mind, sensuality and intellect, or feminine and masculine.

Schneemann accounted for her own sensations in terms of her personal erotic charge, claiming that "when I touch things,

I can feel they get sizzling; tables, chairs, things pour an energy back to me."[22] Even though we tend to describe experiences in terms of individual senses, most of the time multiple senses are used at once. Even as an image is perceived, or a morsel of food tasted, that experience will involve a range of other senses, for example the ambient temperature, texture, smell, sound, light, and awareness of what is happening inside the body. Going beyond the limitations of single-sense descriptions was a goal Schneemann shared with her husband, the composer James Tenney, who was at the time studying theories of the physical properties of sound. This question is at the heart of *Fuses* (1967), the extraordinary 30-minute film that Schneemann made over the course of three years, depicting herself and Tenney making love, the spliced film burned by acid and fire and marked with paint. With *Fuses*, Schneemann was attempting to depict her bodily sensations of sexual pleasure in filmic language: she wanted "the bodies to be turning into tactile sensations of flickers."[23] As *Meat Joy* had done a few years earlier, the film stumped critics, who did not know how to situate this depiction of a natural but usually censored physical act of connection and pleasure inspired by an "equitable, loving relationship"[24] within the binary between pornography and scientific documentary.

In *Meat Joy*, Schneemann set up a situation in which men and women engaged in mutual pleasure and "relational spontaneity." But with its liberated sensuality, *Meat Joy* posed a challenge to the dominant culture in America at the time, which was mainly concerned with economic expansion and international power. It was a time when racial segregation was in place in the Southern US (the Jim Crow Laws were enforced until 1965), when birth control for unmarried women was prohibited in 26 states, and when second-wave feminism and environmentalism were just beginning to emerge. *Meat Joy*'s use of near-naked bodies, gleeful deployment of unashamedly sensory materials, and call to joy produced a work with the power to shock, delight, and confound. Schneemann credited the thinking of the Austrian psychoanalyst and psychiatrist Wilhelm Reich as influential to *Meat Joy*. According to Reich, "sexual energy ... governs the structure of human feeling and thinking."[25] He theorized in his 1933 book *The Mass Psychology of Fascism* that authoritarians and fascists gain power through mass sexual repression, and discussed how this can lead to violence and war. Reich's ideas led Schneemann to imagine *Meat Joy* as a response to current geopolitical events, especially the war in Vietnam. She called it "an erotic rite to enliven my guilty culture,"[26] hoping that it would enable "ecstatic connection ... in reaction to a government shaped by assassinations and militaristic aggressions."[27]

Exposure to raw meat can be uncomfortable, even intolerable, for those who don't consume it, yet in the early 1960s a string of hot dogs or a chicken carcass was a mundane thing, and meat was widely consumed in America, where it was largely untouched by ethical concerns.[i] Schneemann was keen for the work to connect with aspects of everyday experience and to speak to current events, but she did not intend the performance to count as real life. Instead, art could open up a necessary and safe space within which to assert and explore different kinds of behavior, identity, and expression, like the one Adrian Piper later carved out for herself when performing her *Catalysis* pieces on the streets of New York City. Schneemann was clear about the need to differentiate what was art from what was real, and recognized how the failure to do so could lead to condemnation and censorship. And yet some people considered *Meat Joy* a genuine threat to society. Perhaps it was the handling of food that made the performance seem so

i Through the 1900s, meat consumption rose, thanks to the availability of cheap transportation and refrigeration. It wasn't until the early 1970s that concerns about the environmental damage caused by the meat industry led to the popularity of vegetarianism in the US, influenced in part by Frances Moore Lappé's bestselling book *Diet for a Small Planet* (1971).

real to some people that they considered it obscene. At the Paris and New York performances, informants from local police stations and self-appointed "moral decency" groups concealed their presence in the audience, paying careful attention to elements they could use to incriminate the artists. The London performance ended abruptly when the police burst in through one door and the performers escaped through another, to be driven away hiding under blankets in the back of cars. *Meat Joy* was so challenging to some people that in Paris a man from the audience rushed onto the stage and attempted to strangle Schneemann, who "was saved by three older women who had never seen any performance, but were convinced that this assault was not part of it."[28]

As with most performances at the time and some today, the potential commercial value of *Meat Joy* suffered due to its lack of a permanent object to exhibit, preserve, and sell. In 1998, by when she had only sold two works to institutions in the US in 30 years, Schneemann lamented "the total economic neglect" of her work. Today, however, she sits in the pantheon of contemporary art, and in 2017 she was awarded the Golden Lion for Lifetime Achievement at the Venice Biennale. But despite the influence of her work, until very late in her career Schneemann struggled to gain recognition and achieve the level of financial success that seemed to come easily to her male peers, few of whom had taken risks even remotely comparable to those she took. Schneemann probed these issues herself:

Was I just a little too early? Or is it because my body of work explores a self-contained, self-defined, pleasured female-identified erotic integration?

Is that what the culture can't stand? It is interested. It gets tremendous courage, vitality, and feeds itself off this material I provided. But it will not come back and help me. It's almost as if it's saying, "If you've got all that, go feed yourself!"[29]

Schneemann used food as a way to reject established hierarchies and divisions within and between bodies, invoking joy and sensuality as a bulwark against a guilt-ridden culture rife with war, corruption, sexism, and myriad injustices. Her greatest achievement with *Meat Joy* is in having created a work that fed the culture of its time and continues to nourish culture today.

HANNAH WILKE

Chew Her Up and Spit Her Out

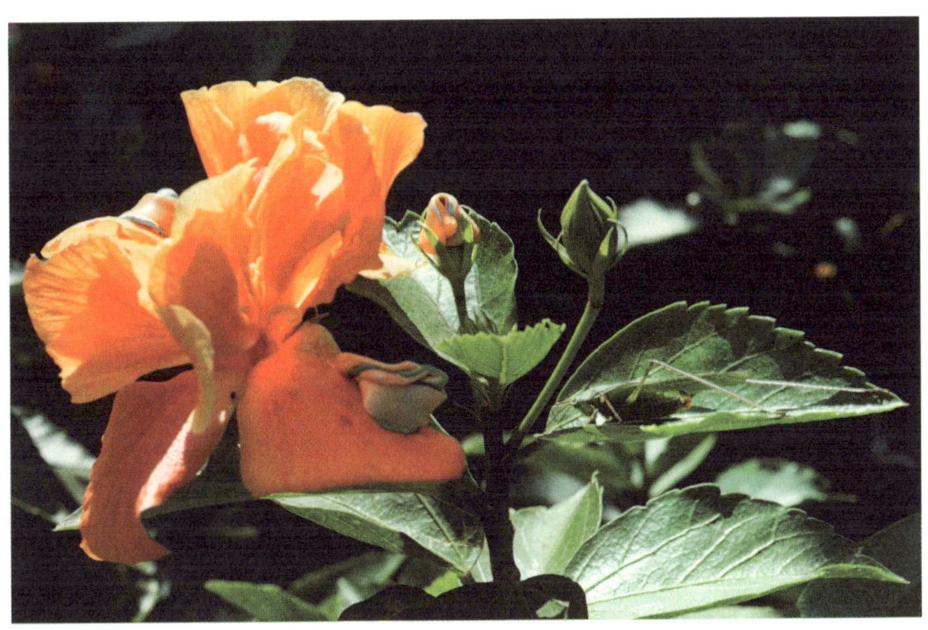

Hannah Wilke, *Gum with Grasshopper* (detail),
California Series, 1976. Archival pigment print, 2019.

A COMPOSITION IN GREENS and oranges: a fulsome hibiscus flower fills the left-hand side of the image, bathed by the sun's warm glow. The bloom is past its best, veined petals already curling back on themselves. Peeking out from the flower is a smooth band of dense-looking material, in the same orange color, bordered by bluish-green satiny edges. In the foreground, slumped on a petal is a similar slick shape, a striped mass of orange and green folded once over itself. Yet another layered wrap of color hugs a tightly closed bud. Each of these small sculptures is a stylized representation of a tiny, plump "cunt." New York-born artist Hannah Wilke used the term deliberately in a bid to destigmatize and reclaim it as a favorable signifier for the female body. Not quite abstract, but not exactly realistic either, her versions are made of chewed gum. Still bright and sweet and juicy, they glisten with the merest residue of saliva. The right-hand side of the image is dominated by fleshy green leaves. One of them cups a grasshopper, richly green but for a few pops of orange on its limbs and body, which match the flower at which it appears poised to leap. With the sun carving out light and shade, the image feels like morning. Do you know this time of day, in summer? The way it portends heat as the coolness of shade creeps up and away from the ground. Its flavors are tutti frutti and ice mint. Can you taste what you see?

The photograph is from Wilke's *California Series* (1976), part of her wider *Sculpture in the Landscape* project, begun around 1975 and featuring the gum sculptures she had been making since 1974 as well as earlier ceramic sculptures.[i] Wilke considered these sculptures "pleasurable objects."[1] For her, the vagina image was "primarily about inner feeling, the feeling of getting beyond oneself that one experiences when making love."[2] They can be seen as part of Wilke's extended creative

i In 1975, Wilke also shot images of gum sculptures in the ocean, suckered to rocks like barnacles and in other natural settings. In 1976, she made the photo montage *California Series* with three of the photos, and she made a postcard of the hibiscus and grasshopper image. The other *Gum in Landscape* photographs were shown posthumously in 2019 at her alma mater, the Tyler School of Art in Philadelphia, in a one-woman show titled Hannah Wilke: Sculpture in the Landscape.

dialogue with the work of Marcel Duchamp, in particular his creation of art infused with a cryptic eroticism and his proclivity for puns and wordplay (Duchamp named his alter-ego Rrose Sélavy, a homophone for "éros, c'est la vie"—eros is life). Wilke's gum vulvas were a woman's reply to Duchamp's "erotic objects," small enigmatic sculptures that include *Wedge of Chastity* (1954, cast 1963), a chunk of bronze implanted in a gum-like lump of pink dental plastic, and *Female Fig Leaf* (1950, cast 1961), cast from the nude, splayed female figure in his sculptural tableau *Étant donnés (Given: 1. The Waterfall, 2. The Illuminating Gas* (1946–66). Viewed through a peephole in a rough wooden fence, this enigmatic work is a sculptural diorama of an outdoor scene lit by a gas lamp held in the hand of a naked body lying on the ground with legs flung wide apart.

Whereas Duchamp's vulval imprint is a representation of the negative space around the female sexual organ, Wilke's gum sculptures are positive renderings of the vulva. But they also operate on a symbolic level. Wilke was fascinated with using the vulva as a way to convey the paradox of that which is both seen and unseen. For her, the vulvar sculpture signaled a space both literal and abstract, which has physical presence and concealed interiority. It was a "metaphysical statement" because it can't be fully comprehended with the eyes, and, as an unknown, she could "abstract it into art."[3]

The status of gum as a pseudo-food was important to Wilke, too. Chewed up and then spat out, gum is a stop-gap that provides neither the sugar rush of candy nor the nourishment of more wholesome food. It is an ersatz treat that delivers a taste sensation but cannot satisfy hunger, and in recent decades it has been reinvented as a virtuous substance purported to clean your teeth. For Wilke, gum was the "perfect metaphor for the American woman ... chew her up, get what you want out of her, throw her out and pop in a new piece."[4]

Yet gum also has an undeniable sensory appeal, from the thrill of unwrapping a stick from its pristine wrapper, to the texture of its patterned surface, its predictable shape and intense aroma: everything is designed to stimulate the senses. Wilke's sculptures exert a magnetic pull–push force on the viewer, evoking taste and inviting touch, but also challenging it with their suggestion of sensitive or raw flesh. As part of her 1975 exhibition at the Ronald Feldman Gallery, New York, she spelled out the connection between her work and the senses by providing a table full of gum for visitors to experiment with, and the instruction to "use all five senses."

Born Arlene Hannah Butter on 7 March 1940 in New York City, her parents were the children of Hungarian and Russian–Polish immigrants. Wilke lived on the Lower East Side of Manhattan as a child and used her first name until she was in her mid-20s. Her father, Emanuel Butter, worked as a labor lawyer and was active in progressive politics,[5] giving Wilke an early awareness of social justice and class issues. But her ambition was to be a star. As a young teenager, in 1954, she had her sister take photographs while she posed nude in her mother's mink stole and high-heeled shoes. Wilke knew from an early age that becoming a star also meant giving oneself up to be consumed by culture. To convey this double-edged destiny, she coined the neologism "starification," a pun on the way one can create oneself as an object of admiration, a star, and the inevitable traumas, or scars, that befall those who enjoy such a status.

Wilke's beauty was often commented upon. "She looks like a rose, but she talks like Voltaire,"[6] wrote Lil Picard in a 1973 issue of Andy Warhol's *Interview* magazine. Her conventionally attractive appearance was held against her by some feminists, who deemed it, and the way she used it in her art, a hindrance to any conceptual or political message she might have conveyed. But Wilke wasn't impressed by such attacks. She freely used her own body and image, liberally sprinkling her work with puns and double entendres. On the occasion of an exhibition of her early ceramic sculptures of boxes shaped like vulvas,[ii] she joked that "when you're beautiful, and I'm resigned to the fact that I am, no one ever looks inside you."[7] The supposed irreconcilability of beauty and moral or political responsibility was highlighted by art historian Linda Nochlin in her seminal 1971 essay "Why have there been no great women artists?" Nochlin wrote that "women are still caught up in their old role as bearers of virtue," a predicament with which Wilke toyed throughout her career.

The gum sculptures were examples of what Wilke called her "one-fold gestural sculptures." They are the most refined versions of the genital forms she had been making since 1960, when she was studying fine art and education at the Tyler School of Art at Temple University in Philadelphia. The early sculptures are rough boxes made from terracotta in which yonic and phallic forms sometimes coexist. To make these, she pushed and pulled the clay, leaving it ragged, and sometimes adding Liquitex to make it look permanently wet. She reworked these forms over several years until by the early 1970s she had devised a simplified one-fold gesture to make them. The one-fold works were confident and versatile, allowing for infinite variation in material, color, and size. Creating them was a ritual throughout Wilke's life. In the late 1970s when her mother, Selma Butter, became ill with cancer, she responded with colorful one-fold works on boards called the *Generation Process Series*, and she later created floor works with sculpture to mark her own cancer diagnosis in 1987. Her proposals for monumental outdoor one-fold sculptures remain unrealized but would undoubtedly be glorious.

Wilke's sculptures sat within the broad church of Post-minimalist art, which emerged in the late 1960s and 1970s,

ii For example, the sculpture *It Was a Lovely Day* (1964).

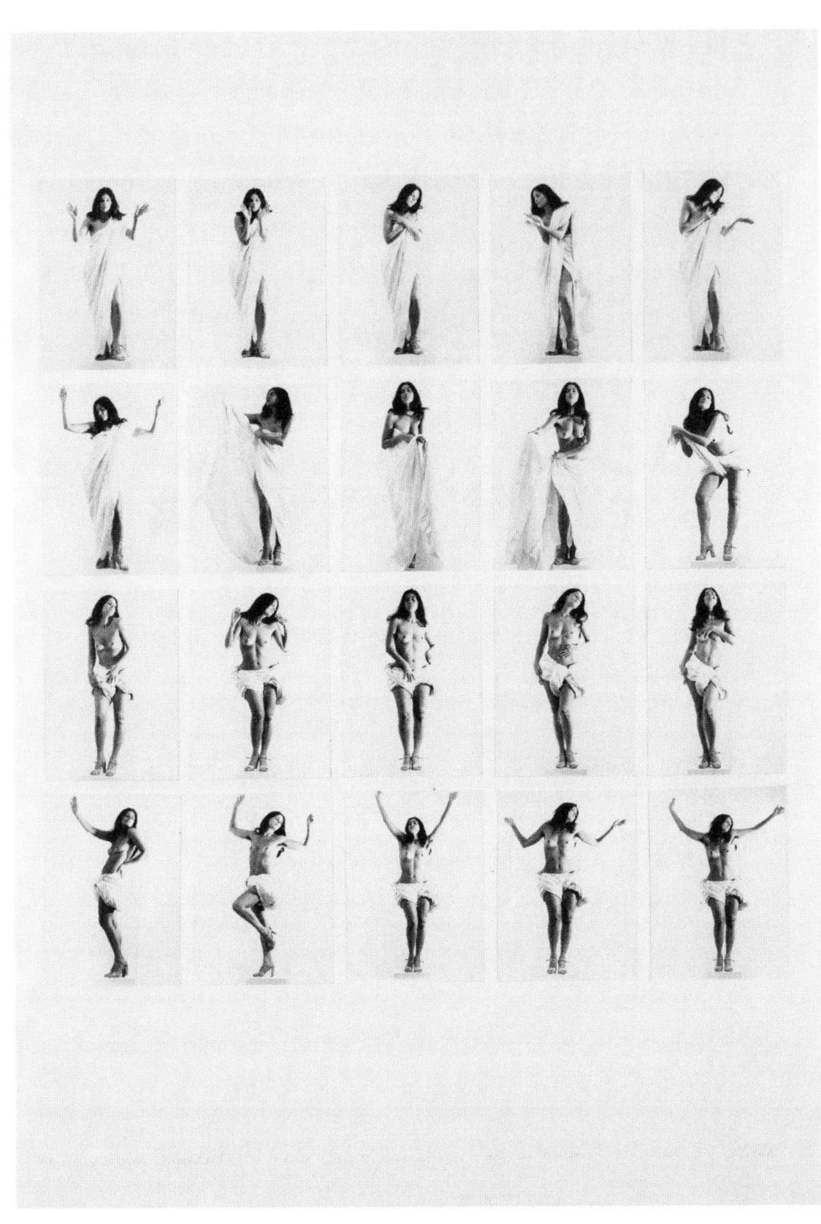

Hannah Wilke, *Super-t-Art*, 1974. Twenty gelatin silver prints framed together and signed "From a performance at the Kitchen, Nov. 1974."

and built on Minimalism's favored strategies of repetition, seriality, and grids and its interest in space, light, and materials. Her art shares an acute physical sensibility with Post-minimal works such as Robert Morris's draped felt pieces, which explored gravity, flexibility, and movement; Richard Serra's splash works, which tested the behaviors of liquids; and Eva Hesse's latex sculptures, which reconciled femininity and abstraction.

As well as using clay, Wilke made one-fold sculptures from unconventional materials including kneadable erasers, Play-Doh, and lint—both gray and tinted with fibers from colored fabrics, which she harvested from a clothes dryer while doing laundry for her partner, the sculptor Claes Oldenburg, in whose *Store Days* happening (1961) Schneemann had participated. Wilke also experimented with a wide range of foods, such as bacon, cookie dough, and chocolate. Her *Untitled (Bacon Fold)* (1976) is simply made from several thick rashers of streaky bacon folded over themselves and presented on a patterned glass plate. The meat is generously marbled with fat, hinting at the mid-century ideal of the nutritious and delicious all-American diner breakfast.

The idea for a sculpture made from chewing gum first came to Wilke in 1974, after a friend remarked that they wished her gray kneaded-eraser sculptures were in color. This led Wilke to the varied colors of chewing gum. One day, she bumped into friends on the street in Manhattan, and offered them some gum. One of them, critic Peter Frank, accepted, and as he chewed the gum Wilke made him promise to return it to her so she could make an art piece from it. Whether it was clay, latex, or bacon, Wilke chose materials for her work based on their sensory qualities, and gum was no different. Gum is made from resin, wax, and elastomer, and closely resembles the textures of plastic and rubber, making it an ideal material with which to mold sculptures that could last beyond the initial hit of flavor and sweetness.

Wilke was interested in the sensory complexity that a certain shape or texture might offer, and using food as a material allowed her to expand on this. Her work sought to translate what was "below the gut level ... into an art close to laughter, making love, shaking hands," something to which food was particularly well suited, given the myriad ways it can affect the body, senses, and emotions by being smelled and tasted, chewed, shared, handled, and preserved as an artwork, all of which Wilke did with chewing gum. But using highly sensual materials was also about enabling something more transcendent, which Wilke expressed as "rearranging the touch of sensuality with a residual magic."[8]

For *Fortunate Cookies* (1974), a work Wilke made for her second exhibition at the Ronald Feldman Gallery, Floor Show, she painted store-bought fortune cookies pink and arranged them on the floor, but not before removing the bad fortunes to protect herself and her audience from inauspicious messages. In the early 1980s, she created a series of 10-in.-high chocolate sculptures for the exhibition Feast Your Eyes at the Pratt Institute. These *Venus Pareve* statues (1982–4), later made in painted plaster, depict Wilke's body from mid-thigh and up, the arms cut off below the shoulders like a classical Venus.[iii] The foods were unorthodox art materials that offered Wilke malleability and suggested sensual pleasure, but they were also highly fragile and vulnerable to natural forces: in 1975 a rat ate a set of cookie dough sculptures she was keeping in her loft.

By using food to create sculptures of the female body, Wilke highlighted how patriarchal culture idealizes women as life-givers who can feed others with their bodies, while at the same time sexualizing them by symbolically aligning them to pleasurable but always ephemeral food. This is evident in the adjectives used to describe a pleasing woman ("sweet," "tasty," "luscious") and in those that refer to an undesirable or uncouth

iii *Pareve* is the Yiddish word for 'neutral'; in the observance of Jewish dietary laws (*kashrut*), *pareve* refers to foods made without milk, meat, or their derivatives, which can therefore be eaten with both meat and dairy, two classes of food that may not be consumed at the same meal.

woman ("sour," "tart"). Food was also part of Wilke's resistance to attempts to carve up the body into independent territories concerned with physical, mental, or sensual life. She wanted to bring these together in "a new language that fuses mind and body into erotic objects" related to "body and feelings, reflecting pleasure as well as pain, the ambiguity and complexity of emotions."[9]

Soon after creating her first gum sculpture, Wilke began work on her *S.O.S. Starification Series* (1974–5), a set of photographs she termed "performalist self-portraits,"[10] in which she reproduces clichéd female poses from advertising and women's magazines. Furnished with various accessories, including hair curlers, a child's toy, a telephone, and a man's necktie, she is alternately cute, ditzy, sophisticated, homely, sultry, and lascivious. In each of the portraits, tiny gum sculptures dot Wilke's skin, appearing on her face, chest, breasts, and fingernails, resembling blemishes, sores, lesions, or scars. For Wilke, they brought to mind ornamentation of the body through scarification rituals that mark rites of passage in some African cultures. Wilke also thought of the scar-like aspect of these chewing gum forms on her skin in relation to her Jewishness, noting that "during the war, I would have been branded and buried had I not been born in America."[11] In addition to the cultural associations the images bring up, Wilke was making herself over as a scarred fantasy of commodity culture that fetishizes materialistic and sexualized femininity. And not everyone was in favor of her approach: for the critic Ann-Sargent Wooster, contravening feminine ideals in the ways Wilke had done was deplorable, and she wrote a vicious condemnation of the work in *Artforum* magazine, accusing Wilke of having "'vulgarly accessorized' and 'crudded up' her 'perfect flesh' with her personal portable leprosy"[12] of chewing-gum sculptures.

Around the time Wilke was creating her *S.O.S. Starification Series*, she appeared in a food-themed performance event curated by the French-born American artist and Fluxus affiliate Jean Dupuy at avant-garde performance art venue The Kitchen in SoHo, New York City. Held in November 1974, *Soup & Tart* featured a dinner of soup, bread, and apple tart served with wine, along with a "menu" of around 30 performers appearing in alphabetical order, including Philip Glass, Joan Jonas, Yvonne Rainer, Richard Serra, and Gordon Matta-Clark—one of the founders of the artist-run restaurant FOOD, who sawed open a wooden box to reveal a house-shaped cake, which he carved into slices. Wilke was the final act of the evening. She premiered *Super-t-Art*, a performance that played on the resonances between appetite for food and lust for the female body. She appeared wearing white high-heeled sandals, her naked body enfolded in a white sheet, and she moved through a series of poses suggesting different cultural and religious archetypes, from goddess, virgin mother and saint, to whore and female Christ crucified for her sexuality. She ran the gamut from innocent and pure, or "sweet," to lustful and wanton, or "super tarty." No matter which pose she adopted, whether her hands were thrown wide with exuberance or her head coyly tilted or tossed back, the context of the evening cast her as an edible woman, offering herself up to be consumed. The audience was mostly quiet throughout the performance, except for a few guffaws from men, but its culmination was eerily silent, perhaps a response to the implied act of "serving" a crucified female body to an audience who were busy eating dinner.

Nakedness, for Wilke, was "fundamentally a gesture of celebration."[13] Throughout her life she played with tropes of the pin-up and the celebrity figure, and referenced art-historical images of Venus, especially Sandro Botticelli's iconic *The Birth of Venus* (*c.*1485), emphasizing their glamor, beauty, vulgarity, and exaltation. These were attributes she embraced in her own life, and during her career she and her art were featured in a range of art publications as well as erotic magazines including *Playboy*, *Penthouse*, *Viva*, and *Oui*. Wilke incorporated her private life as subject matter in these articles, creating herself as a work of art, a character, and a "starification" object. "I become my art; my art becomes me," she wrote in 1975.[14]

In January 1975, Wilke was invited to participate in the exhibition Artists Make Toys at the Clocktower, the gallery that eventually became MoMA PS1 in New York City. Building on her *S.O.S. Starification Series* portraits, she created the *S.O.S. Starification Object Series: An Adult Game of Mastication*. A proposed multiple for which only the prototype was ever made, it includes a box that recalls Marcel Duchamp's famous *Boîte-en-valise*, a portable collection of miniature versions of his best-known works. Wilke's installation contained 28 starification photographs, Xeroxed game instructions, one large starification self-portrait for the wall, 48 numbered playing cards, eight loose photographs from the *S.O.S. Starification Series*, six boxes of Chiclets candy-coated chewing gum pellets in a range of flavors, and 16 packs of stick gum in assorted flavors, including Juicy Fruit, Doublemint, and Big Red. Later, Wilke added 12 gum sculptures in Plexiglas boxes to the prototype game set. Last but by no means least, the work, now in the permanent collection of the Centre Pompidou, Paris, then included the S.O., or Starification Object: Wilke herself. To play the game, gallery visitors would have to rent her for $1,500.

The rules were as follows: each player was instructed to choose a flavor of gum and, while they chewed it, turn over a card that would determine the pose the S.O. would adopt. After chewing their gum, they were to give it to the S.O., who would then sculpt it into a "starification object"—a tiny one-fold sculpture. The instructions were written in a playful, non-threatening way, encouraging players to "Always try something new. Remember, the S.O. will always help you."

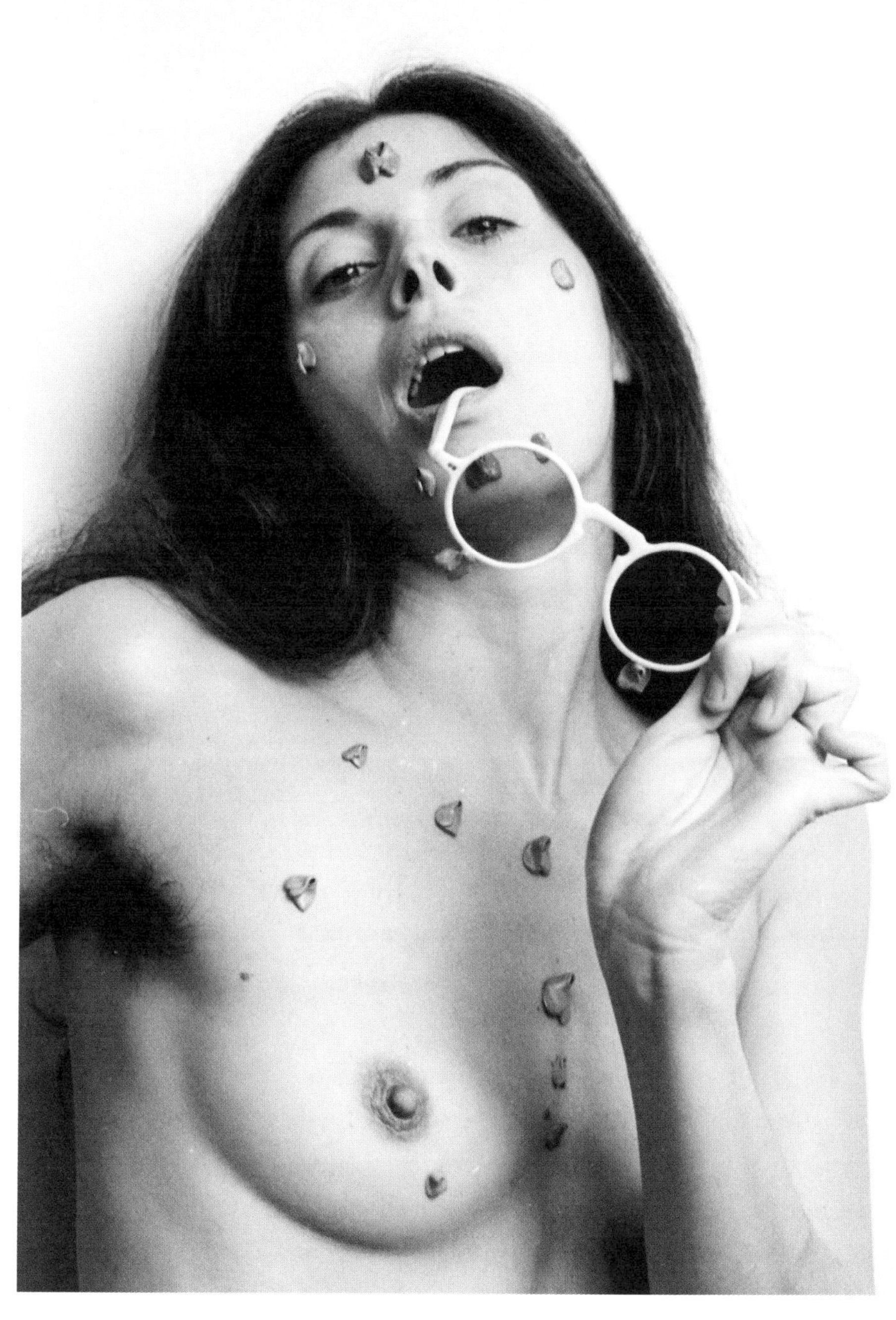

Hannah Wilke, *S.O.S. Starification Object Series*, 1974. Black and white gelatin silver print. Performalist self-portrait with Les Wollam.

After Wilke sculpted the forms, she would return them to the players, who were instructed to place them on the S.O., who became more starified as the game went on. Once the "series" was completed, a gum card would be drawn. The player whose flavor matched the one shown on the card would win the game and receive a photo of him- or herself with the S.O., to be sent later in a brown paper envelope with all the gum from the pose, which they could use to play the game again.[15]

Wilke revisited the interactive aspect of the *S.O.S. Starification Series* in a three-hour-long performance for the exhibition 5 Américaines à Paris (5 American Women in Paris) at the Gerald Piltzer Gallery, Paris, in February 1975. She offered her audience 3,000 pieces of American stick chewing gum, asking them to chew and return a wad to her so she could sculpt it. The finished sculptures were either placed on paper and pinned to the wall or applied to Wilke's naked torso or face. As she accumulated gum cunts on her body, people's attention to what she was doing and how she looked grew, and so did her star—and scar—quotient.

Another version of the game was part of Wilke's performance *My Country 'tis of Thee* (1976), which marked the US Bicentennial Independence Day, at the Albright-Knox Gallery in Buffalo, New York. On this occasion, the communal chewing activity was for an audience comprising adults and children. Wilke had experience with teaching her niece and nephews to chew gum for her. She had also earned her teaching certificate in Philadelphia, and over the course of her life taught for around 30 years, both at two high schools and at the New York School of Visual Arts. Here, the children and their parents supplied her with their just-chewed gum, which she placed on paper and used to build up a frieze around the base of the gallery's neoclassical portico. Three 11-ft-tall cardboard cut-outs of Wilke, bare-breasted in a toga and a laurel crown, looked down on proceedings.

These participatory gum performances provided people with a flavor sensation, a potentially erotic charge, and an opportunity to link chance with creativity. They also flouted conventions around sweets, including the warning typically issued to children not to take candy from strangers, the notion that it is uncouth to chew gum in public places (let alone to spit it out and stick it to civic architecture), and the warning that saliva, held in spent gum, transmits germs and disease. In these games Wilke was also playing with her own body, and because the gum contained residue from the chewers' mouths, she implicated their bodies in the game too, conjoining their biological traces with hers, and preserving them in her art.

Throughout her career, Wilke used her own body and chewing gum to make her message clear, whether it was around the social potential of play or the dangers of extremist ideologies. In 1977, her gum sculptures featured in a poster she designed of a photograph from the *S.O.S. Starification Object Series,* depicting her with her shirt open to the waist, a man's necktie hanging down between her breasts, and starification gum vulvas on her face, neck, and torso. Above and below the image is Wilke's slogan "Marxism and Art: Beware of Fascist Feminism."[iv] She later explained her rationale for the line: "I felt that feminism could easily become fascistic if people believe that feminism is only their kind of feminism, and, not my kind of feminism, or, her kind of feminism, or his kind of feminism."[16] It was partly a response to the accusations of narcissism that had been leveled against her by some feminists. According to Wilke, these were an expression of "fascist feminism," a problematic rehashing of male supremacy that failed to properly account for, among other things, the nourishing capacity of women. Throughout her life, Wilke engaged with the vexed symbolism of women's bodies, not least as potential providers of food, a capacity she attributed to "the physical superiority of woman as the life source."[17]

iv *Marxism and Art: Beware of Fascist Feminism* was made in response to an invitation in 1975 from the Center for Feminist Art Historical Studies for a project entitled What is Feminist Art?, and it was shown as part of an exhibition at the Women's Building in Los Angeles in 1977.

SARAH LUCAS

The Unsavory Aspect of the Usually Discreet

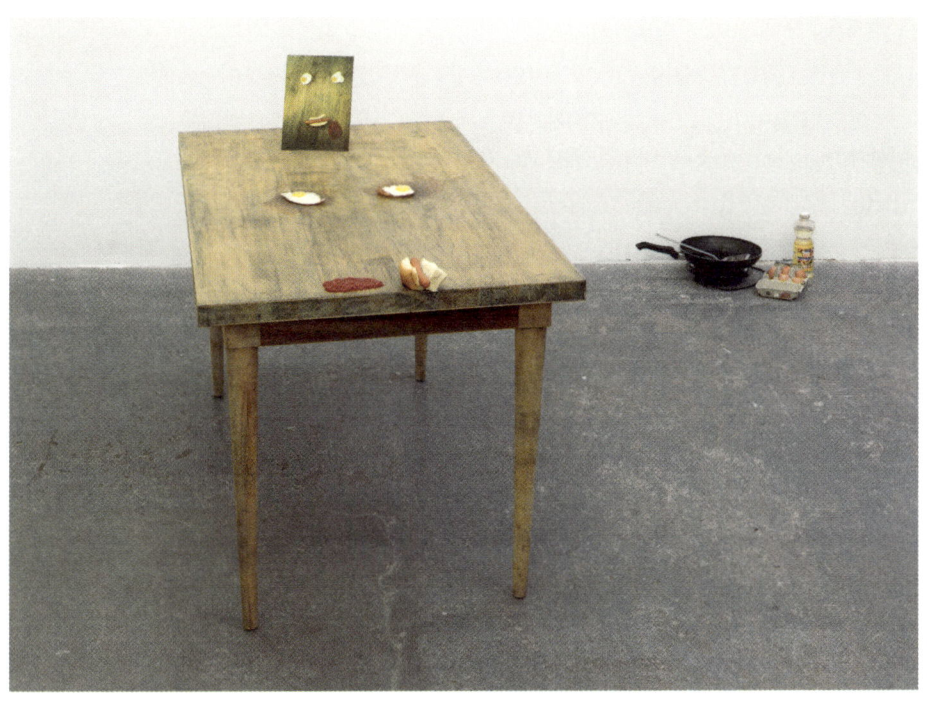

Sarah Lucas, *Fucked*, 1995. Table, eggs, hot dog, photograph, and frying pan.

EVERY MORNING ON HER WAY to open her 1992 solo exhibition The Whole Joke, London-born sculptor Sarah Lucas bought a kebab. When she got to the gallery space—a former shop on Kingly Street in London's Soho neighborhood—she fried two eggs on a portable stove and began putting together a fresh version of her work. The show featured a pair of new sculptures: *Two Fried Eggs and a Kebab*, installed in the shop front visible from the street, and *The Old Couple*, a composition with two chairs, one with a dildo placed upright on the seat, the other harboring a set of dentures poised to bite any backsides tempted to sit on it.

The descriptive title *Two Fried Eggs and a Kebab* leaves a few things out. The sculpture also included a kitchen table on which Lucas arranged the titular food to evoke a female frontal nude, and a photograph propped up at the head of the table. The image is a diminutive work-within-a work, a food-portrait in which the arrangement of the eggs and kebab also seems to stand in for a rudimentary face with a gormless expression. "They're so much like a pair of eyes, aren't they?" Lucas says as she fries eggs in the 1996 BBC documentary *Two Melons and a Stinking Fish*, which follows her around London as she makes her work. We watch her sculpt. She handles the eggs and arranges them directly on the table, explaining how she first stripped the varnish from the wooden surface, which developed dark oil patches where the eggs sat, and later re-varnished it to preserve those stains. When she positions the kebab—a large doner, dry, with no salad or sauce—in its slot, a rough slit hewn out of the wood, she presses it down, using her fingers to widen the pitta bread, slightly tearing it in the process, and poking at the brown strips of cold meat, one of which falls out and lands on the tabletop.

Lucas later incorporated the cooking equipment into a work in its own right. *Fucked* (1995) bears a clear resemblance to *Two Fried Eggs and a Kebab*, but this time it is a body sketched out with a pair of fried eggs and a hotdog in a bun, served up to the viewer on a wooden table. Nearby, the frying pan and portable stove plugged into the wall sit alongside a spatula, eggs, and vegetable oil. The sculpture's ambiguous title, also slang for being drunk, evokes several scenarios. Fried eggs can be a fast, cheap, and nourishing meal whether it is after a hard night's drinking or in advance of a hard day's work. In *Fucked* the female sex suggested by *Two Fried Eggs and a Kebab* has shifted, and the work is more ambiguous. Another sculpture Lucas made around the same time also sets up a food-based still life on and around a table. *Bitch* (1995) is a submissive form facing the floor. A vacuum-packed kipper is nailed to the side of the table, and a t-shirt wrapped around the tabletop hangs heavy with melons poking through holes cut in the fabric. Here, the table legs have the strongest anthropomorphic charge of any of Lucas's table works. With its disparaging substitution of a smelly fish for a vagina and its derogatory title, *Bitch* gives off a nasty air. To portray the female form in this way is to degrade the female body. Or it would be, were Lucas not a woman lacking any apparent sense of shame in her use of sexual and sexist references. She leaves it up to us to choose to become exercised or to laugh along with the joke. While Wilke focused on creating tenderly abstracted vulvas for the benefit of both male and female audience members, describing her work as "a specifically female iconography for both sexes,"[1] Lucas used food to lay out crude and sardonic versions of a range of sexual organs.

In Lucas's sculptures, as in the work of Carolee Schneemann and other artists in this book, the use-value of food as nourishment is traded for its symbolic value and sensory affect. We are not invited to eat the foods in Schneemann's *Meat Joy* or in Lucas's sculptures, but to consider their cultural and conceptual meanings as part of their art. Still life paintings of food invite similar reflections, but Lucas's sculptures make use of actual food, not pictures of food and certainly not noble materials like stone or bronze. Her early arrangements used furniture and food to eschew the traditions of Western art, which required the artist to create a realistic copy of something in the world. Her works feature oily, smelly foods and are prepared by cooking, not carving. She uses ordinary materials we all know, and by introducing them into the gallery environment she disrupts the sensory order and carefully guarded sterility of the fine-art environment. These strange, absurd, and sometimes violent works trigger multi-sensory, visceral responses in the body: revulsion, salivation, or hunger pangs; an urge to sniff the air for the lingering aroma of foods; or a memory of having eaten them. As the artist Angus Fairhurst, her partner for several years in the 1990s, wrote of Lucas's art, "What is normally hidden—the unsavory aspect of the usually discreet—is flaunted."[2] In her irreverence for artistic delicacy and harmony, Lucas flouted the expectation that art must be serious.

Sarah Lucas was born in 1962 in Holloway, North London, to a milkman father and a mother who worked part time as a gardener and cleaner. While studying fine art at Goldsmiths College from 1984 to 1987, she met several of the artists who would become known as the Young British Artists (YBAs), a moniker cooked up by advertising executive and art collector Charles Saatchi, who bought and championed their work. For six months in 1993, Lucas and her friend the artist Tracey Emin ran The Shop, a studio and meeting place on Bethnal Green Road, where they made and sold small editions of their artworks and built their reputations as hedonistic and unruly artists.

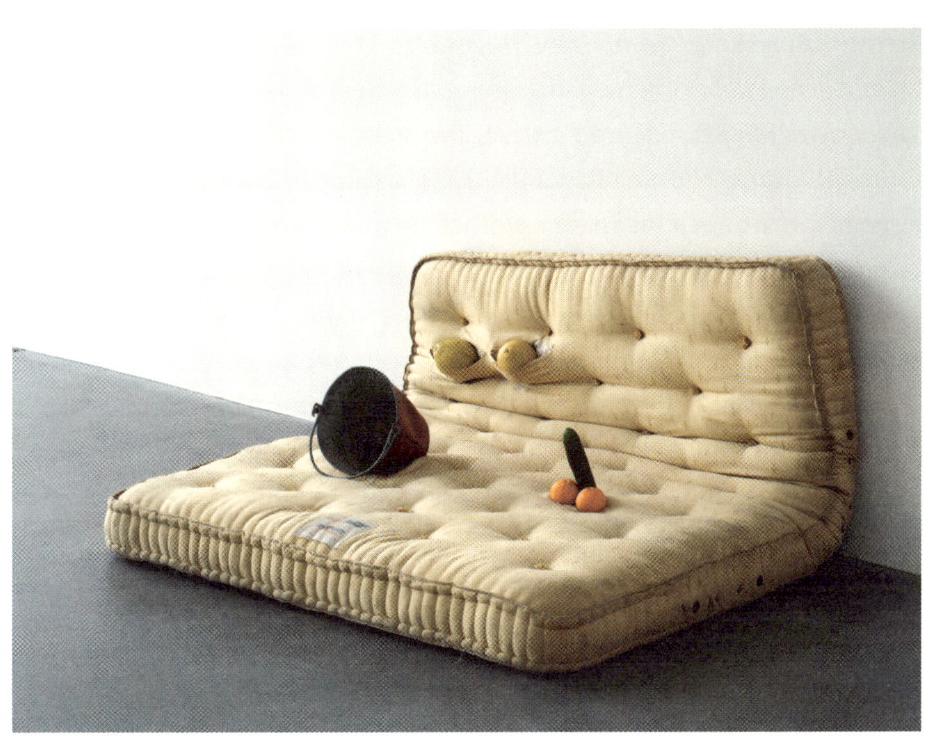

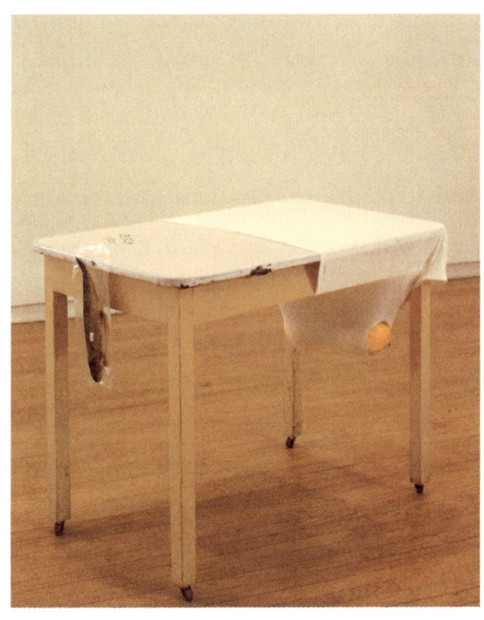

TOP Sarah Lucas, *Au Naturel*, 1994. Mattress, melons, oranges, cucumber, water, and bucket. BOTTOM Sarah Lucas, *Bitch*, 1995. Table, t-shirt, melons, and kipper.

The unglamorous essentials of daily life inspired much of Lucas's work, from the cheap foods available in local convenience stores, to habitual activities like sitting on the toilet—the subject of a series of works including *Human Toilet II* (1997), a nude self-portrait of Lucas sitting on a lavatory holding the cistern on her lap—and lying in bed. The last is the setting for one of her most famous works, *Au Naturel* (1994), which features an old mattress slumped against a wall and a collection of fruit and veg made to signify human bodies. Lucas sliced the mattress's fabric covering, inserted a pair of heavy melons into the slits, and placed an empty metal bucket with its opening facing the viewer in front of the fruit to complete her perfunctory female nude. Beside the bucket, a cucumber pokes out of another hole in the mattress, bolstered by a pair of oranges at its base: the male nude.

Grubby and bare, the mattress connotes slum-like living conditions or homelessness, a reference perhaps to the prevalence of squatting among young artists in the East End of London in the early 1990s. *Au Naturel* is also part of a lineage of candid bed-themed artworks that includes Robert Rauschenberg's *Bed* (1955), one of his early "combines." At the time of making *Bed*, Rauschenberg couldn't afford expensive art materials, so he used the pillow, sheet, and quilt from his own bed, which he mounted on wood supports, scrawled with graphite, and daubed and dripped with oil paint. In 1969, John Lennon and Yoko Ono staged their famous *Bed-In* performances, staying—and eating—in bed for a week in hotels in Amsterdam and Montreal to protest the Vietnam War and promote world peace. In 1998, Lucas's close friend and collaborator Tracey Emin made *My Bed*, which presents the stark reality of a suffering woman's unmade bed, littered with condoms, medicines, blood-stained underwear, empty bottles, and full ashtrays. Like the food in Lucas's sculptures, the situations and objects in these pieces gained new meaning in their transition from the everyday to art.

In Lucas's handling, basic foods and objects can convey a funny, debased, or debauched tone, but they also communicate the artist's astute grasp of our predicament as human animals. In fact, it may be precisely because these materials are considered unsophisticated that they carry such affect. As Lucas told Fairhurst: "The best magic comes out of the things that are the most concrete."[3] Items of food in these sculptures operate as synecdoche: parts we instantly understand as representing whole bodies. In *Au Naturel*, Lucas chose to use fresh fruit and vegetables liable to wither and sag over time, a fate shared by human flesh. The way the mattress sinks and leans, edging ever closer to the ground, also suggests weariness, the heaviness of flesh and fat accumulated on middle-aged bodies, and perhaps also the yawning ennui of some long-term relationships.

If Lucas's tabletop sculptures alert the nose, *Au Naturel* seems more concerned with touch and the sense of space. Standing in front of it triggers an awareness of one's own body in relation to the two figures plotted out on the mattress, a feeling of what it might be like to lie or sit half-up on the mattress with heavy breasts or an erect penis. The horizontal orientation of the mattress—even the part that leans against the wall seems to be heading south—flouts the spatial norm of contemporary art galleries, in which the vertical axis—the wall—is preferred for the display of paintings, which are usually much easier to handle than unwieldy old mattresses and fresh food. On a more detailed level, there is an alluring tactility to the mattress fabric, the skin of the melons, and the cucumber's turgidity. Lucas's food works evoke specific activities, from seducing to fucking, sleeping to cooking, eating, and drinking. But despite the suggestion of action, the works themselves are strangely static. The objects from which they are made are whole, their appearance clear, not streaked or blurred with energetic gestural marks as they are in some paintings. As food portraits they display an uncanny stillness: the apathy of bodies reduced to cucumbers and melons.

Food, speech, and laughter are all intimately associated with the mouth. In Lucas's self-portrait *Eating a Banana* (1990), she glares at the camera as she prepares to bite into the peeled fruit. It's a picture that is both perverse and plain, straightforward and sexual. As Fairhurst pointed out, the image "is not a metaphor but knows it looks like one and plays it for laughs as well as straight."[4] Such deadpan wittiness relies on our familiarity with both sides of the equation: the original being lampooned and the material parodying it. Some foods have especially complex and contradictory cultural associations. While fruits and vegetables are connected with health and vitality, and can be used to signal wholesomeness, virtue, purity, or innocence, they also carry negative connotations, for example when they symbolize the forbidden fruits whose eating gave rise to human sin. Equally ambiguous are processed meat or fried foods. The doner kebab, a food often eaten at the end of a night out drinking, combines hot slices of processed meat with raw onions, cabbage, and garlic sauce to send up a pungent aroma that lingers in the air and on the body. The name is also a British slang term for "vulva," and the kebab itself is a signifier for class and social status, linked in the popular imagination to the diets of students and immigrants. The smoked fish of *Bitch* makes an olfactory allusion to the smell sometimes imputed to vaginas. Lucas's stand-ins for sexual body parts take their cues from slang, not lyrical poetry.

There is a puerile aspect to Lucas's humor, a tittering, awkward immaturity that can't stay away from the object of its sexual fascination. Her works also engage on a visceral level with the rawness, wetness, and stickiness of the sexual act, and the stale condition of marital slump, rather than the romanticized ideal of love. It is not so much sensuality or eros that is on show, but lustiness, which brings with it elements of titillation and squalor. When she was frying the eggs for that first show, Lucas recalls, "a heck of a lot of people came and stood looking in the window and I'd tell them to come in, but they'd just scuttle off. I don't know ... it was good frying the eggs, I felt a bit like a dirty old man."[5] The wittiness of the works pairs with a seedy side, apparent in Lucas's use of sexist tropes, crude imagery, and unflinching directness. They elbow out discussion of high or low culture; instead, it becomes a question of how affecting they are: does a vacuum-packed smoked fish for a vagina make you laugh, retch, or rage? Lucas, who has said that she finds sex embarrassing, seems to enjoy playing at sexism. But is laughing along with her a ploy to avert confrontation, or is it complicity?

Lucas continues to use eggs in her work. In 2017, she first staged her performance *One Thousand Eggs: For Women*, in which 1,000 of Lucas' friends and collaborators threw 1,000 fresh eggs at white gallery walls. Part social event, part protest, it asked women and men dressed as women to handle everyday symbols of fertility and life and to unleash their energies by smashing them into a tacky, gloopy, smelly scramble. Although the event was lively and cathartic, its primary goal was to create art, an intention Lucas underscored when she told participants it was about "being really neat, and making the most beautiful egg painting."[6]

For all their possible meanings and associations, in Lucas's view materials must be allowed to express themselves honestly, whether that has to do with their class associations, smells, or decomposition. "You can't torture them into being something they don't want to be," she has said.[7] Nevertheless, disobedient materials like food need a carer, a role traditionally allotted to women. The rot constantly threatens to set in, so when works like *Au Naturel* and *Two Fried Eggs and a Kebab* are

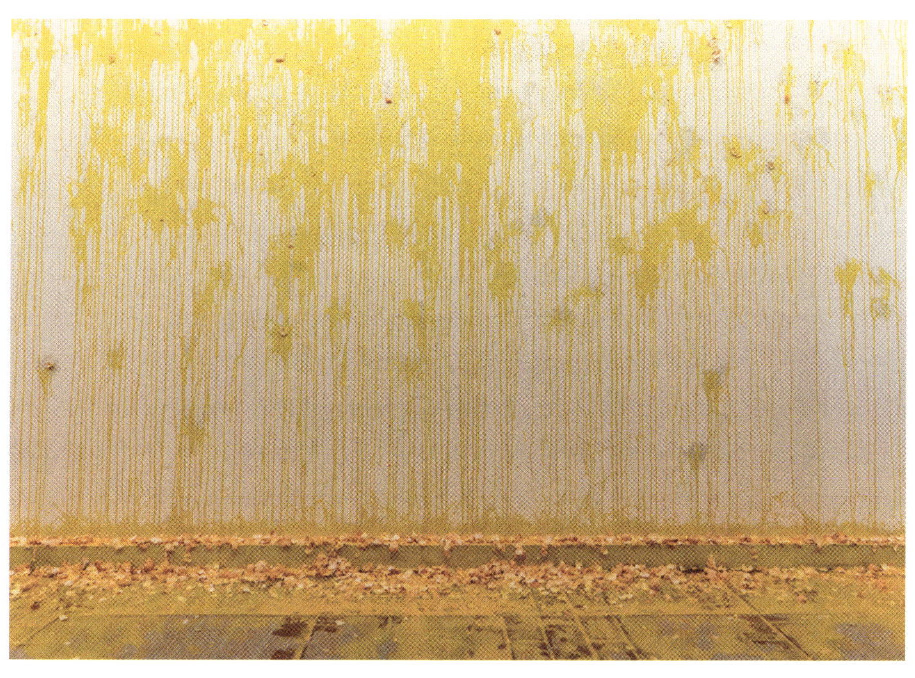

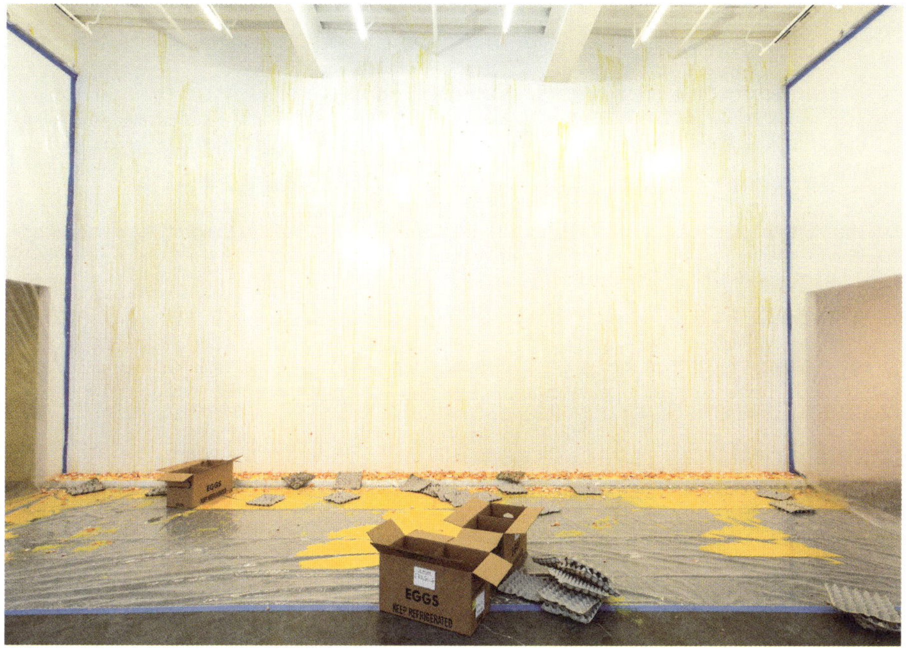

Sarah Lucas, *One Thousand Eggs: For Women*, 2018. Documentation of the performance held at the New Museum, New York.

displayed, Lucas or her assistants dutifully fetch supplies and check for freshness: is the cucumber still stiff, are the melons still firm? This daily ritual of shopping and cooking plugs the art into a system of mundane consumption, relying on a secure and constant supply of ingredients and feminine labor.

In his 1995 essay "Look back in hunger," *New Yorker* critic Anthony Lane wonders why women make such great cookery writers. He suspects it is in part due to the fact that "they realize it is enough to be a great cook, whereas men, larded with pride in their own accomplishments, invariably go one step too far and try to be great *chefs*."[8] Whether women in general have chosen the domestic kitchen because of their humility and sensible nature, as Lane suggests, or because a repressive patriarchy kept them there, this book demonstrates that great women artists have used food as a material in ways unimaginable to their male counterparts. Yet, Lucas recognizes the absurdity in this kind of neat carving up of gender roles, and traces the gender ambiguity that pervades her work back to her childhood, when her father "was the tits" of the family by virtue of his job as a milkman. And as an artist, Lucas has skated over gender categories, obfuscating anatomical references, playing with sexist humor, and enjoying her own masculinity—"I like inserting myself into blokiness,"[9] she has declared.

When Lucas began making work using food in the early 1990s, the second wave of feminism had already been historicized and the third wave was just about to begin. Instead of accepting a moral duty to tackle gender politics in her work, as had previously been expected of women artists, Lucas approached gender from a range of positions, playing with sexist tropes that reduced women to basic foodstuffs, and reconstructing sexual clichés in sculptural form. As Fairhurst described Lucas, "on the surface it was all bitch: tough, uncompromising, unashamedly staking a claim to traditional male territories of bravado, the threat of violence, and the flaunting of the saltier aspects of the body."[10] But there is also indulgence and compassion in Lucas's appraisal of the human body, with its spillages, stains, and smells, and in the sentiments wafting up from her works: affection from *Au Naturel*, vulnerability from *Two Fried Eggs*, and rage from *Bitch*.

As well as being somewhat freed from gender-based expectations of her work, on a practical level Lucas was released from the sacrifices expected of women during the 1960s and 1970s: the obligation to choose between work and motherhood, or between the roles of "beautiful woman and artist ... flirt and feminist," as Lucy Lippard had demanded Hannah Wilke choose. Lucas's ability to play with sexuality, gender, and food was indebted to the work of artists like Schneemann, Wilke, and Piper, for whom risk, play, pleasure, and joy were avowedly political acts, and who demanded the right to deploy ambiguity and complexity in their lives as in their work. The platform built by feminists in the 1960s and 1970s also opened up a space for artists like Lucas to introduce elements of working-class culture into their work, which exposed the ways in which earlier work reflected the relative privilege and class aspirations of the artists who made it.

In the 1990s, Britain was in an economic recession, the result of global factors and years of government policy that led to industrial decline in areas such as coal mining and steel production. One cultural by-product of the recession was the growth of nostalgia for a disappearing working-class culture, for example in the popular television show *Only Fools and Horses ...*, a long-running comedy set in working-class Peckham. Looking through rose-tinted glasses at social and economic conditions was one thing, but Lucas brought her own twist to the trend by both celebrating and denigrating the signifiers of English working-class culture, such as cheap foods and tabloid newspapers, the latter in a series of works consisting of photocopies of salacious tabloid articles. Her works appealed to a wide audience, eliciting recognition, shock, amusement, and outrage. They have been seen as part of a growing sense of "Englishness" as a cultural identity that emerged at the time. With the public visibility of the YBAs, including in newspaper coverage of them staggering out of private members clubs in Soho and drunken appearances on prime-time television shows, came an idea that there might be a particularly English kind of art premised on popular culture. This was at a time when globalization was changing the status of the UK and its four nations. In her study of *Au Naturel*, art historian Amna Malik linked the work to cultural theorist Stuart Hall's claim that globalization had contributed to making "Englishness an ethnicity, which stripped it of its earlier claim to universality—a claim that was the legacy of its colonial rule, eroded once Britain had lost its pre-eminence as an economic and political power."[11]

For the British critic John Roberts, Lucas's work in the 1990s was part of a historical tendency to play out class divisions in the gallery and museum. But, while historically this division meant that high culture was for the benefit of the upper class and the working class were considered "plebs," Lucas and her peers reversed this trend by bringing working-class culture into the most exalted art institutions in the land, including the Royal Academy of Arts and the Tate. According to Roberts, this reversal hinged on the historically attributed sensuous, craving condition of the working class. They were placed at the lower end of both the social and sensory hierarchies, associated with poor foods, bad smells, and animalistic pleasure-seeking. At the opposite end of the scale were the upper classes and their alignment with rationality. Lucas's work, Roberts wrote, enacted the "revenge of a stereotyped proletarian cognition (pure appetite; a body without subjectivity) on the deracinated body of bourgeois culture and the piety of identity politics that has no place for the voluptuous and the transgressive."[12]

The messiness and disorder of works incorporating food are radically opposed to the sterile and static environment of the white cube, the dominant architectural model for displaying art at the time when Lucas made her food-based works. In their perishability, Lucas's sculptures—like the works of Piper, Schneemann, and Wilke—challenge the ideals of order and permanence that haunt the history of art, and affect its contemporary production and display. Although originally made in the informal setting of The Shop, Lucas's work was embraced in the white cube environment. Her sculptures insert everyday sensuality into the pristine white cube, bringing with them their eggy smell and tendency to decay. With their marriage of fresh fruits, eggs, and processed meats with discarded furniture, these sculptures exist in limbo, partway between being wholly inanimate and showing faint signs of life. They are zombie *memento mori*, rising again every time they are replenished with fresh foods. In activating our awareness of smells, hunger, amusement, or disgust, they not only return us to our senses but remind us of our own best-before date.

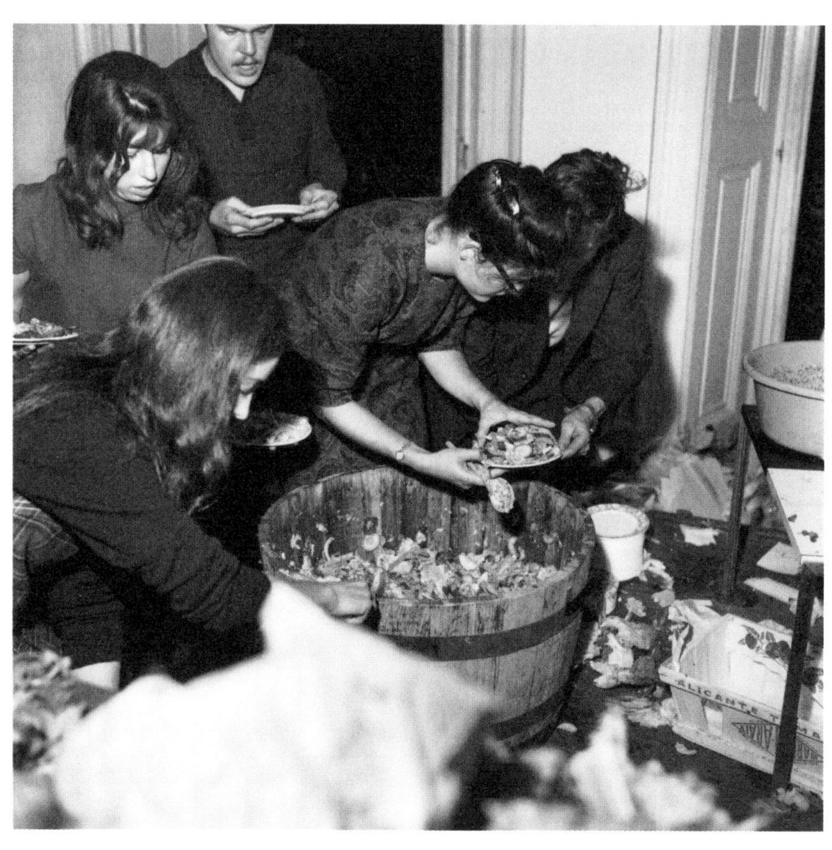

Alison Knowles, *Proposition (Make a Salad)*, 1962. Documentation of the performance at the Festival of Misfits, ICA, London. Gelatin silver print.

ALISON KNOWLES

A Recipe for Art and Life

ON THE EVENING of 20 October 1962, American artist Alison Knowles was in a London taxicab with her husband, the artist Dick Higgins, trying to figure out her next creative move. "Well, what are you going to do?" Higgins asked her, about her plans for the Fluxus concert due to take place the following day at the Institute of Contemporary Arts in London. A small room was booked for the event in the ICA's grand Regency-style building, situated on The Mall, the tree-lined avenue leading from Trafalgar Square to Buckingham Palace. Knowles looked at Higgins and said, "What can I do?" A split second later, she wondered aloud, "Why don't I do something with food? Why don't I make a salad?"[1]

The next morning, Knowles recalled she "had no time to do anything but buy the vegetables ... And meanwhile, of course, people were expecting some huge show."[2] Fluxus performances, or "Fluxconcerts" as they were also known, tended to be put together at the last minute, which contributed to their charm and restless energy. Even though planning was a short-term affair, the group usually had a sense of what they were going to be doing by the time they were presenting. The events brought together individual artists, often with competing aims, and the appearance of unity within Fluxus, the radical experimental performance group founded in 1960 by the Lithuanian American artist George Maciunas, concealed a fractious reality. According to Knowles, "People always thought they were meeting this completely compatible group," but there were often people in the group who didn't get along.

The Fluxus movement drew on the historical precedents of Futurism and Dada, in particular the work of Marcel Duchamp, but the main impetus for the movement came from music and poetry, not art.[3] It was inspired by the way composer John Cage incorporated chance and everyday objects in his music, and dipped into different media, genres, and techniques, crossing the line between performer and audience to produce what Maciunas called "living art."

Artists associated with Fluxus, including Joseph Beuys, Yoko Ono, Nam June Paik, and La Monte Young, came together during Fluxconcerts, the first of which took place in 1962 in Wiesbaden, Germany, followed by several around Europe during 1962–3, including the one at London's ICA. Using whatever materials were available to create performances, Fluxus artists celebrated randomness and DIY approaches, and their democratic anti-elitist attitude meant everyone was invited to attend and take part. The goal was to annihilate the separation between art and life, a boundary that reflected and reinforced social divisions, inequality, and inauthenticity. What better way for Knowles to achieve this than by recruiting food—a material that could infiltrate both art and life?

Fluxus events could be exuberant, funny, and sometimes chaotic. The first execution of *Make a Salad* was characteristically fraught and more than a little vaudevillian, thanks in part to a "little man in a red jacket who served the drinks," who forbade Knowles from using any water to wash the salad because he needed it to wash glasses. When she protested, he raised his voice, whereupon fellow Fluxus artist Robert Filliou came to her rescue with brute force, picking up the barman by his lapels, shaking him and ordering him to "give her whatever she wants."

In Knowles's salad work, the amplified process of preparing the ingredients generates a musical component or a cacophony, depending on the audience's receptivity. She didn't think it would ever be reprised after its first performance, but it soon became one of her most famous and popular scores. It has been performed in museums, theaters, and universities; in outdoor spaces; in upside-down kettle drums; and with the sounds of washing, chopping, grating, and mixing amplified at concerts. At a staging for 300 people in Denmark, as part of a concert funded by the music conservatory, it "turned out to be a very rebellious piece." On that occasion the audience took offence—"some carrots were thrown back"—although some people stayed to watch Knowles and her associates wash and chop the vegetables they had dragged onstage, and toss the salad with a cheese dressing in a barrel donated by Crosse & Blackwell, a maker of preserves. In the end, the vexed audience members succumbed to the powerful draw of free food and were tempted back to eat the salad.[4]

What was it that so offended those concertgoers? Was it the disruption of sensory order: the fact that food, with its uncontrollable smells and risk of mess, had been imported into a space devoted to listening? Or was it that a rudimentary process requiring neither qualifications nor specialist equipment undermined the high art environment? Perhaps making a salad was not considered artful or serious enough for such grand surroundings. Or maybe it was that Knowles had brought an activity into the gallery that ought to have remained in the home. On a practical level, Knowles was feeding people. So was the problem that it was considered uncouth to nourish the lowly body in a space dedicated to more lofty pursuits? The enactment of such a simple task and the amplification of the noises it generated within the concert hall might have struck some as banal, silly, willful, or strange. But introducing the everyday into these spaces and announcing it as art might also have felt wonderful to some. Knowles's performance exposed how cultural conventions are often based on common agreement of their importance, rather than anything inherent in them. Why should an avant-garde salad have less to say about the world we live in than an avant-garde symphony?

The ability to shake off the pressure to make something that would be judged important was key to the development of Knowles's practice: "I made those early performances as real experiences, which weren't disguised as anything else."[5] Akin to a game of charades, Knowles's performances de-dramatize the art-making moment and introduce an element of play into the art-viewing environment. They emphasize the creative potential of simple tasks, behaviors, and movements. In these works, "unconscious, ordinary actions were investigated for performance possibilities."[6] They were—and are—open to everyone; there is no way of getting them wrong.

In 2008, *Make a Salad* gained its largest audience to date when it was performed as part of Tate Modern's Long Weekend performance event. A gargantuan production that combined food, performance, and architecture, it featured vast quantities of salad leaves and vegetables that Knowles had selected from the nearby gourmet emporium Borough Market, and it fed more than 2,000 people. Ingredients were thrown over the side of the footbridge spanning the enormous Turbine Hall of the former power station that houses the museum, landing on a tarpaulin below, where they were showered with jugfuls of dressing, mixed with rakes and scooped up with shovels before being deposited into industrial-scale bowls from which Knowles served audience members. This was a salad on an epic scale, but a grand production is not required for *Make a Salad* to be a success. Knowles is most interested when the work is performed in a simple way, its significance primarily as food: "I prefer it straight; just getting out there and making a salad for people. Participation is guaranteed."[7]

Knowles, who was born in 1933 in New York City, was the only woman among the founding members of Fluxus. She came to the group after studying painting and fine art at Pratt Institute in the mid-1950s and attending a course at Syracuse University taught by the German artist and founder of Black Mountain College, Josef Albers. A self-declared "oddball,"[8] Knowles explored a range of art forms, genres, and techniques, and was especially interested in abstraction. During her student years, she made and published books, drew illustrations, and worked as a commercial artist creating greeting cards and advertisements. By 1958, she felt painting as an artform was too limiting and she destroyed all her canvases in a bonfire.

Around the same time Fluxus took off, the American avant-garde artist and chemist George Brecht developed a format he called the "event score," which consisted of a set of instructions for an artwork that was not rehearsed, and that anyone could create. Knowles was attracted to Brecht's idea and its minimal style[9] and began to create her own event scores, which she defined as "a one or two-line recipe for action."[10] This description of the event score reflects the central position that food and culinary practices would gain in Knowles's work. Beginning with *Make a Salad*, she invited audiences to think of food preparation as an art form worthy of experimentation and, conversely, of art as something that can consist of cooking and enjoying a simple meal.

In the years following the premiere of *Make a Salad*, Knowles developed numerous event scores, which provide a basic structure for an action around which variation can occur. In 1965, she numbered them and brought them together in a small book, *by alison knowles*. The simple and sometimes absurd instructions for action include *Proposition #1: Shuffle*, which invited people to quietly shuffle into the performance area, around and through the audience, and *Proposition #10: Braid*, which asked its performers to find something to braid, such as hair or yarn, and to braid it. In each case, there was an infinite number of ways to perform the event, depending on the performer, available materials, context, and audience. As Knowles explained, *Proposition #2: Make a Salad* "might be made in Indonesia, and you have to work with very different ingredients than you would in New York City."[11] In 1964, her

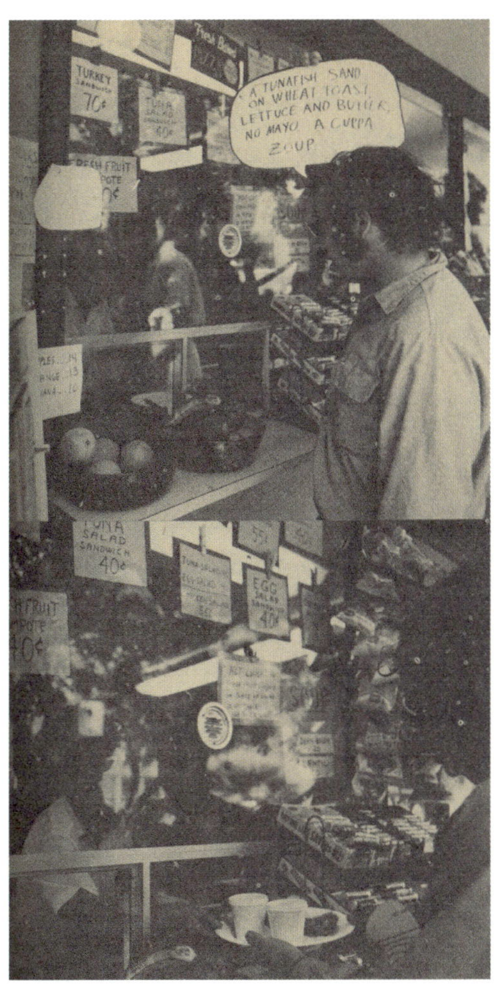

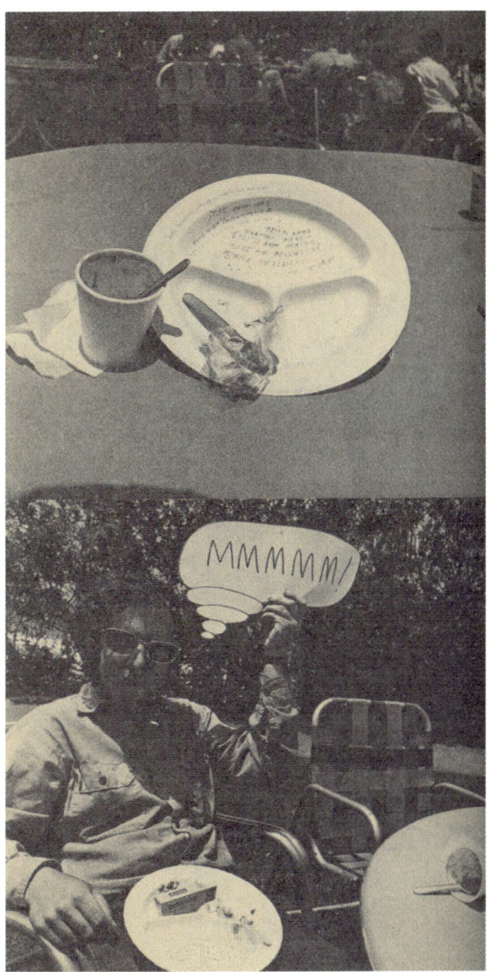

Alison Knowles, *Journal of the Identical Lunch* (detail), 1971.

score for *Proposition #2a: Make a Soup* instructed a culinary variation on *Make a Salad*, and equally left the particulars of the dish up to its maker.

From early on in her career, Knowles was part of a circle of artists, composers, and writers keen to test and stretch the boundaries between creative disciplines. With her friend, the correspondence artist Ray Johnson, who made art through the postal system by mailing people artworks and texts with instructions for activities, Knowles would "play the streets,"[12] picking up objects to be used in artworks at a later date.

Knowles was keen to include "real things" in her work, objects that were not typical art materials, such as the dried beans she used in her *Bean Rolls* (1963) and encouraged people to plant. These were packed in a metal can along with scores, bean stories, and proverbs printed on paper scrolls. Beans were a recurring material in Knowles's life and art. After meeting Daniel Spoerri, "the French artist interested in eggs," she decided that "beans and eggs were the most ancient, the most mysterious foods in the world."[13] Eggs, of course, could be made into salads, but beans too could be used to make art that was interactive and multi-sensory. Knowles made papers with lentils and flax, which she used to create musical instruments, tactile and auditory books, and voluminous crinkled paper costumes that would create sound as the body moved. She incorporated beans that she had been collecting into sonic bases to create *Bean Shakers*, which people could hold and use to produce "sound poetry."[14] In 1963, she premiered her first *Bean Garden*, a large, amplified platform containing dried beans, similar in appearance to a sandpit, through which people could walk, wade, or dance. It provided an unusual sensory connection between food and the body, as well as a live improvised sound performance. These works brought parts of the body often divorced from our food into contact with new and unusual sensations of friction, texture, temperature, pressure, weight, hardness, dryness, and movement. Like the curators of early museums, Knowles was keen for people to note a range of physical qualities as part of the experience of an object.

Knowles's interest in food was part of a recognition of the value of the everyday, by which "daily routine was found to be quite mysterious."[15] But what do we mean by "the everyday," and why was its value not already recognized? If works such as *Make a Salad, Braid,* or *Shuffle* seem slight, short on bombast and artifice, that's the point: they cannot be distinguished from the same actions performed in the context of the home, factory, or street. One of the aims that Maciunas listed in the Fluxus manifesto was to "PURGE the world of dead art, imitation, artificial art, abstract art, illusionistic art." Fluxus was against the spectacularization of art, and art as escapism. This countercultural stance was baffling to those who expected art to transport them away from their everyday lives. And if event scores such as "Make a Salad" were considered banal or unimportant, such an attitude revealed the low value ascribed to the job of keeping people fed, healthy, and happy. Knowles's Fluxus scores connect people to the tactile, auditory, olfactory, and gustatory aspects of life, but they also draw attention to the way we regard domestic labor and those who perform it. As Knowles noted of "Make a Salad," "I was the only woman in the original Fluxus group, so the piece had a dynamic feminist twist as well." Her work investigated the performance capacities of domestic labor, the burden of which remains disproportionately female. But the feminist tenor of her works didn't focus on protest or blame, but on opening up the space within which art could occur, for the benefit of everyone.

In the late 1960s, Knowles again turned to food as a creative catalyst, adopting a daily food ritual that soon became an artwork. "The Identical lunch" was her "noon-time meditation," which involved eating the same lunch every day. It consisted of a solitary meal of a "tuna sandwich on wheat with lettuce and butter, no mayo and a large glass of buttermilk or a cup of soup," eaten at the Riss Foods luncheonette in Chelsea. Although she had always considered food preparation to be a form of meditation, at the time Knowles had young twin daughters at home, and eating lunch out was a way for her to "gather her thoughts and revive her creative energies."[16] At a demanding moment in her life, the lunch generated art from necessary restoration. The work also clearly identified food and time as key components in the predominantly female labor of parenting.

The Identical Lunch took a social turn when a friend of Knowles, the Fluxus artist and composer Philip Corner, joined her in performing the ritual. Corner was interested in finding out whether her lunchtime habit could be "altered into a more formalized performance score."[17] He offered to investigate it along with her and they agreed to eat the lunch at any place where the menu of a tuna sandwich and buttermilk or soup was available, for as long as they wanted to keep performing the score, and to record and compare their experiences. The indeterminacy of duration, location, and timespan left open many aspects of the performance. Eventually, Corner became "obsessed" with the repetition of the score and Knowles grew tired of the lunch,[18] but not before realizing that she could refresh it by opening it up for others to perform and explore in detail. She invited friends including Maciunas, her husband Dick Higgins, poet and artist Emmett Williams, and the Japanese video artist Shigeko Kubota to perform *The Identical Lunch* over the course of two years, paying attention to the details infusing the everyday. The collective performance of the piece revealed the role that food plays in asserting differences of identity and individuality. Some of the differences reflected people's preferences: Higgins did not have soup; others were an expression of their personality—Maciunas thought of "blending all of the ingredients into a super shake."[19] The participants gathered documentation including receipts, drawings, photographs, and notes from their performances, which were published in a one-off issue of the *Journal of the Identical Lunch* in 1971.

Whether it was eating a tuna-fish sandwich, or making a soup or a salad, Knowles's event scores inspired people to find meaning and beauty in their everyday actions. In 2010, on the 50th anniversary of the founding of Fluxus, she tried to identify what was so special about the movement. "Overnight," she said, "object, event, self, and the world of daily occurrence penetrated art from a real world, a world not born in museums or universities, and asking: 'What is the value of maintaining esthetic boundaries anyway?'"[20] The radical intentions underpinning the Fluxus movement were about moving beyond limited conceptions of what could count as art. Knowles did this by using food, something to which everyone can relate on a personal level. Food was a material that also helped her link the spaces of art to the home and to everyday activities that nourish and sustain. As Knowles put it, using food was about "emphasizing the heretofore neglected sensibilities of smell, site, touch and task as a relevant base for art making and performance."[21]

Love Among the Cabbages

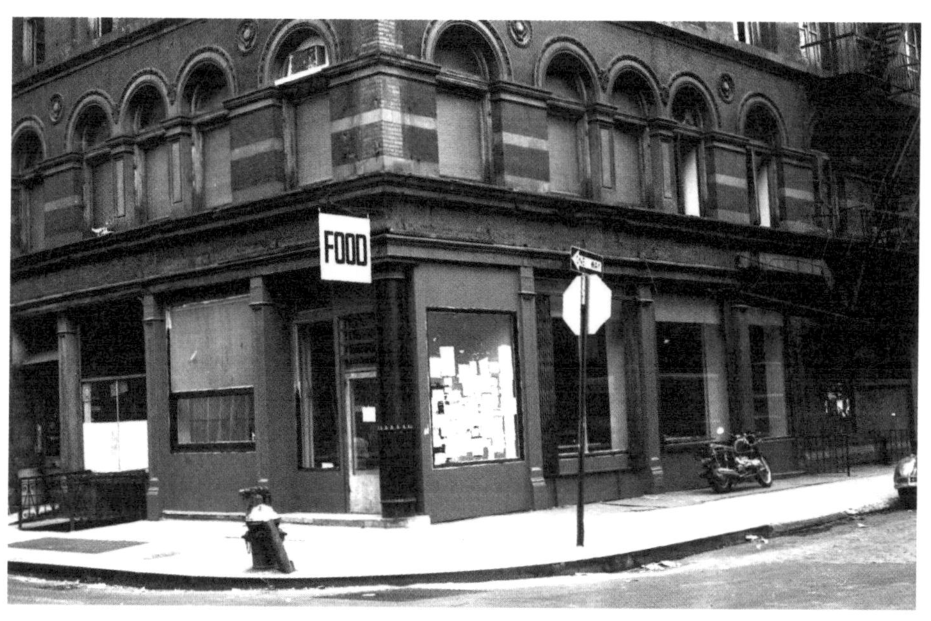

FOOD, New York City, c.1971–2.

ALISON KNOWLES INVITED people to partake in the preparation and appreciation of food as a valid art form, calling attention to the parallels between making food and creating art, and equipping individuals with instructions for doing both. The artist founders of the restaurant FOOD extended this proposition in new directions by providing their creative community with a unique location where the overlap between food, art, and life could be explored and enjoyed in imaginative new ways. Founded in 1971 by artists and friends Tina Girouard, Carol Goodden, and Gordon Matta-Clark, FOOD was located on the corner of Prince and Wooster Streets in New York's SoHo area, among a growing community of artists who had congregated there since the early 1960s. Once it opened, FOOD quickly became a fixture in the local scene, and for three years, Goodden recalls, the restaurant "produced delicious healthy inexpensive meals" and was "a relaxing place for artists to meet, plan events, be stared at by business-types who could go home and say they saw Robert Rauschenberg or Susan Rothenberg, Richard Nonas or Isamu Noguchi."[1] In 1992, Goodden recalled that "both Gordon and I saw FOOD as an 'art piece'"; she viewed it as "a series of life photograph-paintings," while for Matta-Clark it was a "complete work."[2] As a living, breathing workplace and restaurant that emphasized social life and sensual enjoyment, FOOD was a radical departure from studio art destined for exhibitions in galleries and museums.

Before FOOD was established, there had been a trend for artists and performers to take turns hosting dinner parties in their Lower Manhattan lofts. Pioneers in this movement were Tina Girouard and several of her friends from Louisiana, who played with avant-garde composer Philip Glass and specialized in laying on Cajun feasts.[3] At the time, Goodden had recently returned from a trip to Europe and had been throwing big eating parties in her loft, while her then boyfriend, Matta-Clark, had been hosting his own dinners in Chinatown. At a flower-themed spring party hosted by Goodden, he suggested that she open a restaurant, and although he made the suggestion "kind of teasingly," she had been growing tired of feeding people for free and it hit home. She told him she would do it if he was part of it, and the following week she found a site and negotiated the tenants out of their lease.

The trio spent the summer clearing out the space and renovating it according to Matta-Clark's designs, and on Saturday 25 September 1971, FOOD opened. It was a "white, high-ceilinged room ... filled with square oak tables, flanked by 40 or 50 chairs, no two of which are alike." The launch party menu consisted of "garlic soup, gumbo, chicken stew, wine, beer, and homemade breads." That night, everything was free and the trio served "friends, gallery goers, and passers-by until late in the evening." Hospitality and social life at FOOD were as important as what was on people's plates. According to the curator Paul Ha: "Gordon Matta-Clark was one of the first artists who clearly let us know that artists are givers."[4] It was all about showing up and enjoying the food and atmosphere, as an advertisement in the magazine *Art-Rite* made clear: "DON'T CALL, COME IN AND EAT AT food."[5] Although the space was innovative and experimental, according to Goodden traditional gender roles still crept in, and while Matta-Clark offered "the charisma that made it work as well as it did," she "ended up being responsible for its day-to-day existence."[6]

At FOOD, people could eat in good company, with live music and playful menus designed by artists who also cooked and waited on tables crowded with up-and-coming creatives from the fields of dance, music, and architecture. Over the years, more than 300 artists worked in FOOD's open kitchen. Diners might be treated to a meal made by Agnes Denes, Yvonne Rainer, or Donald Judd, or try homemade chili by Robert Rauschenberg, whose assistant, the Japanese artist Hisachika Takahashi, served sashimi at FOOD before most New Yorkers knew what it was, listing it as "raw mackerel with wasabi sauce." Some ideas were outlandish, but that was in the spirit of FOOD: Mark di Suvero's proposal for a sculptor's dinner served by a crane reaching through the restaurant's windows and eaten with screwdrivers, hammers, and chisels was discussed but never realized. A mythical aura surrounded even the meals that were cooked, and curator Alanna Heiss, who worked with many of the FOOD artists, later noted that the restaurant was "a site of a lot of apocryphal stories."[7]

FOOD was a labor of love, or as an advert in the avant-garde art magazine *Avalanche* put it: "Love among the cabbages."[8] Although it was officially founded by five friends, two of the initial group, artist Suzanne Harris and dancer Rachel Lew, left the operation early on, and it was run by Girouard, Goodden, and Matta-Clark. Goodden, who was born in London in 1940 and moved to the US in 1945, was working as a photographer and a dancer with the Trisha Brown Dance Company when she founded FOOD.

Tina Girouard was born in 1946 in DeQuincy, Louisiana, and grew up on her father's rice farm. After studying fine art in her home state, in the late 1960s she moved to New York, where she befriended other artists from Louisiana, including Lynda Benglis and Keith Sonnier, who were central to the Post-minimalist scene.

Gordon Matta, as Matta-Clark was known until 1971, when he adopted his mother's maiden name, was born in New York in 1943, the son of American artist Anne Clark and Chilean painter Roberto Matta. Immersed in the artistic elite from birth, he was the godson of Teeny Duchamp, Marcel Duchamp's wife. While studying architecture at Cornell University, he spent a year at the Sorbonne in Paris in 1968, a time of civil unrest throughout France, with widespread left-wing protests and strikes beginning with the May 1968 student revolts, which decried capitalism,

American imperialism, and consumerism. In Paris, he met the French theorist and filmmaker Guy Debord and was introduced to the Situationist International, a collective of neo-Marxist avant-garde artists and theorists who constructed "situations." These were tools intended to liberate everyday life from the hold of spectacle and the alienation it produced, and they included the *dérive*: drifting walks through urban environments that intended to cut through the political meanings of spaces and invest them with personal, psychological meaning instead. The Situationists also invented the practice of *détournement*, which involved subverting materials—often images—away from their existing ideological functions, for example by taking a martial arts film and replacing its dialogue with discussions of the liberation of the proletariat from bourgeois oppression, as René Viénet did with his 1973 work *La Dialectique peut-elle casser des briques?* (Can Dialectics Break Bricks?).

On his return to New York, Matta-Clark began conducting artistic experiments with alchemical processes, many of which applied cooking to edible materials. With "flame, time and the elements" as his palette, he explored the ways in which food, in particular agar-agar, a seaweed-based gel, could be turned into art, first by spreading it on the more traditional support of stretched canvas, many of which rotted away, and then in experiments that defy traditional media.[9] For *Photo-Fry* (1969), he burned photographs and Polaroids of Christmas trees in a frying pan with vegetable oil and added gold leaf, then boxed up the charred remnants and sent them to friends as Christmas cards. Around the same time as Piper was concocting her volatile mixture of eggs, vinegar, milk, and fish oil for *Catalysis I*, Matta-Clark was combining agar-agar with sugar, salt, yeast, vegetable oils, milk products, eggs, meat, and bouillon cubes, boiling it until it reached a spreadable consistency and then slathering the resulting brew into shallow metal trays, where it would dry and develop microbial cultures, molds, and fungi. He titled these sheets of augmented agar *Incendiary Wafers*, for their tendency to burst into flames, as he discovered on New Year's Day 1971 when one spontaneously combusted. Sometimes, he would pick up the moldy sheet of agar and stick it to the brick wall of his studio, where it would pick up spores and seeds drifting on the breeze. When he exhibited these unruly crinkled skins, which he thought of as building materials that provided environments for living creatures including microbes and fungi, he offered people magnifying glasses to marvel at the elaborate microcosms created by these growths. In 1970, he displayed them in an exhibition at Bykert Gallery, titled Museum. In the glow of whale-oil lamps, agar works of various sizes were hung on the wall, installed to appear as if they were creeping out of boxes, and draped over vine-like lengths of wire. With respect to the exhibition's title, the works Matta-Clark cooked up did invite a kind of multi-sensorial scrutiny that would have been encouraged in the early museum: to get to know a work by handling it and checking its weight and texture, by smelling it, and possibly even by tasting it. His work enticed people to use all of their senses, overcoming the distance that sometimes exists between an artwork and its viewers in a contemporary art setting.

Matta-Clark also showed his work at 112 Greene Street, a local gallery to which FOOD was closely connected. Founded by artist Jeffrey Lew with a group of artists including Matta-Clark, the gallery opened in 1970, and Lew later described it as "the only socialist art system in New York at that time."[10] It would later go on to become White Columns, now New York's oldest artist-run space. After FOOD opened, the two locations "were like brother and sister," Goodden recalled, with FOOD "everybody's kitchen."

According to Lew, Matta-Clark's neighbors reported "a constantly burning stove at his home and studio,"[11] on which he

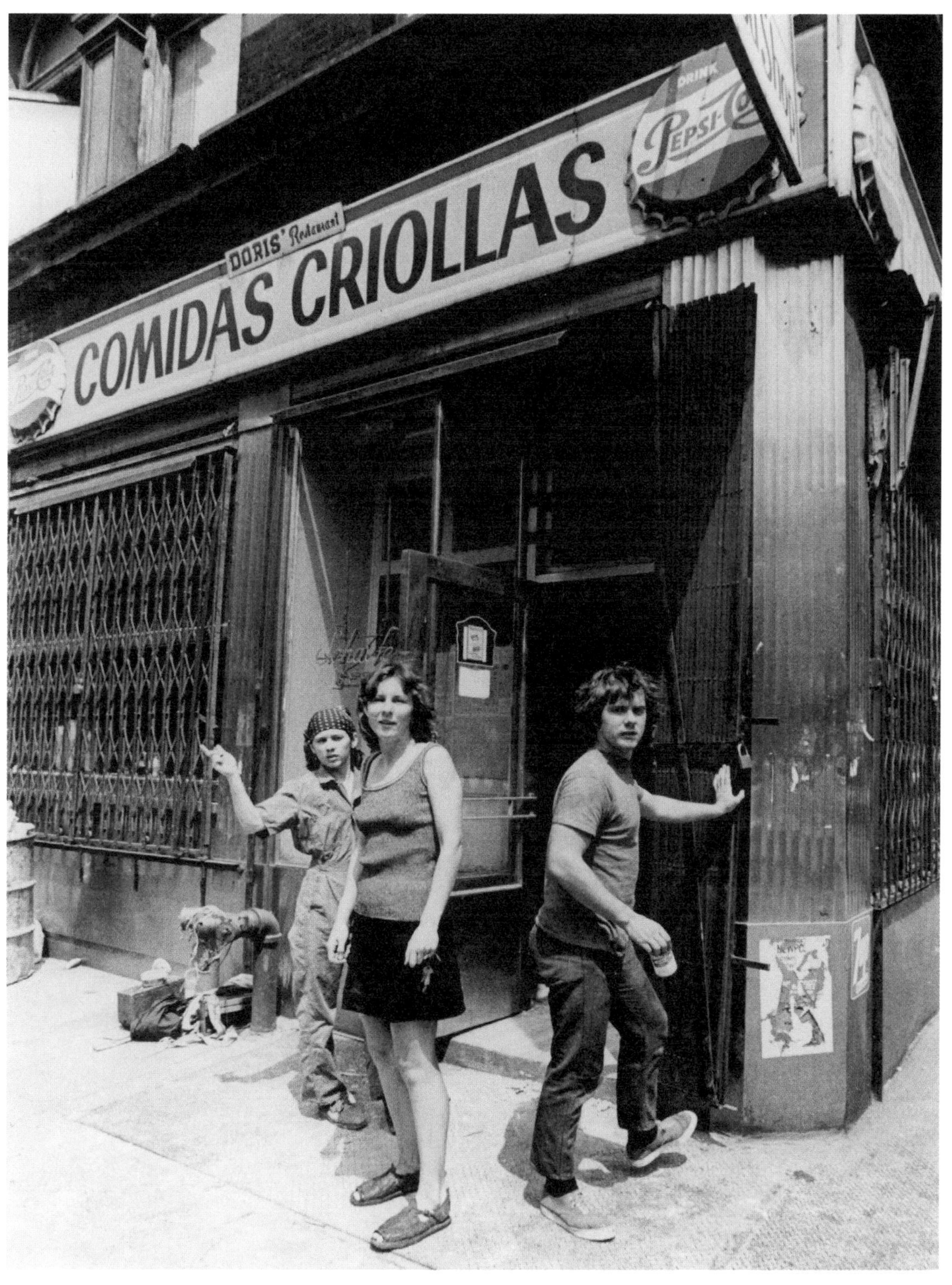

LEFT TO RIGHT Tina Girouard, Carol Goodden, and Gordon Matta-Clark outside FOOD prior to its opening, 1971.

would brew concoctions of V8 and cranberry juices, chocolate-flavored Yoo-Hoo, and sperm-whale oil. During his first studio visit with Matta-Clark, Lew encountered a space teeming with "corks, racks, trays, fermenting bottles." Matta-Clark's radical approach to materials was informed by his own bodily senses, and "every once in a while, he'd taste, feel, smell, or squeeze one of the things. Every sense was taken into account."[12] This included the sense of wonder when Matta-Clark brought a cherry tree into the basement of 112 Greene Street and forced it to flower on New Year's Day 1971. A few months later, as part of the Brooklyn Bridge Event organized by curator Alanna Heiss on 24 May 1971, he spit-roast a whole pig named Jack beside a mixed-media assemblage of abandoned cars and bits of metal, an installation titled *Jacks* in the pig's honor. Under the Brooklyn Bridge, Matta-Clark served 500 barbecued pork sandwiches to friends, guests, and artists, and filmed the event for *Pig Roast* (1971). The following year, he created *Dumpster—Drag-On—Open House* outside Holly Solomon's gallery at 98 Greene Street. A temporary studio, gallery, and kitchen in a shipping container with umbrellas for a roof when it rained, it was also the location for a reprise of the original *Pig Roast*.

FOOD is sometimes attributed solely to Matta-Clark, but it was a collective endeavor, with many artists in addition to the original five pitching in, such as the musician and Philip Glass Ensemble member Robert Prado. This diversity of input was recognized by *New York Magazine*'s restaurant column, The Underground Gourmet, when it gave full billing to those involved, with "Carol Goodden (soups and menu planning), Gordon Matta-Clark (everything), Robert Prado (soups, stews and gumbos), Suzy Harris (vegetables), Tina Girouard (Cajun cuisine), Anne Marshall (dinners), Rachel Lew (guest dinners and factotum)." It was clear to the reviewers that "all the chefs are vitally interested."[13]

The Underground Gourmet gave FOOD a positive review, noting its early cult status: "As we were leaving, a young woman who recognized us said somewhat touchingly, 'Please don't write about this place!'"[14] But advertising, at least in magazines targeted at artists, was a great way for the trio leading FOOD to get the word out and customers in. They also used advertising to perform an auto-critique of their activities. In the spring 1972 issue of *Avalanche*, an ad announcing "FOOD'S FAMILY FISCAL FACTS" poked fun at FOOD's dual status as a business and kinship group, itemizing its budget and listing more than a hundred names involved in the operation. The income somehow miraculously balances with the cost of running the place, while the list of consumables includes an entertaining "7 made up Social Security numbers" and "99 cut fingers."

Although FOOD has been referred to as SoHo's first restaurant, a now-iconic photograph taken by musician Richard Landry (Girouard's husband at the time) of Girouard, Goodden, and Matta-Clark opening the security grilles before they renovated the space puts paid to this idea, since the original sign "Doris' Restaurant" is clearly visible. The Puerto Rican luncheonette advertised "comidas Criollas," or Creole meals, including gumbo, jambalaya, or chicken fricassée. In another version of the image, used as an advertisement in *Avalanche*, the original name of the eatery has been crossed out in thick black marker pen, and "FOOD" printed vertically over the façade.

If the neighborhood of SoHo is now an exemplar of gentrification, at the time it was undergoing a preliminary transformation from an industrial zone, whose workers Doris would have catered to, into a creative enclave, with artists taking over abandoned and derelict warehouses as studio space, pioneering loft living, and forging a vibrant community of friends, collaborators, rivals, and lovers. According to the curator Catherine Morris, it was a place "where neighbors wouldn't care how loud you were, or what kind of things you cooked up in your space."[15] This was before SoHo was declared a historic district; before designer boutiques and unaffordable rents.

The first half of the 1970s were turbulent years across the US, with the continuation of the civil rights movement and protests against the American war in Vietnam; the conservative backlash that lifted Richard Nixon to the office of President in 1968 and saw him re-elected in 1972; and rising populism, which fomented strong sentiment against the countercultural experiments of the 1960s. Americans celebrated the first Earth Day in 1970, while the oil crisis further highlighted the importance of conservation. Nationwide economic stagnation was compounded in New York City by a middle-class flight to the suburbs, and by 1975 the city was all but bankrupt, with infamously high crime rates. But within the chaos, creativity flourished, and the collective and DIY ethos of FOOD was in tune with the activist principles of the time.

FOOD supported this transitional phase by providing healthy meals, jobs, and a space where artists could meet, create, and take risks.[16] Eating there was affordable, with menus featuring soup with bread for just 50–75 cents, stew with bread for $1.25–1.50, or a full dinner for $3.00. People could pay in cash or with meal tickets that cost $9.50 for a book worth $10.[17] Artists could work in the kitchen or serving tables and pick up flexible shifts when they had shows coming up. Best of all, they could "earn a living while working with friends."[18] Goodden thought FOOD would make a profit, but instead it made a loss. She covered this with her inheritance, which she had put up to secure the lease on the building.

Meals at FOOD followed trends in healthy food, Cajun and fashionable world cuisines, and experimental cooking. The menu changed daily and included fresh fish from Fulton Street Market as well as unusual ingredients such as carob, honey, okra, dried shiitake mushrooms, lychees, and pickled ginger. The Underground Gourmet, which described FOOD as "a restaurant commune" found an appealing winter menu consisting of a "first-rate caldo Gallego, a soup made of chickpeas, ham hocks, a leafy green vegetable and onions brewed in a mildly piquant broth ... an alternative was thick lentil soup ... Also on tap that day was a chicken stew served over rice and shrimp, an imaginative combination."[19] Regional and international specialties included gumbos, Kentucky burgoo stew, Greek avgolemono, or egg-lemon soup, and billi-bi, a French cream of mussel soup, all served with thick slices of homemade bread "arranged around a huge mound of fresh yellow butter."[20] Desserts included "a bowl of yoghurt with almonds and sunflower seeds, laced through with thick sweet honey (50 cents)."[21]

On Tuesday nights the menu was vegetarian, and on Sundays meals were made by individual artists, sometimes with astonishing results. Matta-Clark's $4.00 "Matta Bones" menu, conceived as a piece of performance art, consisted of the following:

Oxtail Soup
Green Salad
Marrow Bones
Stuffed Bones
Frog Legs Provençale
Pot Roast Bones
Sliced Peaches
Coffee or Tea

The meal ended with each guest being offered a necklace made from their leftover bones, which had been retrieved from their plates and hastily scrubbed in the kitchen.

According to Goodden, cooking was also a way for Matta-Clark to "assembl[e] people, like choreography."[22] Performance was inherent to the ethos at FOOD, where the open kitchen—an unusual feature in restaurants at the time—was designed so that cooks, servers, and dishwashers were visible and central to the space's activities.

A bright, playful use of language ran through the menus and printed matter associated with FOOD: "velvet chicken in satin sauce," "used car stew," "mock chicken drumsticks or city chicken." Such puns and clever food play also pepper Matta-Clark's practice, but underpinning it all was a radical agenda, outlined in "A Matta's proposal," his reworking of Jonathan Swift's 1729 satire "A modest proposal." Swift's suggestion was that the poor Irish Catholics of his time sell their children to the wealthy to be eaten as a way of ending their misery. In his version, Matta-Clark transposes this idea to the art world, proposing artistic cannibalism. In a letter to his friend and fellow artist Lee Jaffe, he notes, "there are deeper needs and pleasures at steak" than making or keeping money, announcing his mission to "restore the art of eating with love instead of fear." He invites Jaffe to offer himself up as the first of many "treats"—or artists—to satisfy "premordial urges." According to Matta-Clark, Jaffe's sacrifice would mark the beginning of a moment in which cannibalism would provide a balm to capitalism's ills, completing "another phase of social development and resolv[ing] the malaise du siècle."[23]

Matta-Clark's artistic experiments with food were not primarily designed to be edible, but rather to bring out the latent physical and sculptural potential of food as a material. His widow, Jane Crawford, recalls a dinner party for which he cooked a sea bass that:

> emerged from the kitchen encased in a block of aspic nearly three feet long. He unmolded it, then gave the table a good kick, so that the aspic

wobbled wildly and the bass seemed to fishtail upstream. All the guests looked at it with this sort of horror and amazement ... In the end my mundane chicken stew got eaten and everyone was too afraid to touch the fish.[24]

When he wasn't giving fish the illusion of life, Matta-Clark wanted to bring buildings to life with interventions such as his "cuts," which involved slicing through and cutting holes in the walls and floors of old buildings. He made his first cut at FOOD during the summer of 1971, when the team was gutting and rebuilding the space according to his designs. When part of a wall had to be removed, he cut it out as a horizontal section and called it a "wall sandwich." The following year he displayed it as part of a selection of his building cuts at 112 Greene Street. Although that first cut was made for practical purposes, subsequent cuts were motivated by a desire to bring life into depressed and difficult urban spaces, including derelict warehouses on the Hudson River piers. This regenerative ambition was also part of FOOD, but whereas the nourishment and social cohesion provided there represented a way of "filling up," the cuts were a way to introduce negative space into the decaying urban environment, letting energy flow through the previously enclosed space, allowing in air along with the spores, seeds, insects, and birds it carried, as well as inviting people to look through openings to visually connect the spaces inside and outside. Renovations at FOOD continued in the same spirit of experimentation and with a whirlwind energy: after accidentally knocking through a wall into their neighbors' space, Matta-Clark handed them a bottle of scotch through the hole by way of apology. In photographs,

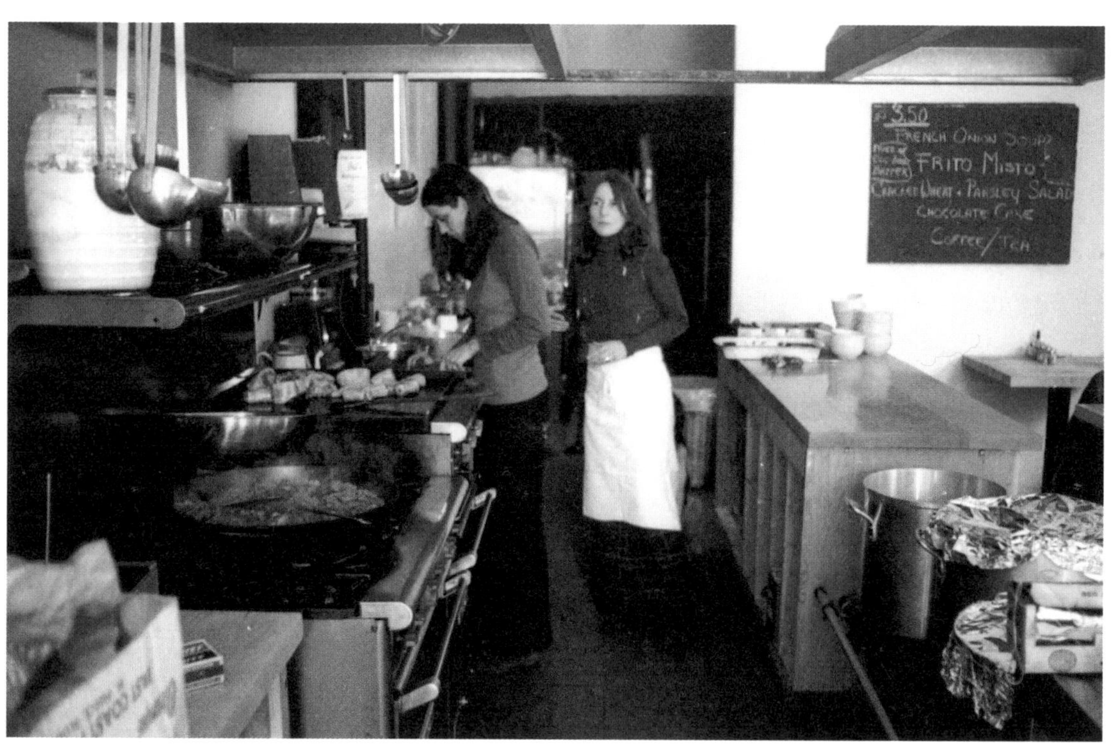

 FOOD, New York City, c.1971–2.

Matta-Clark is usually either grinning or on the verge of cracking a mischievous smile. As Goodden described the dynamic of FOOD, people returned time and time again "for my soups, Gordon's charm, and Tina's Cajun dinners."[25]

Matta-Clark's film *Food* (also known as *A Day in the Life of Food*) (1971–3), made with photographer Robert Frank, is an affectionate portrait of the hard work and playful cacophony that made FOOD. It opens with Goodden on a 4 a.m. shopping expedition to Fulton Street Fish Market. A man with big hair makes coffee on an industrial percolator for fishmongers from Guyana, Greece, and downtown New York. Goodden knows what she wants, discusses the precise caliber of fish she is after, weighs the goods, and confidently barters with the fishmongers: "I don't want to pay over $5 a bushel." The fishmonger knows about FOOD and wants to eat there.

We watch the market-fresh fish arriving at FOOD, where staff gut and scale it, make borscht, and start a duck gumbo for the day's menu, which also features fruit salad with yoghurt, melons, and frozen bananas. In the office, phone calls are made and the FOOD staff share a joint. A title card pops up: it's "Later," and the restaurant is filled with patrons, an accordionist, lovers kissing, loud slurping noises. Matta-Clark plays with the boom microphone, turning it into a cock, a toothbrush. People look stoned, drunk, and happy: they are young and in love; they touch each other, gaze intently across the table. Toward the end of the film, dirty dishes are piled up like Jenga. A hand wipes the menu blackboard, people stack furniture, wash up, count money. They tidy the salt-and-pepper shakers, and oil the bread tins. They mix water into flour, and knead the dough by hand, ready for the next day.

In 2011, *The New Yorker*'s art critic Peter Schjeldahl, who used to eat at FOOD, chronicled the "happy-go-lucky gastronomy" of the time, detailing an event at Matta-Clark's loft, for which "guests were required to bring whole fish from the Chinatown markets," which were chucked into a pot to produce a "dubious stew."[26] Schjeldahl's job was to write about art, not food, so his readiness to reflect on food-based creative experiments shows how influential these were to the culture of the time, even if their importance hasn't been fully credited in the intervening decades.

In 1973, the three principals of FOOD joined with artists Laurie Anderson, Suzanne Harris, Jene Highstein, Bernard Kirschenbaum, Richard Landry, and Richard Nonas to form Anarchitecture, a short-lived but influential group whose purpose was to critique the role of architecture, art, and language in capitalist society. They posed questions around how people build and inhabit their spaces, and how to deconstruct systems of power and entrenched ways of life. FOOD provided them with the inspiration for developing their ideas and practices, with a captive audience of eaters, in a place open to experimentation. By using food as a material, FOOD fueled a way of thinking and creating through the senses. Experiments were grounded in the sensory reality of ingredients, cooking processes, and eating, rather than being based on abstract theories. As Girouard described it, anarchitecture was the "think tank" that "came after FOOD," and the group held weekly meetings at FOOD, 112 Greene Street, and in people's lofts.[27] According to Highstein, "everyone felt free to cross mediums and cook through ideas that ranged from torturing words to making a cheese sandwich."[28]

Although FOOD generally balanced the thrill and edginess of experimentation with the reassurance of a hot, affordable meal, sometimes the gambit did not succeed with the public. For a dinner announced as *Alive*, Matta-Clark hollowed out halved, boiled eggs and filled them with a pool of broth swimming with live brine shrimp. Goodden remembers that "some non-artist customers were furious and claimed there should be a law against us ... We told them guest chef days were no holds barred days and they could leave if they wished. So they did."[29] In other cases, the playful attitude offered something easier to swallow, as with *Robert Kushner and Friends Eat Their Clothes* (1972). In a playful performance that offered a lighter take on the idea of edible people than the one Wilke would put forward with *Super-t-Art* a couple of years later, Kushner, who was FOOD's dessert chef and manager from 1972 to 1974, had nude performers—both men and women—model clothing made from fruit and vegetables attached to crocheted garments, which audience members were invited to nibble on. Leftover produce was later served to diners at FOOD.

In 1974, Goodden and the others still involved sold the restaurant, which continued in one way or another until the 1980s, but it wasn't the same without the involvement of the original team. Both Girouard and Goodden eventually left New York to work on new projects, and Matta-Clark died from pancreatic cancer in 1978, aged just 35. So much of what distinguished FOOD has now become standard in the restaurant industry: the use of new and varied ingredients; the performative staging of food preparation; the notion of "guest chefs"; the experimental approach to designing a dining space and experience. For Goodden, FOOD "was a beautiful, nourishing, vital, stimulating new concept, which was a living, pulsating hub of creative energy—and piles of fresh parsley."[30] Ultimately, the freedom and generosity that made FOOD such a special place were also responsible for its downfall. The capitalism Matta-Clark fantasized about challenging with artistic cannibalism won out in the end. As Goodden put it, "Though we consumed food, FOOD consumed us ... It was a free enterprise which gave food away much too freely."[31] But its true legacy is as a pioneering space that nourished a community with food, and in doing so fueled their creative work. At FOOD, breaking bread also meant breaking old habits and patterns, and coming up with new ways of feeding culture.

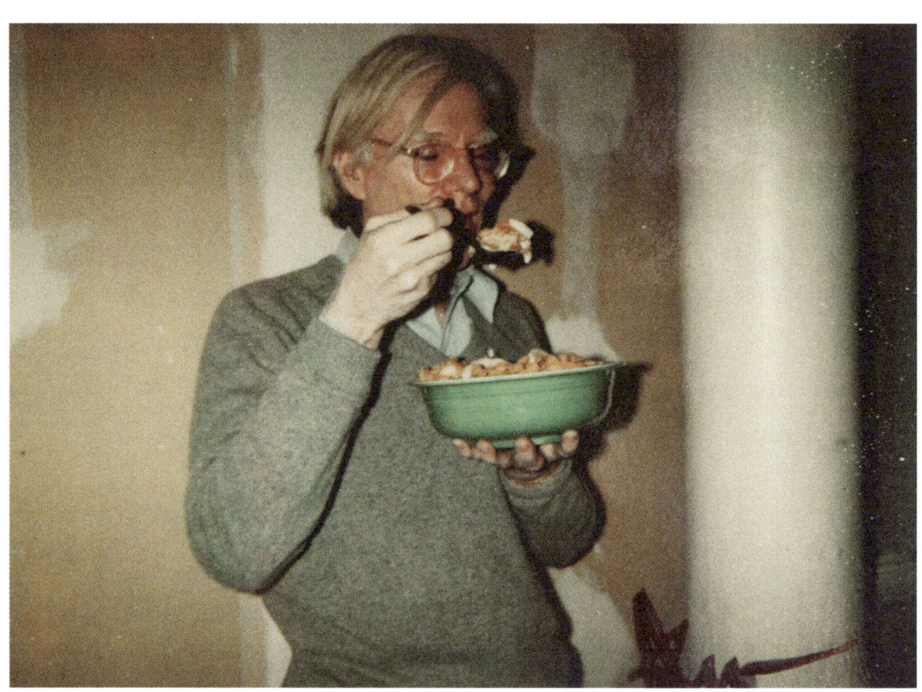

Andy Warhol eating cereal, c.1975.

ANDY WARHOL

Bringing Home the Bacon

FOOD PROVIDED MEALS, jobs, and a sense of community for artists living in Downtown Manhattan. The other artists we've considered so far used food to break down barriers between art and life, whether by combining raw fish, meat, and chickens with near-naked bodies, infusing the streets of New York with the reek of rotten food, or making a salad as a performance. These actions brought the essential substance of food into art, but they were also finite events.

For Andy Warhol, perhaps more than for any other artist in the 20th century, his own life was his art. Food was central to his existence and to his creativity: a material that fed, enlivened, and occasionally troubled him and his art. Warhol crafted his persona in the media, in the art world, and in popular culture over decades, with the same care and detail he brought to his sculptures and screen prints, films, and books. So much of his aura emanates from his story, the grand arcs and mundane details of his life, and the way he himself narrated it: his childhood, his relationship with his mother Julia, and the entourage at his studio, the Factory, and later the Office; his fame, fans, and philosophy; his sexuality, habits, idiosyncrasies, and paradoxes. Warhol's relationship with food, what he did and didn't eat, what he said and wrote about food, are a central part of the work of art that was Andy Warhol's life.

Along with fame, money, and death, food is one of the central themes of Warhol's work. Images of food abound, from the exquisite gastronomic illustrations made during his early years as a commercial artist to his satirical cookbook *Wild Raspberries*; from iconic paintings of packaged goods such as Campbell's soup, Kellogg's cornflakes, and Coke bottles to still-life paintings of fruit and the most reproduced banana in the world for The Velvet Underground & Nico, as well as *Eat* and *Drunk aka Drink*, films he made in the mid-1960s.

Warhol lived a life of detail. He kept records of expenditure down to the penny; preserved all manner of old paperwork, packaging, and products; and recorded his every activity, thought, and emotion in his diaries. To embrace Warhol's relationship with food as a legitimate aspect of his oeuvre is to recognize that the details and sensory experiences of everyday life are as important to culture as grand gestures and abstract concepts. This is something that Warhol and those in his circle knew. In the late 1960s, his associate, Bob Colacello (Warhol once suggested that he should change his name to Bob Cola), noted that:

> people have such a fascination with the little tiny details of what other people do, what they eat and what they drink and what they wear and I suppose that if you keep a record of all those details, of all that trivia, long enough, which is what ... Andy does ... it does add up to a total picture of our time.[1]

In his proclamations about food and its esthetic qualities, Warhol was a sage of the edible on a par with Epicurus, the ancient Greek philosopher of simple pleasures; Jean Anthelme Brillat-Savarin, the author of *The Physiology of Taste* (1825), and the American food writer M. F. K. Fisher. His statements and aphorisms on the subject of food are invitations to meditate on our individual desires, pleasures, and experiences and to chuckle at our inconsistencies, foibles, and propensity to be seduced by our senses. Warhol thought about food a lot. He felt powerful emotions about food and held strong opinions on many food-related topics. He mused on the esthetic, political, economic, and class significance of what is offered to us on a plate, and what we choose to eat instead. His diaries and books include evidence of his conflicted relationship with food, and his public proclamations of gourmandize together with written accounts of his eating habits yield a portrait of a sensualist who was obsessed with the symbolism of certain foods. He succumbed to cravings, was worried about his weight, and, after he was shot by Valerie Solanas in 1968, his health too.

One of the richest sources on Warhol's relationship with food is his 1975 book *The Philosophy of Andy Warhol (From A to B and Back Again)*, which he originally wanted to title simply *THE*. Mainly written in Warhol's voice, it is constructed from numerous conversations Warhol had with Colacello and his close friend and Factory stalwart Brigid Polk (also known as Brigid Berlin), which were organized by the writer Pat Hackett, who also transcribed Warhol's daily phone calls into his diaries. But even though the book appears to be confessional in tone, it is not always clear who is speaking, or whether their words are sincere or intended for effect. This hall of mirrors is typical of Warhol's life and work: his identity was perhaps his greatest work of art, forged and formulated over time, in private, public, and among the motley crew of friends, acolytes, and stars with whom he surrounded himself. As Factory superstar Ondine recognized, self-creation was a fundamental part of Warhol's world: "He allowed me to create myself, and I allowed him to create himself."[2]

Andrew Warhola was born on 6 August 1928 in Pittsburgh, Pennsylvania, the son of Rusyn immigrants from an area of the Eastern Carpathians that is now part of Slovakia. Growing up during the Great Depression, he was a sickly child who suffered repeated attacks of the neurological disorder St Vitus's dance from the ages of eight to ten. Each year the flare-ups, which he called "nervous breakdowns," started on the first day of summer vacation, so the poorly young Andrew would stay in bed, play with paper dolls and listen to the radio. His mother read to him in her strong accent, which even he struggled to understand, and, laying the foundations for a lifelong sweet habit, every time he finished a page in his coloring book, she rewarded his creativity with a Hershey's bar.[3] When Warhol was 13, his father died and, as the youngest son, his relationship with his mother grew even closer. Warhol moved to New York in 1949, and she followed in 1951. They lived together until shortly before her death in 1972.

Warhol's diet as a child reflected the family's poverty and, as he later recognized, contributed to his tendency to seek comfort in food-related rituals. His wholesome breakfast consisted of a bowl of oatmeal, half an orange, and a glass of milk with Ovaltine stirred into it. Lunch, by Warhol's own account, was identical for 20 years: a bowl of Campbell's soup and a cheese sandwich. However, in keeping with the multiple and sometimes contradictory narratives Warhol gave of his own life, he also said that the soup his family ate was not Campbell's—too pricey—but a cheaper concoction made from water, salt, pepper, and ketchup. It was Heinz ketchup, which was famously produced in Pittsburgh by a family that later purchased Warhol's work.[4]

When Warhol achieved success and regularly stayed in expensive hotels, being looked after by cleaning staff caused him a certain amount of discomfort: "I just don't know where to put my eyes, where to look, what to be doing while they're cleaning," he wrote.[5] In an unexpected leap of the imagination, Warhol connected this awkward feeling to his obsession with both candy and money in his adult life, writing "When I was a child I never had a fantasy about having a maid, what I had

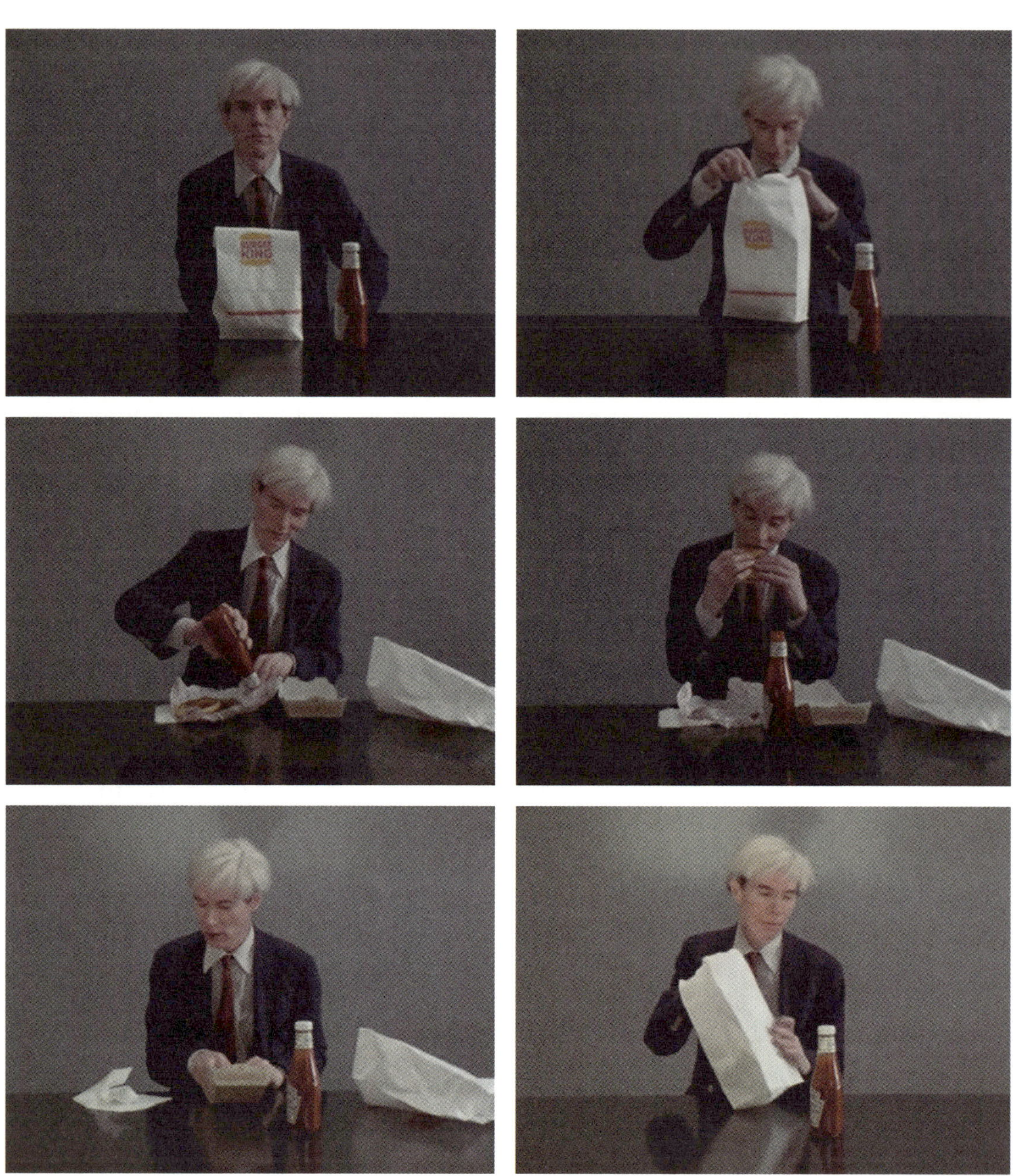

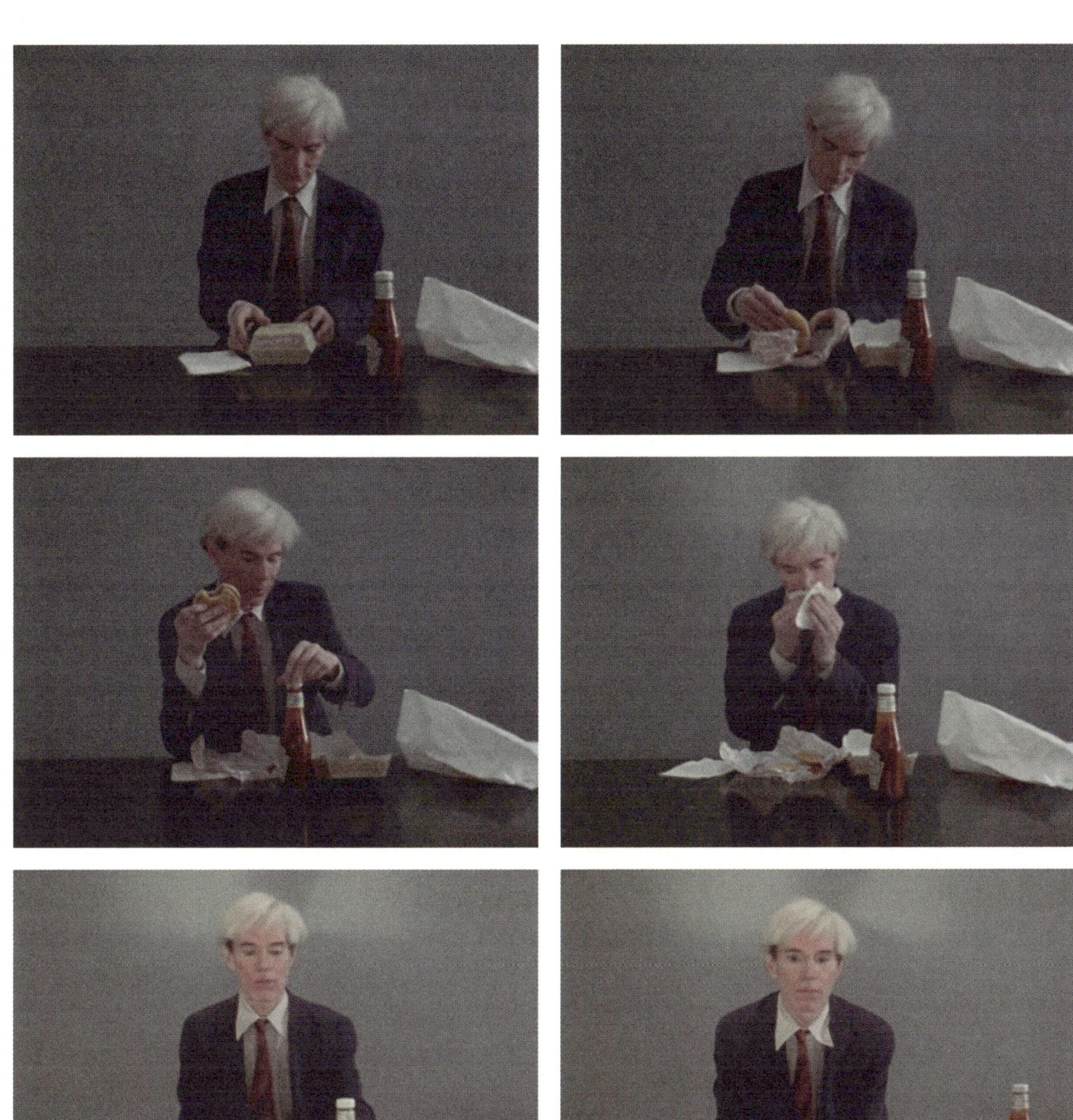

Andy Warhol, *66 Scenes from America*, 1982, directed by Jørgen Leth. Stills of Warhol eating a hamburger.

a fantasy about having was candy. As I matured, that fantasy translated itself into 'make money to have candy' … [When] my career started to pick up … I started getting more and more candy, and now I have a roomful of candy all in shopping bags … instead of a maid's room."[6] In a single paragraph Warhol sketches a parable about the mechanisms of self-consciousness, desire, and acquisition—all in terms of food.

Warhol's sweet tooth guided many of his food choices and inventions, including his minimalist recipe for cake: "You take some chocolate … and you take two pieces of bread … and you put the candy in the middle and you make a sandwich of it. And that would be cake."[7] It would if Warhol were at home, but in the 1950s, when he worked as a commercial artist illustrating fashion magazines and advertisements, he spent a lot of his time at Serendipity 3, a café on East 58th Street where he would have coffee and dessert—the only thing they served. He was such a regular that people thought he was one of the owners, and according to Stephen Bruce, an actual founder of the café, Warhol was addicted to cappuccino, which was at the time "a symbol of subversive sophistication."[8]

Warhol's freedom to consume luxurious foods and play with food imagery in his art was a product of his position as a citizen of the world's wealthiest nation, whose affluence was brought about in part by the new status of the US as a food super-producer. In the years following World War II, new government policies promoted the intensification of farming, new breeds of grain, and nitrogen fertilizers, generating record agricultural yields. This set in motion the development of food-processing technologies, a culture of consumerism and carefree wastage, and a boom in branding and marketing. Following the wartime and post-war austerity of the 1940s, consumer goods, from cars to clothing, candy bars to cosmetics, signified a new America: they were emblems of plenty, choice, and freedom.

Nowhere was this message more directly expressed than in the abundance of food available on supermarket shelves. It was mass-produced, highly processed, brightly advertised, and idealized as glamorous and modern—and for all these reasons it fascinated Warhol and provided inspiration for his art.

The post-war boom in consumerism was fueled by political decisions made prior to the US entering the war on 7 December 1941. Just a year earlier, on 9 December 1940, President Franklin D. Roosevelt had called for the US to become the "arsenal of democracy," and overnight the war industries ramped up, with many factories repurposed to produce airplanes, tanks, guns, and other supplies for the war effort. Over the following four years unemployment dropped, reaching a record low of 1.2 percent in 1944. By the end of the war, the US was in better economic condition than any other country in the world, its prosperity boosted by policies such as the 1944 GI Bill of Rights, which provided money to veterans to buy houses and farms, automobiles and appliances, and to attend college. Factories were reconverted to produce consumer goods; for example, Frigidaire, which had changed its assembly lines to build .50-caliber machine guns and B-20 propellers, now expanded from refrigerators to clothes washers and dryers, dishwashers, and food-waste disposal units.[9] Mass-production methods pioneered by the automobile industry were applied to homebuilding, increasing housing availability and affordability. By the end of the war, Americans had lived under a food rations system for three years, during which time they had been encouraged to invest spare cash in government war bonds. They were now urged to spend those savings to buy goods as a patriotic duty, which boosted the economy even further. With each decade after the war the Gross National Product leapt from $200 billion in 1940 to $300 billion in 1950 and $500 billion in 1960.

The boom in post-war marriages and births increased demand for new housing developments in suburbia, where attitudes and behaviors conformed to images modeled in advertisements for goods made by corporations and sold in new supermarkets. Buying processed, packaged, and branded foods from a wide range of available products was touted as good for the health of the family, economy, and country. In 1959, Vice President Richard Nixon visited the American National Exhibition in Moscow, where he debated the role of women in the proliferating market for home appliances with Soviet Premier Nikita Khruschev. In what became known as "The Kitchen Debate," Nixon claimed that "the right to choose" was the most important part of the American way of life. He extolled the virtues of a consumer cornucopia that offered "many different kinds of washing machines so that the housewives have a choice." Just two years later, in 1961, Warhol began painting a series, *Campbell's Soup Cans*: 32 canvases, one for each flavor of Campbell's soup then available to housewives and artists alike.

After the war, many Americans bought television sets for the first time, which beamed commercials for processed foods directly into people's living rooms. Manufacturers of kitchen appliances provided free recipe booklets featuring processed foods as core ingredients. Seasonal eating started to give way to branded eating. Spending on groceries increased, and new products such as Tupperware and Saran Wrap were developed for saving leftovers. Women were expected to maintain a perfect household at the push of a button, but this automated lifestyle isolated many women, whose chores had traditionally been completed within a social setting. Upward mobility mainly benefited white Americans, causing exclusion along racial and class divisions, a further injustice that helped fuel the civil rights movement among communities who were being short-changed from the benefits of post-war growth.

Warhol was fascinated by what he saw as the democratic nature of consumerism in America. He didn't ascribe value judgments to so-called "low" culture, and embraced all manifestations of contemporary culture, from Hollywood stars to tabloid newspapers, royalty to junk food. For Warhol, the fact that everyone ate the same ultra-processed, branded foods and drank the same sugary sodas was one of the great things about America:

> You can be watching TV and see Coca-Cola, and you can know that the President drinks Coke, Liz Taylor drinks Coke, and just think, you can drink Coke, too. A Coke is a Coke and no amount of money can get you a better Coke than the one the bum on the corner is drinking. All the Cokes are the same and all the Cokes are good.[10]

According to Warhol, the same truth applied to hot dogs, which crossed barriers of class, culture, and tradition. Commenting on Queen Elizabeth the Queen Mother's visit to the United States in 1939, when "President Eisenhower bought her a hot dog," Warhol wrote, "I'm sure he felt confident that she couldn't have had delivered to Buckingham Palace a better hot dog than that one he bought for her for maybe twenty cents at the ballpark ... She could get one for twenty cents and so could anybody else."[11] Actually, it was not the Republican Eisenhower but Democratic President Franklin D. Roosevelt who fed hot

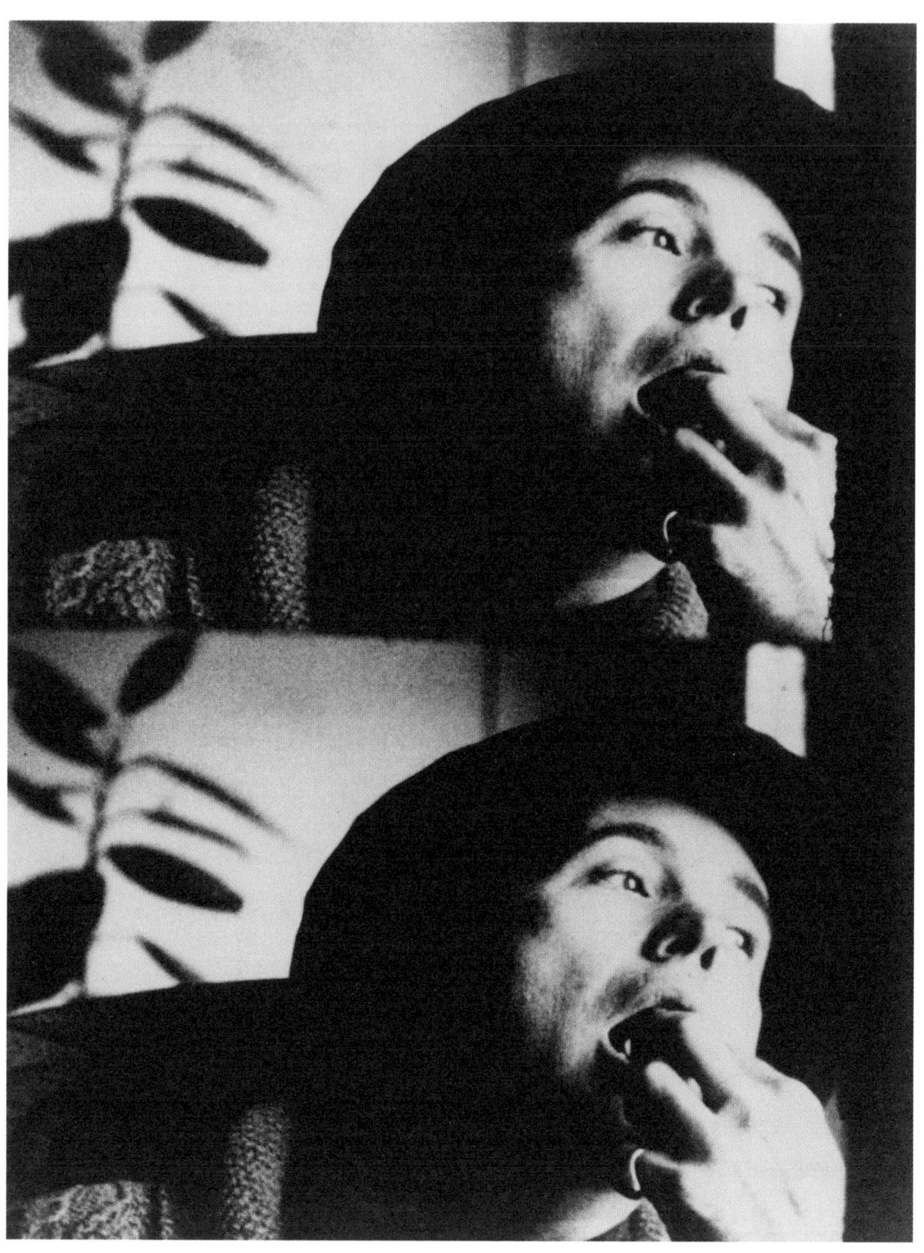

Andy Warhol, *Eat*, 1964.
Film stills.

dogs to Elizabeth and her husband King George VI when they visited. The wieners were presented on a silver tray and eaten off paper plates—and it was a private picnic at the President's country residence in Hyde Park, New York, not the ballpark, but Warhol's point about it being as good (or bad) a hot dog as the Royals could get anywhere else is still valid. In the event, the meal was a success, and the *New York Times* proclaimed: "King tries hot dog and asks for more," also reporting that Elizabeth inquired of Roosevelt how one should eat the thing. "Very simple," he replied, "push it into your mouth and keep pushing it until it is all gone."[12] She opted for a knife and fork instead.

For his appearance in Danish filmmaker Jørgen Leth's 1982 film *66 Scenes from America*, Warhol spent eight minutes eating a Burger King hamburger. In a single, fixed shot he opens the paper bag containing the hamburger, unwraps it, inspects it, and looks bored. He eats the burger in a dispassionate, methodical manner, and, following Roosevelt's instructions, he keeps eating until it is all gone. Conscious of the importance Warhol accorded to design and branding, Leth had asked his assistant to buy hamburgers with plain wrapping. They came back with three hamburgers, two in plain wrapping and one from Burger King. Had they read *The Philosophy of Andy Warhol*, they would have known about Warhol's preference for McDonald's, which he thought had the nicest design. In fact, according to Warhol, McDonald's was even "the most beautiful thing" in cities around the world, including Tokyo, Stockholm, and Florence, and at the time the lack of McDonalds in "Peking and Moscow" meant they didn't have "anything beautiful yet."[13] But it was more than design that drew him to hot dogs and burgers: they were powerful symbols of an unprecedented era of American freedom, wealth, and fun.

In 2019, Burger King ran a television commercial for its Whopper hamburger during the Super Bowl halftime show, featuring a clip of Warhol's appearance in Leth's film with the hashtag #eatlikeandy. It has received more than 3 billion media impressions to date, but popular perception of Warhol as a hamburger eater is at odds with the more idiosyncratic reality of his culinary habits.[14] According to Warhol's biographer Blake Gopnik, Warhol did eat fast food, especially at McDonald's, once it opened across the street from his studio—but receipts show that he also ate plenty of exotic and very high-end meals ... Then once he was shot and his guts got ruined, his favorite nourishment was the insides of chocolate-covered cherries, sucked out of their chocolate coating! So to "eat like Andy" is to eat WEIRD![15]

The fact that Warhol integrated aspects of his food life into his meticulously crafted public persona reminds us of the rich sensual realm of the early museum. Both value the role of a wide range of senses in shaping our picture of the world. The tactile, textural, social, philosophical, palatable, and the distasteful were all welcome in Warhol's world. The result is a lavish menu of options for living, fully invested with playful sensory potential, from his thirst for a quintessentially democratic Coca-Cola to his deadpan instructions for making cake.

During the 1960s, Warhol's Factory was the playground of a diverse cohort of eccentrics, superstars, waifs, and strays who hung out, danced, and sat for screen tests, cultivating individual fame and often misbehaving. At the same time, it was the studio in which Warhol created a prolific artistic output across a range of media. When quizzed about the ever-growing prices for his work, Warhol was fond of telling people that it was because he had "a lot of mouths to feed," and "someone has to bring home the bacon." Among his Factory gang were young people from various social groups, a mix of dropouts from privileged milieus, like the socialite Edie Sedgwick, and others from all different kinds of backgrounds who didn't quite fit in elsewhere. They all contributed to the chaotic energy of the Factory, and helped bolster Warhol's status as a cultural innovator in a decade marked by a loosening of behavioral codes and experimentation in ways of life, drugs, music, and spirituality.

Warhol's films *Eat* (1964) and *Drunk aka Drink* (1965) were made in this context and feature extreme endurance practices related to food and drink. The footage used for *Eat*, a 45-minute portrait of artist Robert Indiana slowly eating a single mushroom, was edited out of sequence and slowed down, resulting in a strange and comic portrait of a man, his cat, and a mushroom. For *Drunk aka Drink*, Warhol's pre-Factory era friend Emile de Antonio offered to drink a quart (just over a liter) of whisky in 20 minutes, boasting "Marine Corps sergeants have been known to die doing that and I am willing to risk my ass for you."[16] The film was shot in the Factory's stairwell, with Warhol's camera peering down at de Antonio, who over the course of an hour became incoherent, sang, ranted, and finally passed out. The next morning, de Antonio phoned his lawyer and told him to forbid Warhol from screening the film, threatening to sue him for 1 million dollars if he ever did. It remained unseen until 2016, when it finally made its New York debut at MoMA. In each film, a seemingly simple act—eating a mushroom or drinking heavy liquor—is made strange by the intense gaze of Warhol's camera combined with very minimal action (a tendency in many of his films, epitomized by *Empire*, his eight-hour-long 1965 film of a static shot of the Empire State Building). The slowness and obsessive focus of these films provide us with time and space to identify with the sensations that make up the experiences depicted—the dissolving of the raw mushroom into a viscous paste, the heat and confusion of staggering drunkenness.

The extreme behaviors of *Eat* and *Drunk aka Drink* have a similar intensity to Warhol's strict dietary restrictions when he was trying to lose weight, a long-term preoccupation that later became a fixation when he was taken on by the Zoli modeling agency in 1981. With a characteristic blend of sentimentality and irony, he announced the "Andy Warhol New York City Diet." When he dined at luxurious restaurants, whose ambiance he preferred to their food, he would order extravagant dishes, leave them more or less untouched and ask the waiter to wrap up his leftovers. He would then deposit the food parcel on the street for someone in need. This stunt, a small scene within the overall performance of his life, spanned the rarefied heights and cruel depths of New York's social hierarchy, and allowed him to attend chic restaurants, stay trim, and participate in humanitarianism.[17] It recruited restaurant staff, fellow diners, and casual passers-by into the creation of an event, which Warhol had devised and even branded with his own name.

In August 1974, Warhol and his team moved from the Factory on Union Square West around the corner to the Office at 860 Broadway, where the third floor of the building became the new headquarters of Andy Warhol Enterprises and his *Interview* magazine. Founded in 1969 by Warhol and the British journalist John Wilcock, *Interview* was touted as "The Crystal Ball of Pop" and featured interviews with artists, musicians, and celebrities done in a natural, unedited style that resembles the conversational tone of *The Philosophy of Andy Warhol*. The boardroom at the new premises was the site of glamorous lunch gatherings for potential advertisers, models, artists, and celebrities, which at first consisted of health food from Brownies Cafe, where Warhol got the carrot juice and tea he drank as he recovered from being shot, but eventually became more decadent, with salmon and caviar sandwiches and an open bar.

The move from the Factory to the Office prompted the creation of Warhol's Time Capsules. Between 1974 and the end of his life in 1987, he made some 610 Time Capsules, which held on average 250 items each. They were a way to make into art the ephemera he had compulsively kept for years and stored in his apartment and studio. Time Capsule number 212, for example, includes two French fry sleeves and two packages of salt from McDonald's; Time Capsule 318 contains an Altoids mints tin, a common item in the Time Capsules, which Warhol may have used for the mints it originally contained, or to store recreational drugs. According to Warhol's friend Richard Dupont, he "always had an Altoids tin full of quaaludes that people had given him hoping to hang out with him."[18]

Perhaps because he had grown up in poor circumstances, or because he had a special ability to see the artistic potential in mundane objects, Warhol was loath to throw anything away, and recycling was important to him. If his New York City Diet was a way of recycling his uneaten food for those less fortunate, the Time Capsules transformed the leftovers of his life into art. In a 1980 interview, Warhol extended this principle to his art, saying it should be resold by collectors because "it's like everything else. I think everything else should be recycled, like leftover food at restaurants. That's what I sort of believe in."[19]

Although he frequented gourmet restaurants and celebrated modern convenience foods in his art, nostalgia for the "carefree" era of the 1940s and 1950s played a big part in Warhol's food life. He loved "the good, plain, American lunchroom or even the good plain American lunch counter" at places like the Chock full o'Nuts coffee shop chain, where he could always get his favorite: a cream cheese sandwich with nuts on date-nut bread. He saw this kind of food as a stabilizing force, writing that "No matter what changes or how fast, the one thing we all always need is real good food so we can know what the changes are and how fast they're coming. Progress is very important and exciting in everything except food." This clash between progressive and reactionary attitudes to food was sublimated in Warhol's plans for the Andy-Mat diner, where comfort food could be eaten in a high-tech setting.

Warhol freely admitted that he was shy, and when it came to mealtimes he preferred to eat alone. To cater for others in the same predicament, he came up with an idea for "The Restaurant for the Lonely Person." It would be a cross between an automat and a private living room, where people would get their food from an automated counter, and take their tray into a booth to eat and watch television alone.[20] The Andy-Mat would be contact-free and sterile, and as a self-service operation it put diners in control of their experience. Chance and risk were minimized, since the menu would always be the same, and although eating at the Andy-Mat would be a solitary experience, diners could indulge their voyeuristic desires, watching each other from a distance, perhaps cruising and occasionally catching sight of the preparation area behind the hatches through which the food was served. Reporting on the initiative in 1977, the *New York Times* saw it as an expression of Warhol's essence as "a 20th century man child, [who] loves junk food."[21]

The idea of the Andy-Mat diner appealed to a group of entrepreneurs who partnered with Warhol to plot its launch. They included Geoffrey Leeds, who had brokered the sale of the old London Bridge and its relocation to the US, architect Araldo Cossutta, and banker C. Cheever Hardwick III. Lest anyone should think the entrepreneurs were taking advantage of Warhol's ability to draw in profits with this move into the fast-food business, Leeds told a journalist that *they* were actually under *his* spell, explaining that "by Andy's sheer passiveness, he harnesses others."[22] As early as 1974, the same year the founders of FOOD finally called it quits, Leeds and Warhol had discussed starting a restaurant, motivated by their shared nostalgia for food from back in the day: if Warhol missed his date-nut cream-cheese sandwiches, Leeds yearned for Schrafft's restaurant chain's "hot lamb sandwiches, their chicken pie and their former prices." They found restaurant culture at the time polarized: "You can't eat out for less than $35 at a little neighborhood restaurant ... the only other option is Burger King or McDonald's."[23] The Andy-Mat would sit somewhere in the middle: "a neighborhood restaurant with a varied menu, simple good food, reasonable prices" and, according to Leeds, "a place where you don't have to be embarrassed to take someone."[24] The business development of Warhol's original idea took it some distance from the cool, solitary automat and television experience he had envisioned. With partners on board, it evolved into something that combined infantilism with high glamor. Still, the ambition to take it global was Warholian enough.

Aristocrat, cookbook author, *Vogue* food columnist, model, muse, and mother figure to Warhol, Maxime de la Falaise McKendry joined the team to design the menu, which included nutritious comfort foods such as a fried-onion tart, shepherd's pie, fish cakes, Irish lamb stew, mashed potatoes, and four assorted mini omelets especially for Warhol. To drink, there would be a choice of champagne or a "nursery cocktail" of milk on the rocks, delivered by waitresses dressed like nannies. Pneumatic tubes would convey orders to the kitchen where the food, all of it frozen, would be reheated. Leeds claimed that "Ninety percent of food in restaurants today is pre-frozen," and the Andy-Mat's own line of frozen food would be made by Flagstaff Corp., which supplied Cunard Lines cruise ships, the Intercontinental Hotel chain, and supermarkets.[25]

An early concept for the interior design was a "sit-down supermarket decorated with frozen food packages," where people could choose from the frozen food section.[26] But in the end,

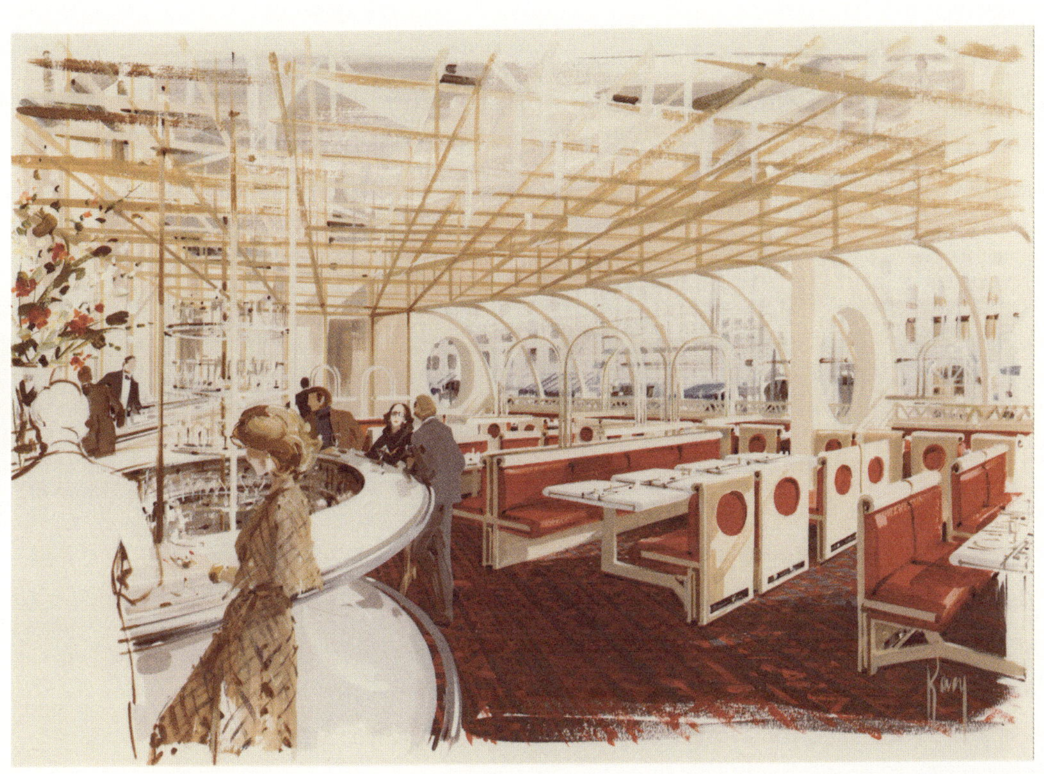

Prospectus for the Andy-Mat diner (detail), 1977.

the 115-seat interior was designed in consultation with Ellen Lehman McCloskey and featured tables and chairs in a block and circle motif, like a child's toy, as well as somewhat sexier red mohair velvet banquettes. A site was found on Madison Avenue at 74th Street, near the Whitney Museum and the Stable Gallery, where Warhol had exhibited his work in the early 1960s, and $1 million capital was raised, but the Andy-Mat was never realized because, according to Gopnik, "Warhol ran into some kind of real estate trouble with the Madison Avenue flagship."[27]

Warhol's life and relationship with food are marbled with contradictions. He yearned for simple, childhood foods and aspired to enjoy gourmet foods. These competing desires produced some of his strangest impulses, some of which he confessed in his writings: "I'll buy a huge piece of meat, cook it up for dinner, and then right before it's done I'll break down and have what I wanted for dinner in the first place—bread and jam." But these contradictions prompt deeper reflection about the role food plays in pleasure and the processing of emotions.

Throughout his life, food was a comfort for Warhol, from the Hershey's bars his mother gave him to reward his creativity when he was ill, to the nursery cocktail he dreamed up for the Andy-Mat diner. When difficult times arose, he would seek solace in food, often eating simple snacks alone. When his relationship with his boyfriend Jed came under pressure after Jed discovered Warhol's *Landscapes*, a secret photographic series of explicit close-ups of male nudes shot with nearly 50 different models, he ate junk food to soothe his nerves. One of the most poignant instances of Warhol turning to food for consolation took place after a public appearance to promote his 1985 book *America* at the Rizzoli bookstore in New York. A girl pretending to request an autograph approached Warhol at the table where he sat signing books, snatched his wig off his head, and threw it over the balcony to an accomplice who ran away with it. Warhol later told his diary the experience was as awful as if he had been shot again. He went home and had a snack consisting of two English muffins with margarine and garlic, and some dried Campbell's soup. None of which, he knew, was "too good for my gallbladder."[28]

In February 1987, shortly before his death, Warhol told his diary, "I had a sharp pain and I guess it was a gall bladder attack."[29] He had been putting off an operation and knew how vulnerable he was to ill health, so he immediately threw away all his junk food. By then his philosophy had morphed from one so often expressed in terms of food, money, and death into one primarily concerned with health. He went from believing that "making money is art and working is art and good business is the best art"[30] to telling his diary that "life is not worth living if you're not healthy. And health is wealth. It's better than money, and companionship, and love, and everything else."[31] A few days after his terrible gall bladder attack, he was rushed to hospital for emergency surgery, and died the following day of cardiac arrhythmia. According to his medical report, Warhol had been anemic and malnourished prior to the surgery.[32] His grave site is visible 24 hours a day, seven days a week, online via webcam. On top of his tombstone are three cans of Campbell's soup, in case he gets a hankering in the afterlife for that mythical childhood lunch.

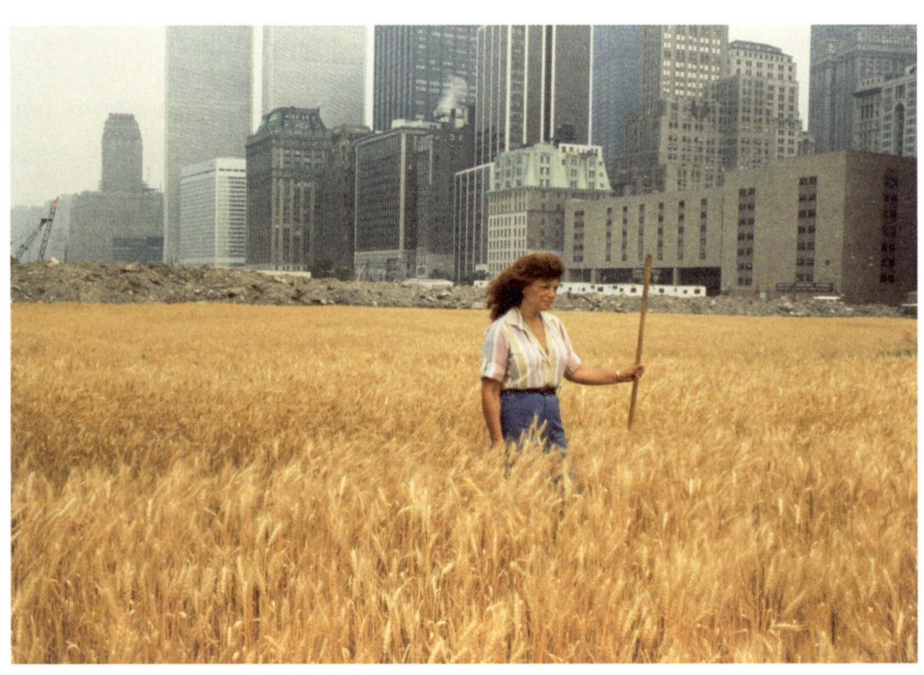

Agnes Denes, *Wheatfield: A Confrontation*, 1982. Documentation of the project at the Battery Park Landfill, Downtown Manhattan.

AGNES DENES

Wall Street Wheat

EARLY ON THE MORNING of 1 May 1982, New York-based artist Agnes Denes arrived at the 92-acre Battery Park landfill site, located at the southern tip of Manhattan Island. She began digging over an area that would eventually stretch to 1.8 acres, to create the first of 285 furrows into which she and her assistants would plant wheat seeds before covering them over with earth. The first of May was the earliest day Denes was able to begin work on *Wheatfield: A Confrontation* and, although she did not choose it for any other reason, the date has some interesting associations. Falling midway between the spring equinox and the summer solstice, in medieval Celtic culture it was the date for the festival of Beltane, which celebrates the beginning of summer, and since the mid-19th century it has marked International Workers' Day. For Denes, however, the primary concerns when creating the work were confronting the misuse of land and addressing world hunger.[1]

Denes's work, for which she cultivated a field of wheat over the course of one summer within a densely packed urban environment, places food at the heart of global supply systems and power structures. Its location, which would later become Battery Park City, was laden with symbolic associations: within view of Wall Street's skyscrapers, it sat between the World Trade Center's Twin Towers, the Statue of Liberty, and the historic immigration hub of Ellis Island. Commerce and freedom—defining themes of American culture—face each other across the site. Although the Public Art Fund, which commissioned the work, initially encouraged Denes to create the project in Queens, where land would be cheaper and more easily obtained, she insisted on realizing it at the Battery Park Landfill, one of the last undeveloped sites on the intensively zoned island of Manhattan. It was a perfect foil for Denes's project, which put into play the magic through which grain, soil, sun, and water are transformed into food.

The landfill had been created with earth removed from the future site of the Twin Towers between 1968 and 1973. Debris from the construction was added at a disconcerting rate: 200 truckloads of "dirty landfill" were dumped between March and May 1982. The ground was a hazardous mess, "full of rusty pipes, boulders, old tires, and overcoats,"[2] and for one month prior to planting, Denes worked with two assistants and up to seven volunteers at a time to prepare the soil. They cleared rocks, metal, and other detritus, flattened the ground with tractors, and added 80 truckloads of soil to create one inch of topsoil across the site. With a $10,000 grant from the Public Art Fund[i] the project was on a tight budget, and Denes worked 16-hour days, making sandwiches each night to give to the volunteers the next day, because she couldn't afford to pay them.[3] After preparing the ground and planting the wheat, they set up an irrigation system, fertilized the crop, sprayed against mildew fungus, and eliminated wheat smut, a damaging fungus that was prevalent across the country at the time. According to Denes, cultivating and harvesting the wheat by hand in her field meant it was the only healthy wheat yield in the country that summer.[4]

It was hard work, but it had a positive effect on those who participated, helping them connect to their environment, understand the fertility of earth, and appreciate the origins of the food they ate. It helped some to balance their emotions, and one volunteer thanked Denes "for allowing her to throw rocks off the field, saving her enormous psychiatric fees, having gotten all aggression out of her system against her ex."[5] The field soon became a local landmark: on one occasion when Denes took a taxi to Wall Street, her driver offered to take her to "see our wheatfield," thinking she was a tourist. There are reports of people weeping when they first encountered the golden expanse thriving at the edge of the built-up financial district. Others cried

i It was the second project in The Urban Environmental Site Program after Alan Finkel's *View for the Catenary Curve* (July 1981–December 1982), a water-tank viewing station framing a section of Brooklyn Bridge in relation to Manhattan skyline, located in Brooklyn's Empire-Fulton Ferry State Park.

when it was harvested, a solemn action performed in front of an audience of volunteers and locals, with a TV crew filming it for NBC's flagship news program *The Today Show*.

Born in Budapest, Hungary, in 1931, Denes says she was born to be an artist and wrote her first poem aged six. She was uprooted at an early age when her family moved to Stockholm and later to New York in 1954, a city she made her home.[6] Growing up in Sweden she had felt "the alienation that people who come into new countries feel," and as a very young artist she identified with migrating birds, which inspired her earliest environmental work, *The Bird Project* (1979). By the time she arrived in the US she spoke five languages, but over time she gradually lost her multilingual abilities.[7] "From the poetry being stilled," she says, "a visual expression was born." She ceased to write poetry and turned her creative efforts toward a visual expression of her philosophical concepts. An independent thinker and creator from a young age, Denes studied science, philosophy, and mathematics, and her goal was to reevaluate human knowledge. Many years of intense study yielded a new art form, "visual philosophy."[8] In 1972, Denes was invited to become a founding member of A.I.R., the first all-female cooperative gallery in the US. Run by women for women "to change attitudes about art by women,"[9] A.I.R. provided space for the creation and exhibition of women's art at a time when it was often ignored or belittled. However, Denes's interests extended beyond the cooperative's feminist agenda, which led her to leave the gallery. Denes's creativity extends to all areas of her life, including cooking, and the team at FOOD invited her for a stint as a guest chef. For Denes, art has always been an open system that can connect with other disciplines to generate new ways of understanding the world. She sees art as a "specialization that need not feed upon itself," but instead opens new vistas for humanity.[10]

Denes envisaged *Wheatfield: A Confrontation* as "an intrusion into the Citadel," since Manhattan's financial district was an expression of the dominating forces of capitalism. The work was also a "Shangri-la," an earthly paradise untethered from its supposedly civilized surroundings, where the natural fertility of the land supported the growth of grain for food.[11] An aerial photograph by the artist shows the field within the landfill, the planted area an ingot of gold surrounded by a churning mass of waste and mud etched with the tracks of farm machinery.

During the summer of 1982, the field of wheat was an idyll for city dwellers, a balm for senses heightened or frayed by the city's intensities, a place to ground emotions and watch new life grow. The field provided unusual sensations for visitors; one imagines them plunging their hands into the earth, weighing and tossing debris, sowing delicate seeds, and feeling the earth under their feet. The wheatfield was never vandalized, which Denes has stated was because "people don't hurt what they love."[12] On NBC's television coverage of the harvest, presenter Jane Pauley asked Denes "Did it hurt a little bit to cut it down?" "Oh yes," she replied, "I lived out there for about four months."[13] Yet even in its absence *Wheatfield* continues to highlight the paradox of eternal impermanence: seasons return each year and nature's cycles continue in spite of human interference.

Denes chose to cultivate a variety known as Hard Red Spring durum wheat, which is planted in spring and harvested in autumn, and which she chose for its ability to grow in the site's poor soil. Spring wheat often has more of the protein gluten than winter wheat, and at 13.5 percent red spring wheat has the highest protein content of all wheat varieties, making it an especially nutritious variety used for bread, croissants, and pizza dough. With its reddish husks, it produces a slightly darker flour and a nuttier, more bitter flavor than white wheat. The grain was harvested in August 1982, and Denes gave some of the wheat to the New York Police Department to feed its horses as a gesture of thanks. Yielding nearly 1,000 pounds of healthy wheat, the harvest was worth very little. It had been cultivated on a parcel of land whose value was then estimated at about $4.5 billion. On the trading floor on nearby Wall Street, wheat was abstracted into a commodity and traded for its commercial value rather than its nutritious properties. By the standards of modern capitalism and from the point of view of property developers, there is a deliberately ironic aspect to *Wheatfield*. Denes states that the project "grew out of a long-standing concern and need to call attention to our misplaced priorities and deteriorating human values," and she intended it to waste "valuable precious real estate." But it went beyond the mismatch between the land's price and its use-value. *Wheatfield* connected to a broad range of values and systems that were key to its meaning. Denes has written that it "represented food, energy, commerce, world trade, economics [and] referred to mismanagement and world hunger."

A constellation of meanings may also be inferred from *Wheatfield*, including the way agricultural practices were politicized during the 20th century, and the impact this had on the availability, quality, and cost of food, which in turn affected lives and livelihoods. Following the disruption that World War I wrought on food production globally, the Great Depression prompted many countries to adopt protectionist policies geared toward self-sufficiency, including milling ratios that set the legal obligation to use a minimum amount of domestic grain. During World War II, agricultural production dropped in most European countries, while in the USA, which saw no military action on the ground, production and demand increased, and prices rose. The main driver in this growth was the Green Revolution: the agricultural counterpart to the consumer revolution that inspired Warhol.

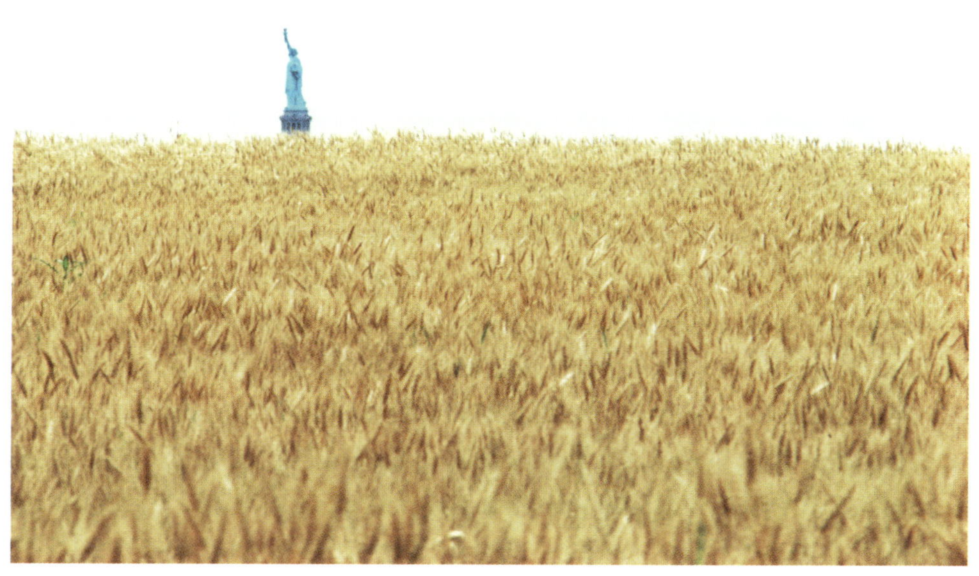

Agnes Denes, *Wheatfield: A Confrontation*, 1982. Documentation of the project at the Battery Park Landfill, Downtown Manhattan.

At the end of World War II, the global population was 2.5 billion and predicted to reach 9 billion by 2015 (an overestimate: it ended up being 7.3 billion). The world would need to dramatically expand its food production systems if there was any hope of avoiding widespread famine. The Green Revolution was the answer, a series of policies that increased rates of grain production, especially wheat and rice, from 1940 to the present day. The main factors in this growth were the development of new, high-yielding varieties of grain and their introduction to developing countries, with Mexico and India particularly successful in their efforts to increase yields. The Green Revolution also turned the US from an importer of wheat into a major exporter. Among the scientists responsible for pioneering the new breeds of grain were the American geneticist Norman Borlaug and the Indian M. S. Swaminathan, who developed short-stemmed wheat varieties with larger grain heads. But these new strains weren't straightforward to cultivate, and they required large amounts of chemical fertilizer and pesticides, and new irrigation systems. Countries without the infrastructure necessary for the new farming practices were disadvantaged because the new strains yielded far less when grown without pesticides and fertilizer, and the diversity of older strains of wheat and rice gave way to monocultures, which are less resistant to diseases and pests. While the Green Revolution fed many people who might otherwise have starved, it also contributed to the global crises in farming and food justice that Denes's work addressed; for example, the challenges of achieving good-quality soil for growing food, and the elevation of food's value as commodity over its function as nourishment.

Wheatfield: A Confrontation may also be seen as a timely response to the way food had been weaponized in the US grain embargo on the USSR, which profoundly changed international trade relations and sowed the seeds for future geopolitical frictions. Initiated by President Jimmy Carter in January 1980, the embargo was a response to the Soviet invasion of Afghanistan on Christmas Eve 1979. As a result, the USSR ceased to import grain from the US and began trading with other countries, mainly Argentina and other South American suppliers, including Brazil. They focused on cultivating wheat in Ukraine, initiating the privatization of farmland and the adoption of free-market prices, all of which added up to Russia becoming the world's largest grain exporter by the middle of the 2010s. The long-term implications of this policy and its ramifications for global food supply chains became painfully obvious when hunger was used as a weapon after Russia's invasion of Ukraine in 2022, notably through the blockade of Black Sea ports from which ships loaded with Ukrainian grain had previously sailed to supply countries around the world.

International relations, and the grain embargo in particular, continued to inform Denes's thinking. To unify the planet under the aegis of wheat, Denes proposed planting three synchronized fields, in Moscow, Beijing, and Washington, DC, plus two in the Diomede Islands in the Arctic Circle during the area's summertime. Her idea was to mix wheat from the US and the USSR to create a hardy hybrid, a symbol of the two antagonistic nations coming together in a generative act. She wanted to celebrate the new breed with a harvest festival for "the miracles of life, growth, endurance and global consciousness."[14]

Additionally, for three years in the late 1980s, samples from *Wheatfield*'s harvest traveled to 18 cities in Europe, Asia, Africa, and the Americas as part of The International Art Show for the End of World Hunger.[ii] People from all over the globe were invited to take seeds home with them and plant them in their local area.

ii Organized by the Minnesota Museum of Art, 1987–1990.

More than a decade before planting *Wheatfield*, Denes had already announced her philosophy and lifelong commitment to ecological issues, presaging today's environmental art movement. In 1968, she created *Rice/Tree/Burial*, her first site work concerned with the environment. The approach brought together her interest in science, which she had studied since a child, with her growing concern for the health of the planet, which she recognized as an issue of global importance that offered scope for artistic innovation. The rice, tree, and burial of the title related to three key themes, which Denes expressed in a trio of ritual acts first performed privately in Sullivan County, New York: planting rice to represent life, chaining trees to represent "interference with life and natural processes,"[15] and burying haiku poetry to represent ideas, human intellectual powers, and creation. The work conceptualized the world as a set of interrelated systems and actions. She repeated the work on a much larger scale during the summer of 1977 at Artpark in Lewiston, New York. The second time, the location included a sacred forest that was also a Native American burial ground. She also planted half an acre of rice 150 feet above the Niagara gorge near the Love Canal neighborhood of Niagara Falls. Decades of dumping toxic chemicals led to an environmental disaster and public health crisis in the 1970s, which caused the rice to grow deformed. Through *Rice/Tree/Burial*, Denes made an active commitment to addressing ecological and environmental issues, life, death, and the forces of nature—the philosophical underpinnings of all her ideas.

As a work that occurred outside the gallery setting, *Wheatfield* marked Denes's ambition to do more than just exhibit artifacts in museums. It was often assumed to be part of the land art movement, whose mostly male protagonists, such as Michael Heizer and Robert Smithson, created vast and highly ambitious interventions, or earthworks, in remote locations using materials sourced from the earth itself. Such works challenged expectations around the scale, location, material, and duration of artworks. But their sheer might and the perception that they disrupt the landscape has led to criticisms of these works as expressions of machismo and ego, the result, some say, of a heroic artist's will to leave his mark on a site. Equally ambitious in terms of scale and labor, *Wheatfield* is the creation of a gentle intervention in the land with a philosophical meaning and societal importance. It transcends time, space, and the formal inventions of contemporary art.

Wheatfield lives on in individual and collective memory, a natural utopia amid glass and concrete. The work was reenacted in London in 2012 and in Milan in 2015, but the original setting's symbolism, with the Twin Towers rising proudly in the background, is hard to match. With the terrorist attacks of 11 September 2001 and the destruction of the towers, Denes's work gains added poignancy.

Denes's wheatfield was a paradise on earth, a philosophical statement, and a warning to future generations. It used food to connect the lived sensory experience of raising a crop with global economic and political systems. In agriculture, rational order is imposed on fertile nature to produce something sensuous, nutritious, and, to a certain extent, unpredictable. Although the original wheatfield came to an end with its harvest, by circulating seeds from the original plants around the globe Denes inserted the work back into an ongoing process of sowing, growth, and harvest, reminding us that food is always a cyclical entity and never just an end in itself.

FELIX GONZALES-TORRES

An Endless Supply

AS DENES DEMONSTRATED with her wheatfield, the food we eat originates in seasonal and agricultural cycles. As our cooking and eating habits have diversified, further rhythms and patterns have appeared, brought about by food's connection to personal or social rituals, and sometimes by economic, political, or environmental events. Foods appear at different times of the day or on certain dates, then disappear until the next occasion. In 1990, the Cuban-born American artist Felix Gonzalez-Torres began making a series of artworks using confectionery—a food loaded with festive promise—which were similarly notable for the way they appeared, disappeared, and reappeared.

Pursuing a strand of his work comprising sculptures made of multiple components that viewers were encouraged to take away with them, in 1990 Gonzalez-Torres created *"Untitled" (Fortune Cookie Corner)*, a pile of 10,000 fortune cookies available for people to take, read, and eat, until the pile was gone. The pile was then replenished and the cycle of offering, acquisition, and depletion began again. It was the first in a series of sculptures he called the "candy works," made from a range of sweets such as Italian hazelnut chocolate Baci, or kisses, black rod licorice, cough drops, and white mints, variously wrapped in clear cellophane, branded packaging, or colored foil. Although they all use sweet components, Gonzalez-Torres built in a great variability to these works. With ideal weights ranging from 42 to 700 lb, and in some cases consisting of merely a handful of candies, the candy works are diverse in scale and volume. Depending on how long the works have been exhibited and how many people have chosen to pick up one or more candies (or to experience the work without taking any at all), there may be many or no candies present. Additionally, since the owners or borrowers of these works have the right to decide when, how, and to what extent they replenish the candy, the sculptures will diminish at different rates. As he installed the works,

Gonzalez-Torres poured thousands of individually wrapped candies onto the ground and arranged them into glittering carpets or heaped them against walls and in corners of galleries and museums, where the shimmering allure of the foil-wrapped treats attracted people, tempting them to pick one up and eat it. These works disaggregate as their component parts disappear into pockets and bags, move through the digestive system, and are dispersed into the world beyond the gallery.

In the gifting of his work, Gonzalez-Torres offered people a free sensory experience of something sweet. Candy provides an innocent pleasure that can provoke a sense of childlike delight, and part of the appeal of the candy works is their ability to spark joy. But the works were also meant to bring feelings of reflection, grief, mourning, and commemoration into a public setting. In 1991, Gonzalez-Torres's used candy to create a portrait of his partner, Ross Laycock, who died from AIDS-related illness in January 1991. Constituted of candies in variously colored wrappers, the sculpture *"Untitled" (Ross)* (1991) was conceived as a physical equivalent for Laycock. Its ideal weight of 175 lb matches Laycock's weight when he was healthy, though its overall dimensions can vary with each installation. While this weight can be seen to relate to Laycock's healthy body weight, and the dwindling pile of candies stands in for the terminally ill body as it wastes away, Gonzalez-Torres's intended for new meanings to arise over time as his work was installed in different contexts and configurations. The ideal weight of 175 lb can also be interpreted as a generalized or approximate weight of a healthy individual, and it was the same weight Gonzalez-Torres used in another portrait he made the same year, *"Untitled" (Portrait of Dad)* (1991). Two other candy works, both titled *"Untitled" (Lover Boys)* (1991), have ideal weights of 355 lb, the combined weight of Gonzalez-Torres and Laycock when they were both healthy. One of these works consists of candies in silver wrappers, while the other is made up of blue-and-white spiral candies, the two colors spun together in a state of fusion.

For Gonzalez-Torres, who died from AIDS-related illness five years after Laycock, in January 1996, staging the disappearance of posters and candies was a response to his partner's, and later his own, physical decline. He wanted the works to operate as sympathetic objects onto which he could transfer the painful process of deterioration and loss as a way to protect himself against their devastating impact. Looking back on his motivations for making these works, he referenced Sigmund Freud's idea that we rehearse our fears in order to lessen them. By refusing to give his works a fixed form and instead allowing them to be "changing, unstable, and fragile" things that gradually reduce to nothing, Gonzalez-Torres was staging a kind of "letting go" that he felt looming over him. It was his attempt "to rehearse my fears of having Ross disappear day by day right in front of my eyes."[1]

As stand-ins for suffering bodies, the piles of candy call to mind the Christian Eucharist. Reaching for a candy, unwrapping it, and putting it in one's mouth initiates a process of assimilation into the body of the eater in much the same way that the body and blood of Christ are supposed to bring about a communion in the members of a congregation. There is a transfer of energy from the artwork into our bodies, but it is less a matter of calories than of emotion and empathy.

Between 1991 and his death in 1996, Gonzalez-Torres created 20 of these candy works, designating some of them as tributes to people he cared about, including Laycock, his father, and his close friend the artist Roni Horn. Other candy works related to issues that affected Gonzalez-Torres's personal life, public opinion about freedom of expression, and, with the red, white, and blue wrapped Bazooka bubblegum of *"Untitled" (Welcome Back Heroes)* (1991), American military operations abroad.

Felix Gonzalez-Torres was born in 1957 in Guáimaro, Cuba. He moved to Madrid in 1971 and then lived in Puerto Rico. In 1979, he went to New York. There, he studied art and photography at schools including New York University, where he also taught in the late 1980s. Between 1987 and 1994, he was a member of the art collective Group Material, which initiated community education and cultural activism projects. Gonzalez-Torres's own art uses Minimalist tropes such as a monochrome palette, the practice of leaving works untitled, and the use of industrially produced materials, geometric forms, and strategies of repetition. But his Minimalist tendencies were a strategy: as an openly gay man and a Latino, using them was a way of appropriating established art styles of the dominant macho white American art world of the 1980s and 1990s in order to infiltrate it. "It's almost like being in drag," he told the writer Nancy Princenthal in 1994 of his adopted esthetic.[2]

From a distance, Gonzalez-Torres's works might be mistaken for one of Carl Andre's metal floor pieces, a Donald Judd stack, or a slumped corner sculpture by Lynda Benglis. But by using food to create works that gradually disappeared, his works disrupt the conventions of the modern art gallery. He rejected traditional artistic media such as stone, bronze, or oil paint, which were laden with meaning and redolent of dominant power systems. Instead, he used ephemeral materials that disappeared into people's hands and mouths, and whose meanings were not fixed. They helped Gonzalez-Torres's work infiltrate the "cracks in the 'master narrative'" and tell a different story.[3]

The items in Gonzalez-Torres's works were intended to perish and be replaced, even those that were not to be consumed as food. His "light strings" were sculptures fashioned from lightbulbs and suspended from the ceiling or draped around a space. When the bulbs burned out, fresh ones would be put in their place and the work would gain a new lease of life. The list of materials for the candy works stipulates an "endless supply" of sweets, and each work is authenticated by a certificate of ownership that specifies where edible provisions can be sourced, and how to ensure they are exactly right. The certificate for the fortune cookie piece, for example, allows that fortune cookies can be obtained from a range of producers provided the messages they contain are optimistic—a concern for the emotional wellbeing of the viewer that Gonzalez-Torres shared with Wilke.[4]

Because monetary value would be difficult to assign to disappearing piles of renewable stock, Gonzalez-Torres conceived of his evanescent works as "a threat to the art-marketing system." And, although empty candy wrappers sometimes litter the floor around the works and outside museums where they are installed, some people choose to save the candies they pick up, arresting the intended disintegration of the work and breaching the boundaries of the museum so that the art comes to exist both inside and outside the institution.

But his selection of materials was about more than resisting patriarchal modes of creation and display; there was also a pragmatic reason for choosing everyday objects. As he told the artist Tim Rollins, in the late 1980s when painting was the preferred medium and commanded the highest prices, artists had to fight for wall space to display their canvases. The floor of the gallery was often free, a "marginal space" that Gonzalez-Torres claimed for his stacks and piles. And since they could be made and remade *in situ*, the works also freed him from the costs and constraints of renting a studio. As he told the artist David Reed, he didn't have or need one, since he was "just a kitchen-table artist."[5]

Gonzalez-Torres also chose candies and cookies to get his message across because he knew it would be difficult to sensationalize these supposedly innocuous treats, even though he intended the work to have an erotic charge. "You put it in your mouth and you suck on someone else's body," he said. "For just a few seconds, I have put something sweet in someone's mouth, and that is very sexy."[6] He was keenly aware that in the early 1990s any work that carried messages related to homosexual love and AIDS risked being mired in controversy, but he also knew that, thanks to his use of sweets, any "homophobic senator is going to have a hard time trying to explain to his constituency that my work is homoerotic or pornographic."[7] The ingredients in his works were banal enough to pass under the radar, their true meaning undecidable. For Gonzalez-Torres, this unknowable quality was a kind of "in-betweenness," which he equated with a pleasurable sense of danger and with his personal experience as a gay man at a time when this was stigmatized and he was "forced by culture and by language to always live a life of in-between."[8]

Part of Gonzalez-Torres's aim for his work was to provide space and time for people to pause and think. He credited the influence of the avant-garde German playwright Bertolt Brecht in helping him achieve this aim. Brecht, who had experienced trauma as a medical orderly during World War I, was staunchly opposed to naturalistic art. His plays avoided illusion, narrative, and plot, and consisted instead of episodes that would wake passive audiences from their stupor. Through devices such as direct address to the audience, minimal sets, props used as symbols such as a soldier's gun, simple white lighting, and fun in the form of satirical songs, spectators would be activated and inspired to think. They would then be better equipped to respond to situations in their lives and motivated to effect social change in the world. These tactics can also be found

in Gonzalez-Torres's candy works, with their minimal design, symbolism of the body, and initial air of fun, as well as the way they directly engage people's bodies in the transmission and dissemination of a personal, moral, and political message. As Gonzalez-Torres summarized when discussing the experience of his work, "You should not have had a catharsis, you should have had a thinking experience."[9]

"Without a public," Gonzalez-Torres said, "these works are nothing, nothing."[10] They depend on the presence and interaction of audiences willing to touch, smell, and eat the art. Each person completes the works in their own unique way, and we read them according to our societal and individual conditioning, our cultural and personal histories. Rather than imposing a specific way of viewing the work, the candy works confront people with their own power. To take or not to take? And if so, which one? Pleasure granted or pleasure deferred? These works help us encounter ourselves through our decisions: Am I the kind of person who picks up candy from the floor? Is it different because it is art, because it is in a gallery? When I pick this up, what is it that I am picking up?

As they disappear into our mouths and the hardened sugar melts on our tongues, the sweets return us our own bodies to supply context and meaning to our experience within the wider world, which Gonzalez-Torres viewed as a world of language, symbols, and laws. When picking up a candy, we might wonder what this food, this art, this sensuous experience means. On the level of individual reception, Gonzalez-Torres wanted his candy sculptures to catalyze a range of effects, from the sensations of grabbing, unwrapping, tasting, dissolving, swallowing, and digesting to a sugar rush and the unfolding of "some action ... some movement ... some travel in the mind."[11] He recognized a fundamental relationship between our bodies and the systems that govern society, and knew that our bodies are "defined not just by the flesh, but ... by language, first of all." Bodily pain, decay, and pleasure are "related to the law or to a symbolic order ... and our rejection or our acceptance of that order."[12] As the feminist cultural theorist and social activist bell hooks wrote of the candy works' ability to transport us, this "counter-hegemonic art requires that we identify not with the artist as iconic figure or with the beautiful art object, but rather that we identify ourselves as subjects in history through our interaction with the work." This can only happen if we start with the bodily senses, with the transition from looking to touching, smelling, and tasting, as it is enabled by food. It may be fleeting and subtle or lingering and intense, but, as hooks puts it, Gonzalez-Torres's work "restores the primacy of our bond with flesh."[13]

If the shape of the candy piles changes over time, so does their meaning. The charge they hold now is different from the one they held in the early 1990s, when a diagnosis of HIV was tantamount to a death sentence. Today, the virus can be treated, though it still cannot be eliminated. It is also common knowledge now that the virus is not transmitted by sharing food and drink, but when Gonzalez-Torres first created the works, ignorance and stigma around HIV and AIDS translated for some into an absolute terror of contact with HIV-positive people and those close to them.

Eating other people's food is still often perceived as carrying a risk of contamination, however, either with microbes or with the traces of an unfamiliar culture. In 2020, during the coronavirus pandemic, the artist's estate initiated a global version of *"Untitled" (Fortune Cookie Corner)* (1990), inviting 1,000 people around the world to recreate the work in private and public places. The project revived questions around the dangers of microbial and cultural contamination, stigma and isolation, the safety of accepting food from strangers, and the role of art in times of crisis. It took the work out of the gallery and into accessible spaces such as urban streets, airports, and parks at a time when many public places were closed; and into people's private homes. Images of mounds of fortune cookies in different settings were circulated via social media, further removing the work from its typical context in the contemporary art gallery, but also multiplying opportunities for it to disrupt the flow of everyday life, command people's attention, and generate new meaning. As London-based art critic Hettie Judah observed of people's interactions with the fortune-cookie pile she installed on a bench outside her house, "I had no control over how the artwork was understood or received. Everyone who encountered this unexpected cookie mountain in these weird times interpreted it their own way."[14] I visited that iteration of the work on one of my first forays across the city after a strict lockdown. What struck me most was the way this pilgrimage helped me reconnect with the richness of physical proximity with friends and art at a time when this was fraught with insecurities. I also wondered what this global manifestation of his work might mean to Gonzalez-Torres.

His hope was that once his works had infiltrated the institutions of culture, they would function in the same way as a virus, appearing and disappearing as "manifestations," and replicating within its host. Viral behavior was something Gonzalez-Torres could use to attach himself to institutions, insert the messages he wanted to make about love, grief, injustice, and death, and then watch them "replicate together with the institutions."[15] Such activism might eventually shift the status quo toward tolerance and justice.

By implanting a gesture of generosity into his work, Gonzalez-Torres also forced galleries and collectors, who usually hold positions of power, to replicate his original gift on their own account. The fact that each visitor can claim a piece of Gonzalez-Torres's art and become its owner undermines the conceit of sole ownership that underpins the art market. That privilege still exists, but at a great cost. In 2015, one of Gonzalez-Torres's candy works was sold at auction for a record $7.6 million.

Nevertheless, the plentiful supply of candy poses a threat to the ideal of scarcity that contributes to the value of art. If an artist has only created a handful of works related to a particular subject, theme, or time period, or when a successful artist dies, the work is likely to go up in value. A sculpture like *"Untitled" (Placebo)* (1991), on the other hand, consists of approximately 40,000 candies in silver wrappers and can be endlessly replenished. There is no original candy that can be prized over any other candy. To paraphrase Warhol's pronouncement about Coca-Cola: in a Gonzalez-Torres candy work, all the candies are the same and all the candies are good. Scarcity gives way to abundance and a potentially infinite number of instances of the work. The "art" aspect of the work resides in Gonzalez-Torres's idea. It exists potentially anywhere, and nowhere in particular. He was clear that these works, with their dynamic of evanescence and manifestation, were "indestructible because they can be endlessly duplicated." We can take one candy or a handful, but we can never take the artwork. It lives on as an idea and a promise. Like the food that furnishes our lives, the candy in Gonzalez-Torres's work is part of an endless cycle of supply and consumption.

ZOE LEONARD

Decomposition as Process

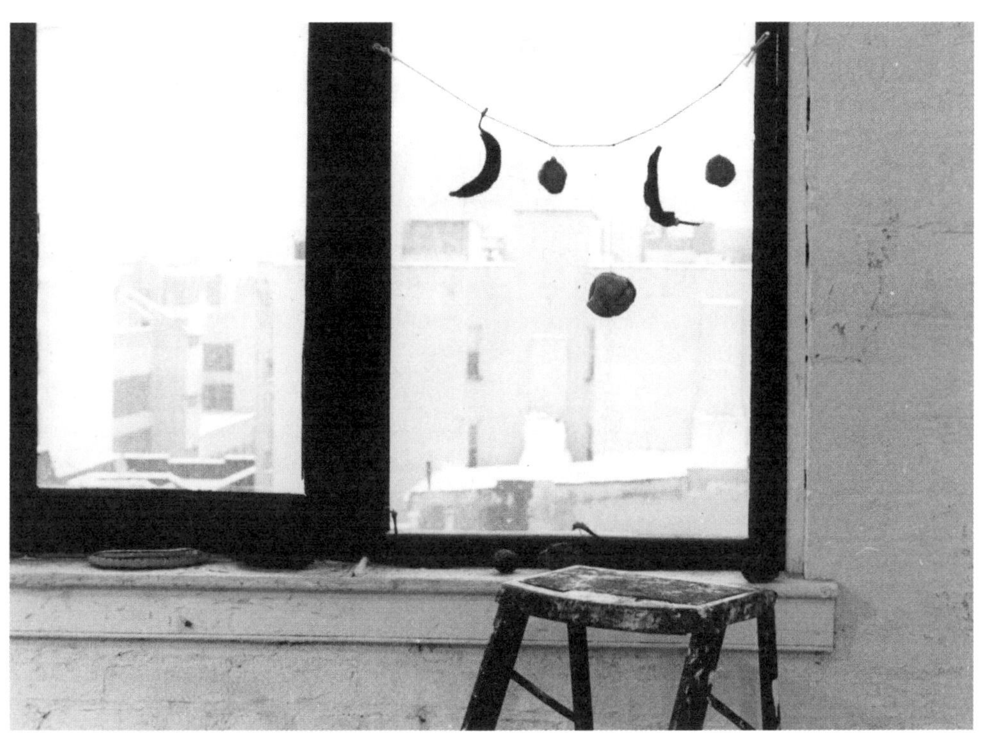

View of Zoe Leonard's studio, New York, 1995.

FOOD IS IMPERMANENT, susceptible to pests, and subject to disintegration. While some artists may be comfortable for their work to bear these entropic tendencies, museums are less so. The ideology of the museum, geared toward the preservation of culture for future generations, acts out its anxieties about the deterioration of objects by controlling. It strictly monitors which works of art become part of collections, and painstakingly preserves those that do, sometimes at the expense of their true meaning. By using food to make art, artists show us that such attempts to avoid the physical demise of artworks are doomed to fail, because they ignore the universal law that all matter—whether food, canvas, or the human body—eventually returns to dust.

From 1992 to 1997, the American artist Zoe Leonard created *Strange Fruit*, a group of 297 fruit skins that she repaired after peeling, using a range of binding materials such as thread, wire, buttons, string, hooks, sinew, and zippers.[i] Leonard started the work in New York, and developed the series while she stayed in Provincetown, a town at the tip of the Cape Cod peninsula in Massachusetts, which has a long history of artist communities, then continued it over two years when she lived in Alaska, where friends mailed her fruit that was not locally available. While she sewed, Leonard says, her thoughts turned to "the friends I'd lost, all the mistakes I've made. The inevitability of a scarred life."[1]

She had begun making the objects shortly after her friend, the artist David Wojnarowicz, died from AIDS-related complications, aged 37. The process of mending fruit skins began as a way for Leonard to think about him and evolved into a meditation on wider questions around loss and healing, and the "intensely human" act of fixing something broken.[2] And since the process of restoring the shape of a shredded fruit skin ultimately could not mend "any real wounds,"[3] it helped Leonard reckon with the impossibility of bringing back what was already gone.

i The full list of materials is orange, banana, grapefruit, and lemon skins, thread, buttons, zippers, needles, wax, sinew, string, snaps, and hooks.

The sundered fruit skins sewn back together recall an unforgettable 1989 photograph of Wojnarowicz pictured with his mouth sewn shut with black thread, taken by German photographer Andreas Sterzing. *Silence = Death* is titled after the most famous slogan of the activist group ACT UP (AIDS Coalition to Unleash Power), of which both Wojnarowicz and Leonard were members. ACT UP campaigned for urgent political and social action in the face of the AIDS epidemic that decimated the gay community in the mid-1980s and early 1990s.

The act of sewing something back together was a motif in Wojnarowicz's work and also appeared in his *Untitled (Bread Sculpture)* (1988–9), a loaf of white bread cut in half, the two portions connected with a zigzag of red thread. The stitched bread loaf rests on newspapers folded to display the financial stocks and shares pages. If Leonard's use of food and thread signal a process of quiet remembrance and healing, in Wojnarowicz's hands they convey a red-hot rage at the devastating effects of silence and self-censorship, while those in power continue to focus on profit.

As an act of mourning, making *Strange Fruit* helped Leonard "pay homage to what remains," and each sculpture honors the uniqueness of its organic material.[4] A banana skin split along its full length is brought back together with a zipper, whose metallic teeth and red cloth edges are inserted into the peel to present a wobbly grin. Lemons evoke breasts repaired after the excavation of a tumor, a ladder of stitches circling the nipple. Some of these "strange fruit" are accessorized: one banana is adorned with a row of buttons; another resembles a delicate purse held together with pink thread. The mending follows the path of the peeling action; putting clothing back on the way it came off. New hybrids arise. One banana snakes its way out of a quartered orange, the two fruits sutured together. Another has sprouted a tiny plastic doll's arm. An orange with baseball stitching sits next to a hand of bananas desiccated into a leathery mitt, to sketch out a tableau of childhood games shriveled with age. As they dried, the skins took on new shapes, tensing and curling against gravity. They moldered and slumped around their central void, not too proud but not ashamed either.

Over the years of their creation, Leonard tested out different ways of displaying the individual fruits, arranging them in her studio on windowsills, suspended in front of the window, on shelves and in small piles on the floor. Later, the pieces came together as a large installation, displayed on the ground, where they are extremely vulnerable to clumsy, distracted, and self-involved feet. The work sits like a congregation of survivors, each fruit an individual whose personality and back story we can't help but surmise. The disposition of the fruit skins on the floor also recalls a particular type of ancient still life, which the Roman architect Vitruvius called *xenia*. These images of flowers, fruit, food, and crockery were created in domestic settings as decorations or homages to guests, but also for cultic and votive purposes. Some were gifts to gods, while others, such as floor mosaics representing scraps of food left over from a meal, were intended for the "shades" of the house—the spirits or ghosts of dead people residing in the underworld. In addition to these pictorial offerings, any actual food remains that fell to the floor would be left there for the benefit of the shades.

Born in 1961 in the small town of Liberty, New York, Zoe Leonard grew up in New York City from the age of two. She left high school early and began taking photographs of friends in the New York City art scene, developing her creative practice independently of academic training. She uses sculpture, installation, and photography to explore the politics of representation in the museum and in society at large. Leonard's most widely circulated work is her 1992 poem, "I want a president," inspired by poet Eileen Myles's bid for US president, which gained renewed acclaim during the run-up to the 2016 US presidential election. As well as being a member of ACT UP, Leonard is one of the founders of the feminist activist group fierce pussy, a collective of queer women artists formed in 1991, who bring lesbian identity and visibility into the streets with poster campaigns.[ii]

In contrast to fierce pussy's work, which Leonard has described as "very loud and very verbal," *Strange Fruit* "is very, very silent" and comes "from a deeply private, nonverbal, even nonvisual place."[5] This quietude manifests in the way the work communicates to its audience, via sensory rather than conceptual channels: its tactility and evocation of smell, taste, gut feelings, and memories. The work opens up a pathway for the transference of grief and healing through bodily awareness and experience. Linking its effects to her own trauma, Leonard described the process of working on the objects as "a way to sew myself back up."[6]

Strange Fruit borrows its title from one of the most devastating songs of the 20th century: the anti-lynching protest ballad written in 1937 by Abel Meeropol, which in Billie Holiday's haunting version became an anthem of the civil rights movement. Leonard's friend, the writer, artist, and activist Gregg Bordowitz, suggested using the title for her array of sutured fruit skins, adding a layer of meaning to the word "fruit," in terms of its metaphorical use to refer to a lynched person but also as a gay slur. Despite its confrontational title, Leonard does not consider *Strange Fruit* an activist piece, but a deeply personal work that speaks to a broad audience about both grief and discrimination.

Throughout history, art has been used as a catalyst for personal and public mourning and healing, whether through an intimate portrait of a loved one, or a public monument commissioned to commemorate those lost in war or catastrophic

ii Their posters promoted lesbian rights in forthright language and with a wry sense of humor. One campaign featured snapshots of the group's members as children with tag lines such as "Dyke," "Lesbian," and "Lover of Women."

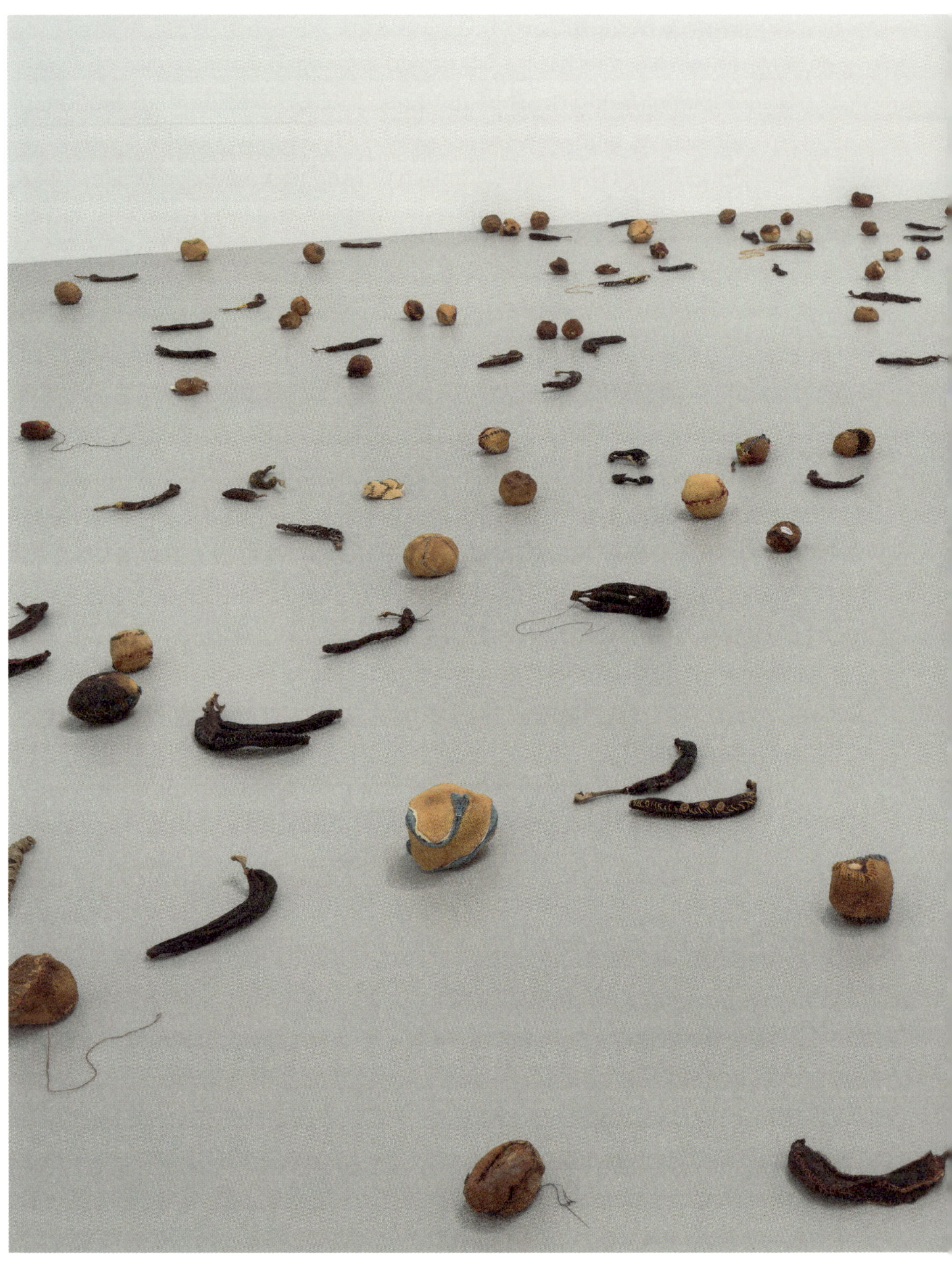

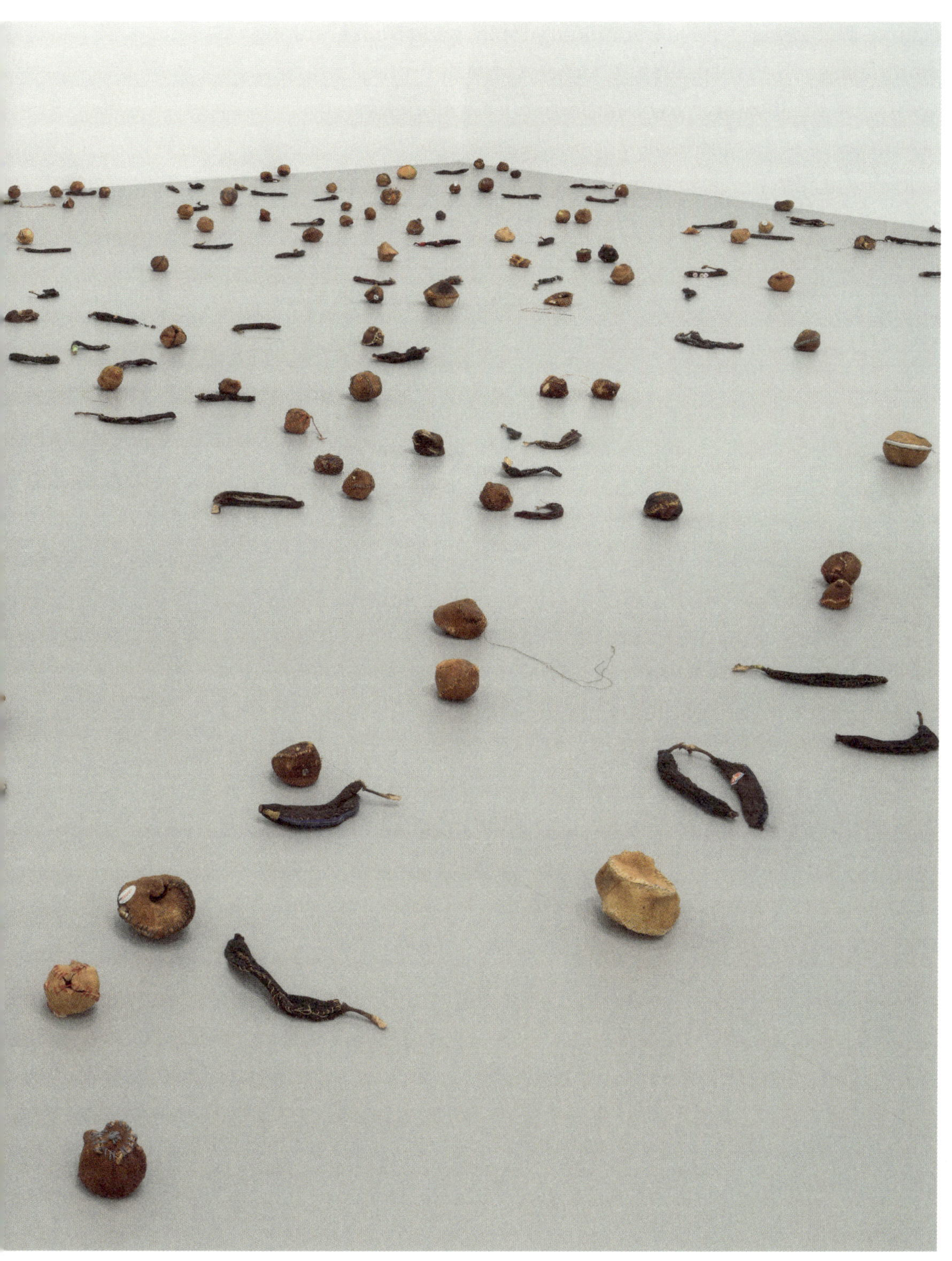

Zoe Leonard, *Strange Fruit*, 1992–7. Orange, banana, grapefruit, and lemon skins, thread, buttons, zippers, needles, wax, sinew, string, snaps, and hooks. Installation view, Whitney Museum of American Art, New York, 2018.

events. These works have traditionally been made from enduring materials, such as oil paint or enamel, stone or bronze, which symbolize the intention to never forget. This ambition for permanence is diametrically opposed to the ephemeral nature of food. Yet, as Gonzalez-Torres and Leonard both understood, food has a special ability to embody the vitality and fragility of life and therefore to convey the experience of loss. As Leonard's fruit skins make clear, we are not so different from the food we eat: over time, our plump skins will wither and ultimately we will decompose just like uneaten food.

As the sewn fruit pieces were exhibited, some were acquired by art collectors. The ongoing decay of the organic material at the heart of these works led to questions and concerns over how such perishable food-based sculptures should be shown and preserved. Leonard's gallerist at the time, Paula Cooper, suggested there might be ways to make the works more durable by preventing further decomposition, and Leonard agreed to experiments by the German museum conservator Christian Scheidemann, who treated several of the fruit skins with chemicals to preserve them. But when he presented his first trial with a banana skin to Leonard, she immediately knew that arresting the process of entropy was the wrong thing to do.[7] The attempt made clear to her that the very essence of the piece is to decompose. In 1997, she stated that "time is a co-creator of the work; decomposition is understood not as damage but as process."[8]

The search for a way to honor the inherent vulnerability of *Strange Fruit* continued, and Leonard envisioned it occupying a permanent exhibition space where it could gradually decay without being disturbed and where visitors could bear witness to its changes over time. In 2001, the Philadelphia Museum of Art, which acquired the work, exhibited the fruit skins for a six-month period. They were in good company alongside the museum's outstanding collections of works by Duchamp, whose use of found objects, or "readymades", related to Leonard's use of everyday foods, and Cézanne, whose late-19th-century still lifes of fruit had revolutionized the genre.[9]

Although it came to own the work, the museum also had misgivings about its impermanence and was initially resistant to the idea of giving it an acquisition number because, as curator Ann Temkin pointed out, "How can you give a number to something that won't always be there?" When the museum eventually acquired *Strange Fruit*, it agreed with Leonard that it would try to show the sculptural installation as often and for as long as possible, and on a regular schedule. Leonard worked with curators to determine a way of showing individual elements within the group in such a way as to accommodate their fragility and conceptual integrity. Leonard maintains a close dialogue with the museum and has installed the work each time it has been shown, including in 2018, as part of her retrospective at the Whitney Museum of American Art in New York, where she included pieces that had been crushed, arranged into small piles of dust and debris.

Despite some efforts to loosen the rigid conventions governing their collections, for example with the emphasis in recent years on finding ways to acquire works of performance art, museums are still largely committed to ideals of material stability and durability. *Strange Fruit*, like many of the food-based works in this book, eludes traditional expectations for art to be permanent and stable, obedient and rational. Paradoxically, in its ongoing process of decay, which is staged for all the senses, *Strange Fruit* remains alive, while it exposes the fantasy that art—or anything—can last forever.

Art

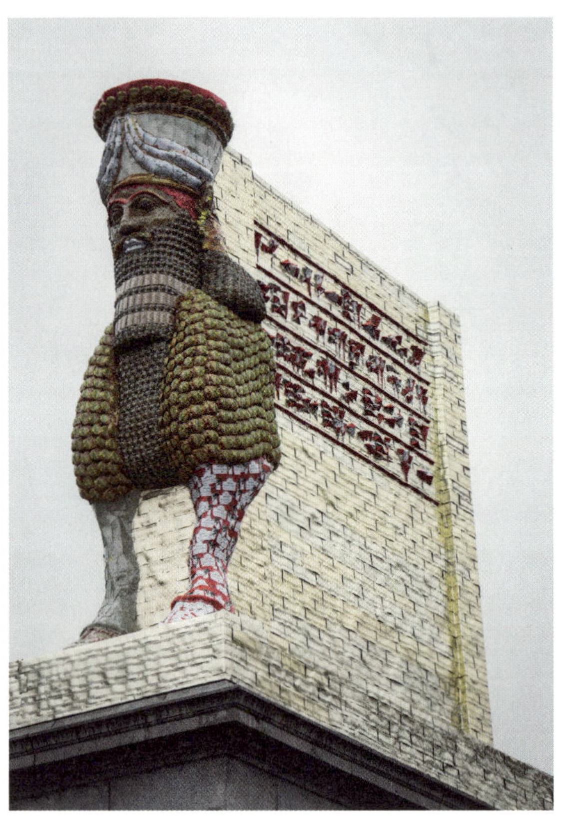

and Food

Today

Michael Rakowitz, *The Invisible Enemy Should Not Exist*, 2018. Trafalgar Square, London, UK.

The decades from the 1960s to the 2000s were a time of intense experimentation, in the realm of art as in wider society. Artists expanded the possibilities of media such as performance and video, while around the world biennials were launched and unprecedented international links forged; the art market went through several cycles of boom and bust; and so-called "fine art" increasingly crossed over with popular culture. These shifts took place in the context of important social developments, from the civil rights movement to feminism, growing recognition of LGBTQIA+ rights, and a progressively urgent environmentalism, while the advent of the internet and social media changed the ways in which people and corporations access information, each other, and art. Against this background, the artists in this book took important risks with their individual creative practices, adopting new strategies in conceptual art, animated by fresh philosophical, political, and material tactics, using food in ways that have surprised and inspired audiences and artists from subsequent generations.

Working with food was, and still is, an unusual approach to making art. It brings into the art space something familiar from ordinary life, which exists in shops and supermarkets, refrigerators and ovens, on our kitchen tables, and in our mouths and stomachs. The artists in this book used food to open up new and sensory ways of experiencing art and the world. Their art challenged accepted hierarchies, both sensory and social. It broke through the boundaries of culture by exploring, among other things, how food can bring sensuality to politically and conceptually motivated work, how perishable ingredients sit within the repertoire of traditional media, and how ordinary actions count as art.

More recently, incorporating food into artworks has been a way for artists to address a range of issues pertinent to our own time, and to foster awareness and empathy for past and suppressed injustices. Such uses of food bring new purpose to art and, to use Adrian Piper's term, they catalyze new reactions.

Food presents a paradox. On the one hand it provides a gateway to embodiment via the senses, infiltrating our nostrils with its scents, its flavors lingering in our mouths, causing our stomachs to churn or cry out for nourishment. The presence of food in an art context can have a visceral impact, awakening disgust or queasiness, or it can help ground us in a present moment or place, allowing us to tune in to our immediate needs, to realize what a particular sensation is trying to tell us about something seemingly unrelated. On the other hand, food can be used as an instrument for exerting economic or political influence, for example in the way corporations aggressively market unhealthy foods to vulnerable groups including children, or government food policies serve private interests over public health, or in the monocultures that devastate ecosystems, or the wars that ruin entire food industries.

Since the early 2000s, the Iraqi–American artist Michael Rakowitz has created a series of interlinking projects related to the food of his Arab–Jewish Iraqi heritage and the military conflicts in Iraq. His works give credence to Knowles's revelation that cooking and feeding have a place within the realm of art. In 2003, Rakowitz started *Enemy Kitchen*, an initiative whose origins he traces back to 1991 when, watching the televised invasion of Iraq during the Gulf War, his mother, Yvonne, commented that there were no Iraqi restaurants in New York. In a bid to compensate for this lack, Rakowitz and Yvonne began gathering Baghdadi recipes from friends and relatives, and teaching them to diverse audiences, including army veterans and school children. Through its activities, the Enemy Kitchen opened up conversations about Iraq that were not connected to the war per se, but "attached to food, to culture, to shared humanity."[1] Like FOOD more than 30 years earlier, the Enemy Kitchen was an experimental space that fostered creativity, mutual support, and community through food and cooking. In 2012, the Enemy Kitchen metamorphosed into a food truck on the streets of Chicago, staffed by Iraqi refugee chefs and assisted by sous-chefs from the community of US Army veterans who had served in the Iraq War. This inverted the power dynamics set up during the invasion of Iraq and meant that American soldiers now took their orders from Iraqi nationals.[2]

Alongside the Enemy Kitchen, Rakowitz created a series of works inspired by Iraqi dates, a fruit that in the 1970s accounted for Iraq's second-largest industry after oil. The date industry severely declined as a result of the Iran–Iraq War of 1988, and its demise was accelerated by the 2003–11 Iraq War. In 2004, when Rakowitz purchased a can of date syrup for his mother from his local Middle Eastern grocery, the shop owner commented that Yvonne would love the Baghdadi product. The can, however, was labeled "product of Lebanon," belying

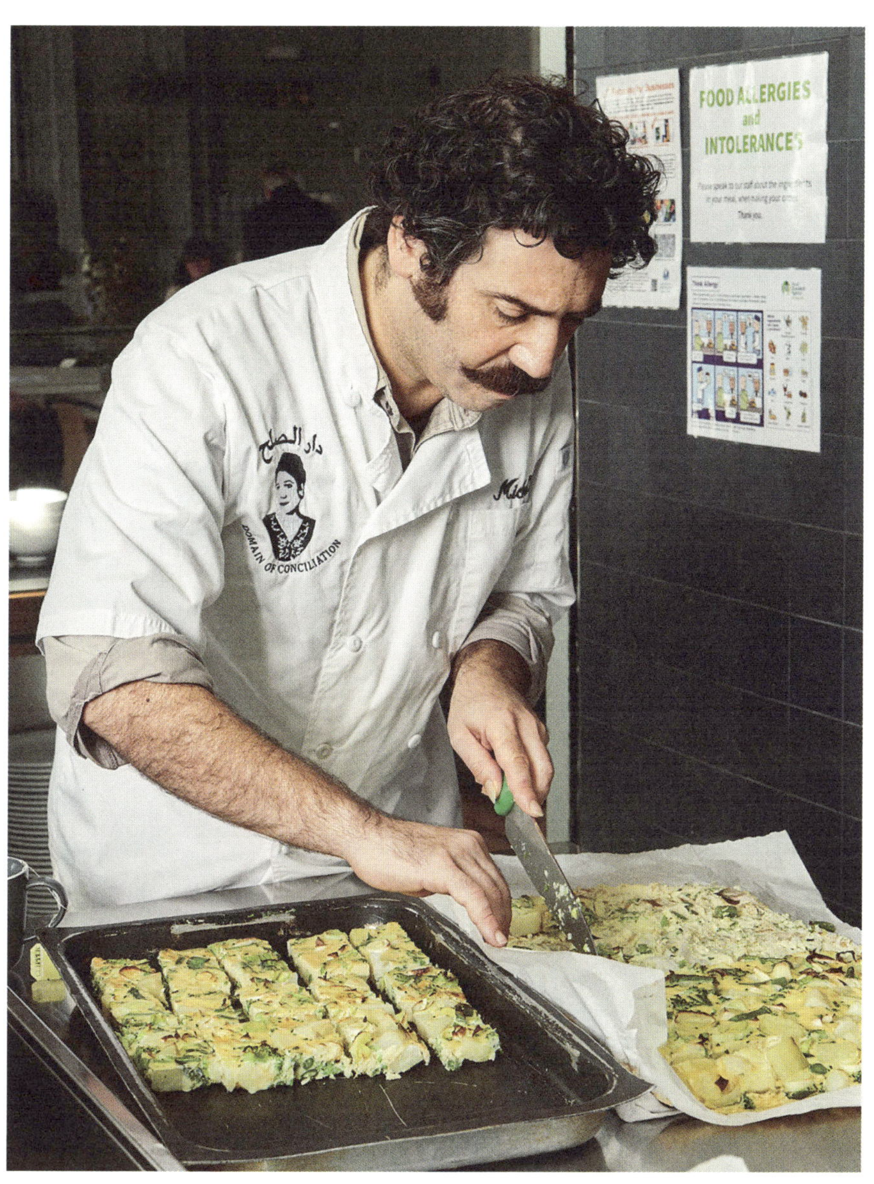

Michael Rakowitz cooking at
Refettorio Felix, London, 2018.

its true origins. As Rakowitz discovered, this was a subterfuge that applied to many "veiled and absent products" from Iraq that disavowed their provenance because of US trade sanctions and xenophobia.

In 2006, the artist revived Davisons & Co., the import–export company that his maternal grandfather had set up in New York in 1947 after fleeing the persecution of Jews by Iraqi authorities, which had ceased trading in the 1960s. Titled *Return*, Rakowitz's import–export business-as-artwork occupied a shop front in Brooklyn and offered free shipping to Iraqis living in the US who wished to export items to Iraq. Under its aegis, Rakowitz also attempted to import a ton of fresh dates from then war-torn Iraq. The process was tortuous, and the shipment was halted at the Jordanian border, then sent back to Baghdad and later to Damascus, where the produce was declared spoiled. Although a smaller quantity of fresh dates was eventually airlifted out of Baghdad, for Rakowitz "the overall transaction served as a surrogate for a larger tragedy."[3]

Around that time, Rakowitz began creating *The Invisible Enemy Should Not Exist*, an ongoing series of sculptural reconstructions that sought to "reappear" some 7,000 artifacts looted from the National Museum of Iraq during the 2003 invasion and stolen or destroyed in the aftermath of the conflict. Rakowitz's versions of the objects are made from the packaging of Middle Eastern foodstuffs including date syrup and date cookies, as well as local Arabic newspapers published in the US. They link disposable food containers with iconic statuary, showing, as Warhol did with his reverence for popular foods in art and life, that the mundane and the transcendent are linked through food, and both have a part in defining culture.

The largest of Rakowitz's reconstructions is the Lamassu, a 9th-century BCE winged protective spirit that was originally part of the stone gate of Nineveh (now Mosul) before it was destroyed by ISIS in 2015. From March 2018 to March 2020, the new Lamassu, made from 10,000 empty cans of Iraqi date syrup, stood on Trafalgar Square's Fourth Plinth, London's foremost site for public art commissions, where it was flanked by monuments to British military leaders and victorious battles. In connection with the commission, Rakowitz authored a cookbook of Iraqi–Jewish recipes featuring date syrup. Titled *A House With a Date Palm Will Never Starve* (2019), its ambition was "to extend the space of the Lamassu beyond the Fourth Plinth into your cupboards and bellies," to transmit a message with food, just as Gonzalez-Torres did with his candies, in the hopes of reprogramming attitudes toward Iraqi food and culture so that ultimately the disappeared date palms might be replanted in Iraq.[4]

As Rakowitz realized while watching the 2003 invasion of Iraq live on television, "our whole history was under attack, and everything we knew about Iraq was suddenly a counter-history."[5] Food offers a means for challenging official histories, by feeding in the stories of those who were silenced or treated as invisible. For Rakowitz, working with food is part of "piecing together an idea of Iraq that can only have existed through the stories and the culture that has been transmitted to me."[6]

The artist Kara Walker has similarly used food as a way to piece together suppressed histories. Her work, which has often taken the form of cut-paper silhouettes and animations that deploy racist tropes for the retelling of slave testimonies and depictions of abuse common to plantation life, aims to challenge dominant narratives around slavery and the mythos of America. In 2014, Walker departed from these media to create her first monumental sculpture, a colossal sugar figure whose full title delivers a precis of the artist's intentions and the context for the work:

A Subtlety,
or the Marvelous Sugar Baby,
an Homage to the unpaid and
overworked Artisans who have
refined our Sweet tastes from the
cane fields to the Kitchens of the
New World on the Occasion of
the demolition of the Domino
Sugar Refining Plant

The Sugar Baby, as the work came to be known, was a sphinx with the kerchiefed head of a "mammy," the stereotyped black nursemaid who nurtures white children, and exaggerated breasts, buttocks, and vulva reminiscent of highly sexualized images of black women in popular media. She was 75 ft long by 35½ ft tall and constructed from 40 tons of refined sugar, whose pale hue contrasted with the dark, molasses-coated walls of the former sugar shed she occupied at the Domino Sugar Refinery. The factory had been active in Williamsburg since 1882 and was due to be demolished shortly after the sculpture was dismantled. Every weekend between May and July, the Sugar Baby and her coterie of sugar candy attendants were New York's

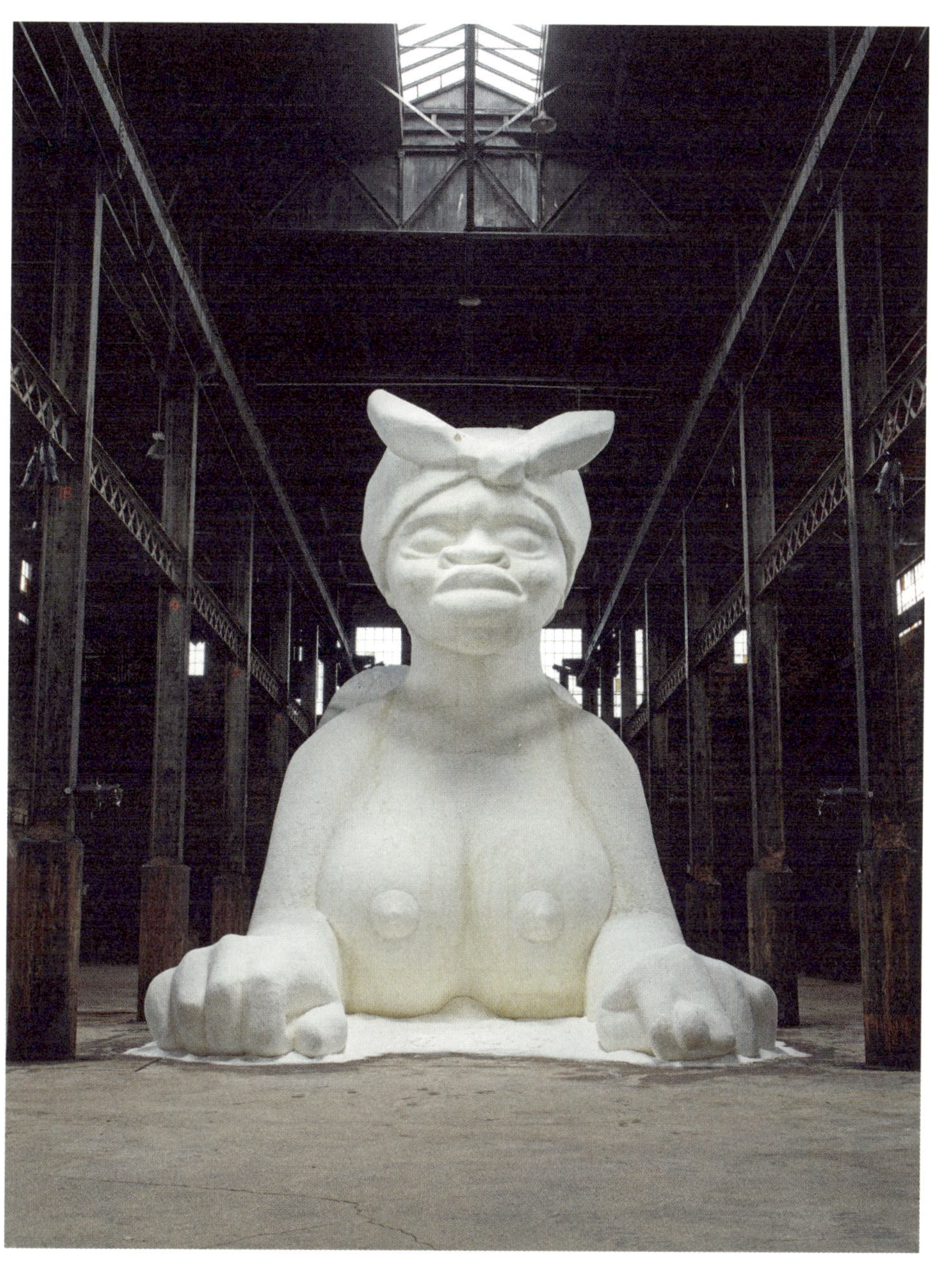

Kara Walker, *A Subtlety, or the* Marvelous Sugar Baby, *an Homage to the unpaid and overworked Artisans who have refined our Sweet tastes from the cane fields to the Kitchens of the New World on the Occasion of the demolition of the Domino Sugar Refining Plant*, 2014. Polystyrene foam and sugar.

hottest attraction. People lined up outside the factory to visit the sweet sphinx, and as the temperature rose the sugar began to ferment, simultaneously decaying and breeding new life. The smell of rot combined with the sickly sweet aroma of the walls produced an odor that Walker described as "grassy, pungent, almost nauseating." Some 130,000 people made the pilgrimage to the Sugar Baby, responding with a mixture of tears, worship, surreptitious tasting, selfies, and mockery. The food from which she was made enticed visitors to use all their senses in experiencing, exploring, and understanding the work, promoting a multi-sensory approach similar to that of the early museum.

As Wilke had done with chewing gum, and Gonzalez-Torres with wrapped candies, Walker demonstrated how sweetness can harbor a range of meanings and provide useful camouflage for the delivery of a message. She wanted the work to "entice and repel," as its presence, material, and form evoked themes and issues ranging from slavery and its economics to the conception of the New World, the hardships of the plantations, and the botany of sugar cane. All these were "refined" by Walker into "something iconic and easily digestible that also speaks about the destruction of humanity that this beautiful, tasty substance has come to represent, has come to be."[7] In the sugar shed, a space layered with the sticky by-products of sugar refining accumulated over the decades, the installation "literally sugarcoat[ed] history."[8] For Walker, the dark environment provided a useful contrast to the visually focused white cube galleries in which her paper-cuts, drawings, and videos have typically been shown. In the sugar shed, a multi-sensory sculpture made from one of the most common ingredients in contemporary food was able to "invert this paradigm and maybe call into question the desire for the refined—to ask what is lost in the process of refining."[9]

The sugar industry was part of the first global commerce, an unprecedented system of capitalist exploitation that furnished colonial powers with food at an incalculable cost to individuals, communities, and the environment—and with a seemingly unending aftermath. The duo Cooking Sections, composed of spatial practitioners Alon Schwabe and Daniel Fernández Pascual, who trained in architecture and performance, use food in art contexts as a tool for developing new knowledge and solutions related to climate change. Harking back to Denes's agricultural investigations into an "eco-logic," Cooking Sections' long-term projects focus on issues such as the transformation of food production from a seasonal to a year-round activity, the evolution of landscapes to support new farming techniques, and the environmental impact of accelerated production across a range of industries. The central axis of their practice so far has been CLIMAVORE, an ambitious ongoing project with strands in multiple sites, from the Pacific Coast to the Persian Gulf. Cooking Sections defines a CLIMAVORE as someone who explores how to eat as climate changes. To do justice to such a complex topic, Schwabe and Fernández Pascual cast their research nets wide, and delve deep into the hidden relationships between global systems, from farming to finance, deserts to waterways, by traveling widely and spending time learning from local communities. The tangible outcome of their research includes sculpture, installation, video, and performance, but also books and lectures, and is not limited to informing audiences; they also set up what they call "alternative metabolic systems": new ways of facilitating the transfer of energy from the weather and soil into food in such a way as to regenerate traumatized ecologies.

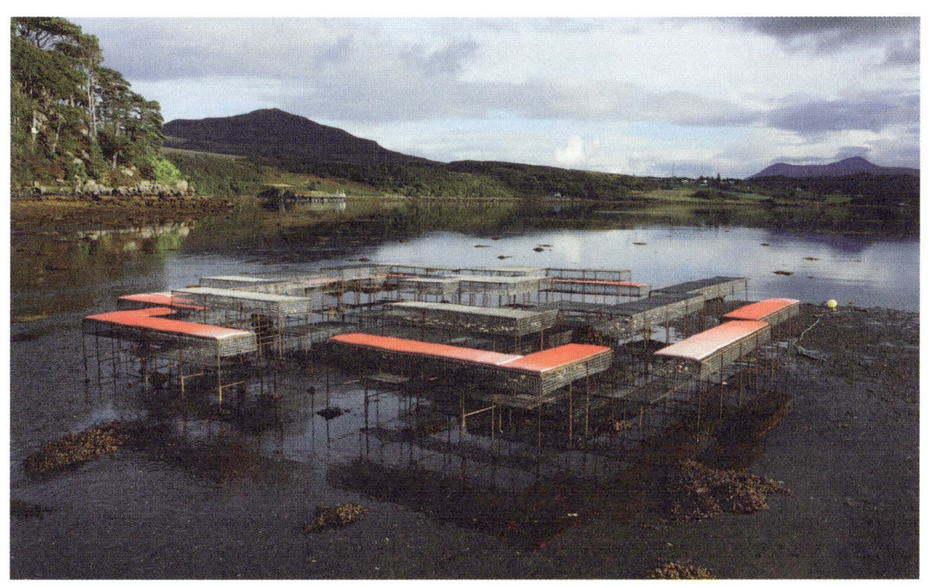

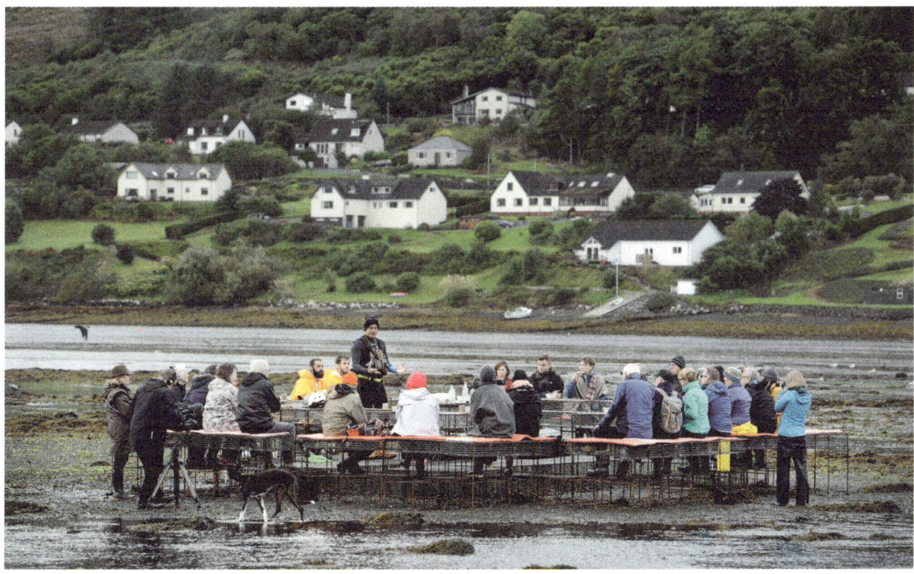

Cooking Sections, CLIMAVORE:
On Tidal Zones, Isle of Skye, 2017.

These aims are embodied in their ongoing project, the CLIMAVORE Station on the Isle of Skye, in Scotland, which they initiated in 2017 to respond to environmental damage on the island stemming from intensive salmon farming, the UK's most valuable food industry. The farming produces countless deformed and sick animals infested with sea lice, and pollutes the water with vast quantities of toxic fish manure that kills off other marine life. On Skye, Cooking Sections collaborated with local businesses and residents to initiate the transition from damaging aquaculture to regenerative practices. They now raise oysters and seaweed on the island, which are potentially cheap sources of protein that clean the water by filtering it and are important ingredients in Climavore recipes.

A central concern of Cooking Sections' work is environmental justice, particularly for those on the front line of climate change—the people who live and work in coastal areas and places affected by desertification, flooding, and toxic leakages, for example. They tackle these issues by working with and training local people in sustainable practices. Like the founders of FOOD, who employed artists to staff their restaurant, Cooking Sections recognize that communities need to sustain themselves through work as well as creativity. On Skye, an apprenticeship program trains local students from Portree High School to become CLIMAVORE cooks, and provides work experience at restaurants around Skye, whose chefs have replaced the farmed salmon dishes on their menus with CLIMAVORE recipes.

Their video *Salmon: A Red Herring*, commissioned for an exhibition at Tate Britain in 2020, chronicles color shifts in animals caused by eating synthetic or toxic substances generated by agriculture, pollution, or climate events. Cooking Sections call these "chromatic alterations," and they include a colony of bees producing iridescent red honey after feeding on waste from a candy factory, and a pink sparrow appearing in a Scottish garden, likely after feasting on salmon feed loaded with synthetic dye. As part of their exhibition, Cooking Sections also worked with Tate Eats, the catering company responsible for Tate's four museums, which committed to stop serving farmed salmon at Tate cafés and restaurants in perpetuity. It now serves CLIMAVORE dishes instead, introducing the notion of eating in response to climate change to a wide public. Cooking Sections see this commitment from Tate as "an action that other organisations can follow as part of a divestment from farmed salmon."[10] The artwork here manifests as a new range of food production techniques and options, as well as long-term food policy reform that benefits from the same enduring status as any artwork, ancient or modern, accessioned into Tate's permanent collection.

The earliest depictions of food in art translated the devotional practice of leaving scraps for the shades that haunted the home into lifelike mosaics that would appease and please them, so that humans could live harmoniously alongside the realm of the spirits. In contemporary times, art made with food brings the bodies, senses, and minds of the living to a fuller experience, to contend with past events, challenge their impact on the present, and explore new ways for the future. Perhaps not that much has changed after all.

Endnotes

I EAT THEREFORE I AM

[1] Bourdain A. (2001) *A Cook's Tour: In Search of the Perfect Meal*. Bloomsbury Press, London, p. 240.

[2] Breuer L., Champagne L., Ehn E., Foreman R *et al*. (2012) Belief. *PAJ: A Journal of Performance and Art* 34(1), p. 20.

COMING TO OUR SENSES

[3] Smith B. (2017) *The Uncommon Senses*. BBC. https://www.bbc.co.uk/programmes/b08km812/episodes/player.

[4] Classen C. (2007) Museum manners: the sensory life of the early museum. *Journal of Social Science* 40(4), p. 897.

[5] Classen C. (2007), p. 906.

[6] Classen C. (2007), p. 907.

[7] Classen C. (2007), p. 897.

[8] Classen C. (2007), p. 902.

[9] Classen C. (2007), p. 903.

[10] Classen C. (2007), p. 905.

[11] Classen C. (2007), p. 903.

[12] Classen C. (2007), p. 905.

[13] Levey, M. (1969) *A Brief History of the National Gallery*. Pitkin Pictorials, London, p. 8. Cited in Classen C. (2007), p. 914.

[14] Drobnik J. (2006) *The Smell Culture Reader*. Berg, Oxford, p. 69.

ADRIAN PIPER: POWER IS BAD
FOR THE LINING OF THE STOMACH

[1] Piper A. (1996) Xenophobia and the indexical present II. In: *Out of Order, Out of Sight*, vol. 1, *Selected Writings in Meta-Art 1968–1992*. MIT Press, Cambridge, MA, p. 261.

[2] Piper A. (1996), p. 261.

[3] Platzker D. (2018) Adrian Piper: unities. In: Cherix C., Butler C., and Platzker D. (eds), *Adrian Piper: A Synthesis of Intuitions: 1965–2016*. Museum of Modern Art, New York, NY, pp. 31–49.

[4] Bowles J. P. (2011) *Adrian Piper: Race, Gender, and Embodiment*. Duke University Press, Durham, NC, p. 91.

[5] Bowles J. P. (2011), p. 91.

[6] Bowles J. P. (2011), p. 91.

[7] Bowles J. P. (2011), p. 90.

[8] Bowles J. P. (2011), p. 91.

[9] Bowles J. P. (2011), p. 91.

[10] Bowles J. P. (2011), p. 91.

[11] Piper A. (1996), p. 261.

[12] Piper A. (1996), p. 261.

[13] Piper A. (2007) Sol, 1928–2007. Adrian Piper Research Archive. http://www.adrianpiper.com/art/sol.shtml.

[14] Piper A. (2007) Sol, 1928–2007. Adrian Piper Research Archive. http://www.adrianpiper.com/art/sol.shtml.

[15] Piper A. (2006) Letter to Daniel Marzona. Adrian Piper Research Archive. http://www.adrianpiper.com/marzona.shtml.

[16] Piper A. (1974) We asked a number of artists to respond to this: make a political statement. *Art-Rite*, No. 6.

[17] Bowles J.P. (2011), p. 251.

[18] Bowles J.P. (2011), p. 1.

[19] Piper A. (2012) News. Adrian Piper Research Archive. http://www.adrianpiper.com/news_sep_2012.shtml.

[20] Bowles J. P. (2011), p. 178.

[21] Lippard L. and Piper A. (1972) Catalysis: an interview with Adrian Piper. *The Drama Review* 16(1), p. 78.
[22] Bowles J.P. (2011), p. 28.
[23] Bowles J. P. (2011), p. 181.
[24] Bowles J. P. (2011), p. 181.
[25] Lippard L. and Piper A. (1972), p. 77.
[26] Bowles J. P. (2011), p. 181.
[27] Bowles J.P. (2011), p. 178.
[28] Bowles J. P. (2011), pp. 178–179.
[29] Bowles J. P. (2011), p. 137.
[30] Piper A. (1996), pp. 151–154, cited in Velasco D. (2018) Reveries of a solitary dancer. *Artforum* 57(1), pp. 204–217.

CAROLEE SCHNEEMANN: GO FEED YOURSELF!

[1] The Allen Ginsberg Project (2017) Michael McClure —interview continued. https://allenginsberg.org/2017/10/sun-o-22/.
[2] Esslin M. (1976) *Antonin Artaud: The Man and His Works*. John Calder, London, p. 83.
[3] McPherson B. R. and Schneemann C. (1979) *More than* Meat Joy*: Performance Works and Selected Writings*. McPherson, Kingston, NY, p. 62.
[4] Archives of American Art (2009) Oral history interview with Carolee Schneemann, 2009 March 1. Archives of American Art, Smithsonian Institution, Washington DC. https://www.aaa.si.edu/collections/interviews/oral-history-interview-carolee-schneemann-15672.
[5] McPherson B. R. and Schneemann C. (1979), p. 64.
[6] Fitzgibbon C. and Schneemann C. (2015) Interview with Carolee Schneemann. *BOMB*, No. 132, p. 132.
[7] Archives of American Art (2009).
[8] McPherson B. R. and Schneemann C. (1979), p. 64.
[9] McPherson B. R. and Schneemann C. (1979), p.76.
[10] McPherson B. R. and Schneemann C. (1979), p.76.
[11] McPherson B. R. and Schneemann C. (1979), p. 270.
[12] McPherson B. R. and Schneemann C. (1979), p. 63.
[13] McPherson B. R. and Schneemann C. (1979), p. 64.
[14] Gioni M. (2015) More than *Meat Joy*: Carolee Schneemann in conversation with Massimiliano Gioni. *Mousse*, No. 48, pp. 4–9. https://www.moussemagazine.it/magazine/carolee-schneemann-massimilano-gioni-2015/.
[15] Fitzgibbon C. and Schneemann C. (2015), p. 136.
16 Schneemann C. (1991) The obscene body/politic. *Art Journal* 50(4), p. 31.
[17] Gioni M. (2015).
[18] Schneemann C. (1991), p. 31.
[19] Fitzgibbon C. and Schneemann C. (2015), p. 133.
[20] Fitzgibbon C. and Schneemann C. (2015), p. 133.
[21] Schneemann C. (1991), p. 28.
[22] Archives of American Art (2009).
[23] Serra M. M. and Ramey K (2007) Eye/body: the cinematic paintings of Carolee Schneemann. In: Blaetz R. (ed.), *Women's Experimental Cinema: Critical Frameworks*. Duke University Press, Durham, NC, p. 110.
[24] Gioni M. (2015).
[25] Kate Haag K. and Schneemann C. (1977) An interview with Carolee Schneemann. *Wide Angle* 20(1). Reproduced in Schneemann C. (2003) *Imagining her Erotics: Essays, Interviews, Projects*. MIT Press, Cambridge, MA, p. 28.
[26] Schneemann C. (1991), p. 29.
[27] Schneemann C. (2014) Response to a reappropriation request. *PAJ: A Journal of Performance and Art* 36(1), p. 8.
[28] Schneemann C. (1991), p. 31.
[29] Haug K. (1998), pp. 20–49.

HANNAH WILKE: CHEW HER UP AND SPIT HER OUT

[1] Picard L. and Wilke H. (1973) Hannah Wilke: sexy objects. *Interview*, January.
[2] Princenthal N. (2010) *Hannah Wilke*. Prestel Publishing, New York, NY, p. 22.
[3] Picard L. and Wilke H. (1973).
[4] Berman A. (1980) A decade of progress, but could a female Chardin make a living today? *Art News* 79(8), p. 77.
[5] Fitzpatrick T., Kochheiser T., Goldman S. and Pollock G. (2009) *Hannah Wilke: Gestures*. Neuberger Museum of Art, Purchase, NY, p. 51.
[6] Picard L. and Wilke H. (1973).
[7] Princenthal (2010), p. 19.
[8] Wilke H. (1976) Intercourse with ... Excerpts from Writing by Hannah Wilke. http://www.hannahwilke.com/id15.html.
[9] Wilke H. (1976) Intercourse with ...
[10] Kochheiser T. H. (1989) *Hannah Wilke: A Retrospective*. University of Missouri Press, Springfield, MO, p. 167.
[11] Princenthal (2010), p. 21.
[12] Wooster A.-S. (1975) Hannah Wilke, Ronald Feldman Gallery. *Artforum* 14(4), p. 74.
[13] Princenthal (2010), p. 69.
[14] Wilke H. (1976) Letter.
[15] Fitzpatrick T. *et al.* (2009), p. 49.
[16] Fitzpatrick T. *et al.* (2009), p. 51.
[17] Princenthal (2010), p. 64.

SARAH LUCAS: THE UNSAVORY ASPECT OF THE USUALLY DISCREET

[1] Princenthal (2010) *Hannah Wilke*. Prestel, New York, NY, p. 22.

[2] Gioni M. and Norton M. (eds) (2018) *Sarah Lucas: Au Naturel*. Phaidon, London, p. 22.

[3] Gioni M. and Norton M. (eds) (2018), p. 23.

[4] Gioni M. and Norton M. (eds) (2018), p. 23.

[5] Freedman C. (1994) A nod's as good as a wink: in conversation with Sarah Lucas. *Frieze*, No, 17. https://www.frieze.com/article/nods-good-wink.

[6] Lucas S. (2017) Video taken in Easter. Contemporary Fine Arts, Berlin.

[7] Gioni M. and Norton M (eds) (2018), p. 20.

[8] Lane A. (2008) Look back in hunger. In: Remnick D. (ed.), Secret Ingredients: *The New Yorker Book of Food and Drink*. Modern Library, New York, NY, pp. 153–4.

[9] Gioni M. and Norton M. (eds) (2018), p. 12.

[10] Gioni M. and Norton M. (eds) (2018), p. 22.

[11] Malik A. (2009) *Sarah Lucas: Au Naturel*. Afterall Books, London, p. 9.

[12] Roberts J. (1996), Mad for it! *Third Text* 10(35), pp. 29–42.

ALISON KNOWLES: A RECIPE FOR ART AND LIFE

[1] Archives of American Art (2010) Oral history interview with Alison Knowles, 2010 June 1–2. Archives of American Art, Smithsonian Institution, Washington DC, p. 26. https://www.aaa.si.edu/collections/interviews/oral-history-interview-alison-knowles-15822.

[2] Archives of American Art (2010), p.26.

[3] Archives of American Art (2010), p. 20.

[4] Montano L. M. (2000) *Performance Artists Talking in the Eighties*. University of California Press, Berkeley, CA, p. 173.

[5] Montano L. M. (2000), p. 174.

[6] Knowles A. (2012) Belief. PAJ: A Journal of Performance and Art 34(1), pp. 20–21.

[7] Montano L. M. (2000), p. 174.

[8] Archives of American Art (2010), p. 11.

[9] Archives of American Art (2010), p. 20.

[10] Obrist, H. U. and Sasinopoulos K. (2022) *140 Artists' Ideas for Planet Earth*. Penguin, London, Introduction.

[11] Archives of American Art (2010), p. 25.

[12] Archives of American Art (2010), p. 25.

[13] Montano L. M. (2000), p. 174.

[14] Archives of American Art (2010), p. 17.

[15] Knowles A. (2012), pp. 20–21.

[16] Woods N. L. (2014) Taste economies: Alison Knowles, Gordon Matta-Clark and the intersection of food, time and performance. *Performance Research* 19(3), p. 159.

[17] Woods N. L. (2014), p. 158.

[18] Woods N. L. (2014), p.159.

[19] Woods N. L. (2014), p. 159.

[20] Knowles A. (2012), pp. 20–21.

[21] Knowles A. (2024) Fluxus. Alison Knowles. https://www.aknowles.com/fluxus.html.

FOOD: LOVE AMONG THE CABBAGES

[1] Donoso P. (ed.) (2016) *Gordon Matta-Clark: Experience Becomes the Object*. Ediciones Polígrafa, Barcelona, p. 25.

[2] Waxman L. (2008) The banquet years: FOOD, a SoHo restaurant. *Gastronomica* 8(4): p. 28.

[3] Kennedy R. (2007) When meals played the muse. *New York Times*, 21 February. https://www.nytimes.com/2007/02/21/dining/21soho.html.

[4] Matta-Clark G., Muller M., Ha P. and Morris C. (1999) *FOOD: An Exhibition by White Columns, New York*. Westfälisches Landesmuseum für Kunst und Kulturgeschichte Münster/Verlag der Buchhandlung Walther König, Cologne, p. 7.

[5] FOOD (1975) Advert. *Art-Rite*, No. 9.

[6] Waxman L. (2008), p. 28.

[7] Matta-Clark G. *et al.* (1999), p. 29.

[8] FOOD (1972) Advert. *Avalanche*, No. 6.

[9] Matta-Clark G. *et al.* (1999), p. 23.

[10] Matta-Clark G. *et al.* (1999), p. 19.

[11] Sørensen L. and Chickey D (eds) (2012) *112 Greene Street: The Early Years (1970–1974)*. Radius Books, Santa Fe, CA, p. 165.

[12] Matta-Clark G. *et al.* (1999), p. 23.

[13] Glaser M. and Snyder J. (The Underground Gourmet) (1972) Food, glorious food. *New York Magazine*, 3 January, p. 65.

[14] Glaser M. and Snyder J. (1972), p. 65.

[15] Matta-Clark G. *et al.* (1999), p. 18.

[16] Cowan S. (2018) The future did not have to be luxury condos: revisiting Gordon Matta-Clark. *The New Yorker*, 18 March. https://www.newyorker.com/culture/culture-desk/the-future-did-not-have-to-be-luxury-condos-revisiting-gordon-matta-clark.

[17] Matta-Clark G. *et al.* (1999), back cover.

[18] Matta-Clark G. *et al.* (1999), p. 16.

[19] Glaser M. and Snyder J. (1972), p. 65.

[20] Glaser M. and Snyder J. (1972), p. 65.
[21] Glaser M. and Snyder J. (1972), p. 65.
[22] Kennedy R. (2007).
[23] Matta-Clark G. *et al.* (1999), p. 14.
[24] Kennedy R. (2007), p. 1.
[25] Donoso P. (ed.) (2016), p. 22.
[26] Schjeldahl P. (2011) Proto SoHo. *The New Yorker*, 9 January. https://www.newyorker.com/magazine/2011/01/17/proto-soho.
[27] Matta-Clark G. *et al.* (1999), p. 42.
[28] Matta-Clark G. *et al.* (1999), p. 42.
[29] Kennedy R. (2007), p. 3.
[30] Kennedy R. (2007), p. 4.
[31] Lee P. M. (1999) *Object to Be Destroyed: The Work of Gordon Matta-Clark*. MIT Press, Cambridge, MA, p. 72.

ANDY WARHOL: BRINGING HOME THE BACON

[1] Rossi A. (dir.) (2022) *The Andy Warhol Diaries*. Netflix.
[2] Mulroney L. (2013) I'd recognize your voice anywhere. In: Schleif N. (ed.), *Reading Andy Warhol*. Hatje Cantz, Berlin, p. 281.
[3] Warhol A. (1977) *The Philosophy of Andy Warhol (From A to B and Back Again)*. Harvest Books, New York, NY, p. 22.
[4] Gopnik B. (2020) *Warhol: A Life as Art*. Allen Lane, London, p. 6.
[5] Warhol A. (1977), p. 102.
[6] Warhol A. (1977), p. 103.
[7] Warhol A. (1977), p. 175.
[8] Gopnik B. (2020), p. 146.
[9] Rechtin M. (2008) Frigidaire kept GM's bottom line cool. *Automotive News Detroit* 83(6325A), p. 86.
[10] Warhol A. (1977), p. 101.
[11] Warhol A. (1977), p. 101.
[12] Eschner K. (2017) When Franklin Delano Roosevelt Served hot dogs to a king. *Smithsonian Magazine*. https://www.smithsonianmag.com/smart-news/when-franklin-delano-roosevelt-served-hot-dogsking-180963589/.
[13] Warhol A. (1977), p. 71.
[14] Gopnik B. (2020), p. 912.
[15] Gopnik A. (2024) Blake Gopnik on Andy Warhol. Warholiana. https://warholiana.com/post/182580130406/andy-warhols-real-diet-does-burgerking-realize.
[16] Gopnik B. (2020), p. 420.
[17] Warhol A. (1977), p. 69.
[18] Gross M. J. (2007) Factory boys. *New York Magazine*, 5 October, p. 4. https://nymag.com/arts/art/season2007/38966/.
[19] Barton G. (1980) Andy Warhol at The Villa by Barton G. Vaultmagazine. https://www.youtube.com/watch?v=E4lUuotDZRw.
[20] Warhol A. (1977), p. 160.
[21] Kron J. (1977) Andy's automat. *New York Times*, 12 May, p. 49. https://www.nytimes.com/1977/05/12/archives/andys-automat-no-campbells-on-the-menu-at-andy-warhols-automat.html.
[22] Kron J. (1977), p. 49.
[23] Kron J. (1977), p. 49.
[24] Kron J. (1977), p. 49.
[25] Kron J. (1977), p. 49.
[26] Kron J. (1977), p. 49.
[27] Gopnik B. (2020), p. 705.
[28] Rossi A. (dir.) (2022).
[29] Rossi A. (dir.) (2022).
[30] Warhol A. (1977), p. 92.
[31] Rossi A. (dir.) (2022).
[32] Rossi A. (dir.) (2022).

AGNES DENES: WALL STREET WHEAT

[1] Denes A. (2022) Conversation with the author, 19 February.
[2] Denes A. (1990) The dream. *Critical Inquiry* 16(4), p. 928.
[3] Jacobs K. (2018) The woman who harvested a wheat field off Wall Street. *The New York Times Style Magazine*, 14 June. https://www.nytimes.com/2018/06/14/t-magazine/agnes-denes-art.html.
[4] Luke B. and Carrigan M. (2019) Agnes Denes: environmental art pioneer. *The Art Newspaper*, 11 October. https://www.theartnewspaper.com/2019/10/11/agnes-denes-environmental-art-pioneer-plus-rembrandt-velazquez-and-de-hooch.
[5] Denes A. (2022).
[6] Luke B. and Carrigan M. (2019).
[7] Luke B. and Carrigan M. (2019).
[8] Luke B. and Carrigan M. (2019).
[9] Edelson B. (1977) A.I.R. Gallery exhibition announcement for Mary Beth Edelson. https://artsandculture.google.com/asset/a-i-r-galleryexhibition-announcement-for-mary-beth-edelson-marybeth-edelson/dwH_Q5HzcOutAw.
[10] Denes A. (1990), p. 920.
[11] Denes A. (1990), p. 928.
[12] Luke B. and Carrigan M. (2019).

[13] Denes A. (1982) *Today*, 16 August. NBC.
[14] Denes A. (1993) Notes on eco-logic: environmental artwork, visual philosophy and global perspective. Leonardo 26(5), p. 390.
[15] Denes A. (1993), p. 388.

FELIX GONZALEZ-TORRES: AN ENDLESS SUPPLY

[1] Rollins T. and Gonzalez-Torres F. (1993) Interview by Tim Rollins. In: Bartman B. (ed.), *Felix Gonzalez-Torres*. Art Resources Transfer, New York, pp. 5–31. https://www.felixgonzalez-torresfoundation.org/attachment/en/5b844b306aa72cea5f8b4567/DownloadableItem/639385f3fa829db6a90469fb.
[2] Princenthal N. (1994) Felix Gonzalez-Torres: multiple choice. *Art + Text*, No. 48, pp. 40–45.
[3] Rollins T. and Gonzalez-Torres F. (1993).
[4] Deitcher D. (1997) *Contradictions and Containment, Felix Gonzalez-Torres: Catalogue Raisonné*. Cantz Verlag, Ostfildern-Ruit, p. 323.
[5] Jacob, M. J. and Grabner M (eds) (2010) *The Studio Reader: On the Spaces of Artists*. University of Chicago Press, Chicago, IL, p. 119.
[6] Searle A. (2000) All this, and free sweets too. *The Guardian*, 6 June. https://www.theguardian.com/culture/2000/jun/06/artsfeatures1.
[7] Bleckner R. and Gonzalez-Torres F. (1995) Interview: Felix Gonzalez-Torres by Ross Bleckner. *Bomb Magazine*, No. 51, pp. 42–47. https://bombmagazine.org/articles/1995/04/01/felix-gonzalez-torres/.
[8] Obrist H.-U. and Gonzalez-Torres F. (1994) Interview: Felix Gonzalez-Torres and Hans-Ulrich Obrist. The Felix Gonzalez-Torres Foundation. https://felixgonzalez-torresfoundation.org/attachment/en/5b844b306aa72cea5f8b4567/DownloadableItem/5fb82a0d5fc138093dcc0e1c.
[9] Rollins T. and Gonzalez-Torres F. (1993).
[10] Rollins T. and Gonzalez-Torres F. (1993).
[11] Rollins T. and Gonzalez-Torres F. (1993).
[12] Obrist H. U. and Gonzalez-Torres F. (1994).
[13] hooks b. (1995) Subversive beauty: new modes of contestation. In: *Art On My Mind: Visual Politics*. The New Press, New York, p. 49. https://www.felixgonzalez-torresfoundation.org/attachment/en/5b844b306aa72cea5f8b4567/DownloadableItem/5f6a10395fc13852548b456c.
[14] Judah H. (2020) Fargo the horse and the great global fortune cookie giveaway. *The Guardian*, 10 June. https://www.theguardian.com/artanddesign/2020/jun/10/fargo-the-horse-and-the-great-global-fortune-cookie-giveaway-felix-gonzalez-torres.
[15] Obrist H. U. and Gonzalez-Torres F. (1994).

ZOE LEONARD: DECOMPOSITION AS PROCESS

[1] Blume A. and Leonard Z. (1997) Interview by Anna Blume. In: *Secession: Zoe Leonard*. Secession, Vienna, p. 17.
[2] Blume A. and Leonard Z. (1997), p. 17.
[3] Blume A. and Leonard Z. (1997), p. 17.
[4] Blume A. and Leonard Z. (1997), p. 17.
[5] Blume A. and Leonard Z. (1997), p. 17.
[6] Blume A. and Leonard Z. (1997), p. 17.
[7] Blume A. and Leonard Z. (1997), p. 18.
[8] Quabeck N. (2019) Intent in the making: the life of Zoe Leonard's "Strange Fruit". *Burlington Contemporary*, No. 1. https://contemporary.burlington.org.uk/journal/journal/intent-in-the-making-the-life-of-zoe-leonards-strange-fruit/pdf.
[9] Quabeck N. (2019).

MORE THAN THE EYES: ART AND FOOD TODAY

[1] Rakowitz M. and friends (2019) *A House With a Date Palm Will Never Starve*. Art/Books, London, p. 15.
[2] Rakowitz M. and friends (2019), p. 15.
[3] Rakowitz M. and friends (2019), p. 16.
[4] Rakowitz M. and friends (2019), p. 17.
[5] Rakowitz M. and friends (2019), p. 15.
[6] Khatchadourian R. (2020) Michael Rakowitz's art of return. *The New Yorker*, 24 August. https://www.newyorker.com/magazine/2020/08/24/michael-rakowitzs-art-of-return.
[7] Walker K. (2021) Kara Walker talks with Thelma Golden. *The New Yorker Radio Hour*, 13 October. The New Yorker and WNYC Studios. https://www.wnycstudios.org/podcasts/tnyradiohour/articles/kara-walker-talks-thelma-golden-podcast.
[8] Walker K. (2021).
[9] Walker K. (2021).
[10] De Wachter E. M. (2020) Cooking Sections: eating for the planet. *Art Quarterly*, winter. https://www.artfund.org/explore/get-inspired/features/cooking-sections-and-the-recipe-for-a-healthy-planet.

Index

Bibliography

Als H. (2014) The Sugar Sphinx. *The New Yorker*. https://www.newyorker.com/culture/culture-desk/the-sugar-sphinx.

Archives of American Art (2009) Oral history interview with Carolee Schneemann, 2009 March 1. Archives of American Art, Smithsonian Institution, Washington DC. https://www.aaa.si.edu/collections/interviews/oral-history-interview-carolee-schneemann-15672.

Archives of American Art (2010) Oral history interview with Alison Knowles, 2010 June 1–2. Archives of American Art, Smithsonian Institution, Washington DC, p. 26. https://www.aaa.si.edu/collections/interviews/oral-history-interview-alison-knowles-15822.

Berman A. (1980) A decade of progress, but could a female Chardin make a living today? *Art News*, 79(8), pp. 73–79.

Bleckner R. and Gonzalez-Torres F. (1995) Interview: Felix Gonzalez-Torres by Ross Bleckner. *Bomb Magazine*, No. 51, pp. 42–47. https://bombmagazine.org/articles/1995/04/01/felix-gonzalez-torres/.

Blume A. (1997) Interview by Anna Blume. In: *Secession: Zoe Leonard*. Secession, Vienna, p. 17.

Bourdain A. (2000) *Kitchen Confidential*. Ecco Press, New York, NY.

Bourdain A. (2001) *A Cook's Tour: In Search of the Perfect Meal*. Bloomsbury Press, London.

Bowles J. P. (2011) *Adrian Piper: Race, Gender, and Embodiment*. Duke University Press, London.

Breuer L., Champagne L., Ehn E., Foreman R et al. (2012) Belief. *PAJ: A Journal of Performance and Art* 34(1), pp. 15–33.

Chianese R. L. (2013) How green is earth art? Regeneration on Tree Mountain. *American Scientist* 101(5), pp. 350–351.

Classen C. (2007) Museum manners: the sensory life of the early museum. *Journal of Social History* 40(4), pp. 895–914.

Classen C. (2017) *The Museum of the Senses: Experiencing Art and Collections*. Bloomsbury Publishing, London.

Classen C. (2020) The senses. Encyclopedia.com. https://www.encyclopedia.com/international/encyclopedias-almanacs-transcripts-and-maps/senses.

Columbia D. P. (2020) Times just past. New York Social Diary. https://www.newyorksocialdiary.com/times-just-past.

Cooking Sections (2018) *The Empire Remains Shop*. Columbia University Press, New York, NY.

Cowan S. (2018) The future did not have to be luxury condos: revisiting Gordon Matta-Clark. *The New Yorker*, 18 March. https://www.newyorker.com/culture/culture-desk/the-future-did-not-have-to-be-luxury-condos-revisiting-gordon-matta-clark.

Curtis H. (2015) Fifty years since Carolee Schneemann's *Meat Joy* (1964). *Performance Research* 20(2), pp. 118–120.

Denes A. (1990) The dream. *Critical Inquiry* 16(4), pp. 919–939.

Denes A. (1992) Wheatfield/Tree Mountain. *Art Journal* 51(2), pp. 22–23.

Denes A. (1993) Notes on eco-logic: environmental artwork, visual philosophy and global perspective. *Leonardo* 26(5), pp. 387–395.

Dezeuze A. (2002) *Meat Joy*. *Art Monthly*. http://www.artmonthly.co.uk/magazine/site/article/meat-joy-by-anna-dezeuze-2002.

Donley A. (2021) The fall and rise of Russian wheat. *World Grain*. https://www.world-grain.com/articles/16273-the-fall-and-rise-of-russian-wheat.

Dupont R. (2007) Factory boys: as told to Michael Joseph Gross. *New York Magazine*. https://nymag.com/arts/art/season2007/38966/.

Ender E. (2020) Agnes Denes (1931–). *The Architectural Review*. https://www.architectural-review.com/essays/reputations/agnes-denes-1931.

Fiore J. (2012) *112 Greene Street: The Early Years (1970–1974)*. David Zwirner, New York, NY.

Fitzgibbon C. and Schneemann C. (2015) Interview with Carolee Schneemann. *BOMB*, No. 132, pp. 130–137.

Fitzpatrick T., Kochheiser T., Goldman S. and Pollock G. (2009) *Hannah Wilke: Gestures*. Neuberger Museum of Art, Purchase, NY.

Flahive G. (2020) Andy Warhol is here to save restaurants. Medium. https://medium.com/@gflahive/andywarhol-is-here-to-save-restaurants-285be3f94b43.

Frye B. L. (2015) Andy Warhol's pantry. *Akron Intellectual Property Journal* 8(1), pp. 18–49.

Gioni M. (2015) More than *Meat Joy*: Carolee Schneemann in conversation with Massimiliano Gioni. *Mousse*, No. 48, pp. 4–9. https://www.moussemagazine.it/magazine/meat-joy-carolee-schneemann/.

Gioni M. and Norton M. (eds) (2018) *Sarah Lucas: Au Naturel*. Phaidon Press, London.

Glaser M. and Snyder J. (1972) Food, glorious food. *New York Magazine*, January, pp. 65.

Goodman E. E. (2017) Sweet and sour and *Super-t-Art*. *Performance Research* 22(7), pp. 82–91.

Gopnik B. (2020) *Warhol: A Life as Art*. Allen Lane, London.

Guggenheim (2019) Collection online: Zoe Leonard. Guggenheim. https://www.guggenheim.org/artwork/artist/zoe-leonard.

Hobbs R. (1982) Earthworks: past and present. *Art Journal* 42(3), pp. 191–194.

hooks b. and Ferguson R. (eds) (1994) *Subversive Beauty: New Modes of Contestation*. Museum of Contemporary Art, Los Angeles, CA.

Jacob M. J. and Grabner M. (eds) (2010) *The Studio Reader: On the Space of Artists*. University of Chicago Press, Chicago, IL.

Jacobs K. (2018) The woman who harvested a wheat field off Wall Street. *The New York Times Style Magazine*, 14 June. https://www.nytimes.com/2018/06/14/t-magazine/agnes-denes-art.html.

Johnson C. (2013) *Femininity, Time and Feminist Art*. Palgrave Macmillan, London.

Kennedy R. (2007) When meals played the muse. *New York Times*, 21 February, p. F.1.

Knowles A. (1965) By. *A Great Bear Pamphlet*. Something Else Press, New York, NY.

Kron J. (1977) Andy's automat. *New York Times*, 12 May, p. 49.

Kwon M. (2006) The becoming of a work of art: FGT and a possibility of renewal, a chance to share, a fragile truce. In: Ault J. (ed.), *Felix Gonzalez-Torres*. Steidl, Gottingen, pp. 281–314.

Lippard L. and Piper A. (1972) Catalysis: an interview with Adrian Piper. *The Drama Review* 16(1), pp. 76–78.

McAloon J. (2018) Sarah Lucas got women to throw 1000 eggs at the wall. Elephant. https://elephant.art/sarah-lucas-1000-eggs-for-women.

McLaughlin J. (2009) Landscape art and the city. *Building Material* 19, pp. 142–145.

Malaguzzi S. (trans. Phillips B.) (2008) *Food and Feasting in Art*. Getty Publications, Los Angeles, CA.

Malik A. (2009) *Sarah Lucas: Au Naturel*. Afterall Books, London.

Mead R. (2009) The art doctor. *The New Yorker*, 4 May. https://www.newyorker.com/magazine/2009/05/11/the-art-doctor.

Mead R. (2018) The animal and the edible in Sarah Lucas's self-portraits. *The New Yorker*, 16 September. https://www.newyorker.com/culture/photo-booth/the-animal-and-the-edible-in-sarah-lucas-self-portraits.

Moore A. and Wacks D. (2005) Being there: the Tribeca neighborhood of Franklin Furnace. *Drama Review* 49(1), pp. 60–79.

Morgan R. C. (1997) Carolee Schneemann: the politics of eroticism. *Art Journal* 56(4), pp. 97–100.

Morris C. (trans. Assmann N. et al.) (1993) *Food: An Exhibition by White Columns*. Westfälisches Landesmuseum für Kunst und Kulturgeschichte, Münster.

Mulroney L. (2014) I'd recognize your voice anywhere. *Bulletin of the Serving Journal*. https://www.servinglibrary.org/journal/8/id-recognize-your-voice-anywhere.

Nelson M. (2019) The reënchantment of Carolee Schneemann. *The New Yorker*, 15 March. https://www.newyorker.com/books/page-turner/the-re-enchantment-of-carolee-schneemann.

Nickas B. (2012) Somebody has to bring home the bacon. Slate, 3 July. https://slate.com/ human-interest/2012/07/somebody-has-to-bring-home-the-bacon-a-history-of-andy-warhols-relationship-with-food-from-lucky-peach.html.

Nickas B. (2012) The Andy Warhol New York City diet. Slate, 4 July. https://slate.com/human-interest/2012/07/the-andy-warhol-new-york-city-diet-part-2-of-a-history-of-the-artists-relationship-with-food-from-lucky-peach.html.

O'Neill-Butler L. (2019) Land of the living. *Artforum* 58(2), p. 180.

Obrist H.-U. and Gonzalez-Torres F. (1994) Interview: Felix GonzalezTorres and Hans-Ulrich Obrist. The Felix Gonzalez-Torres Foundation. https://felixgonzalez-torresfoundation.org/attachment/en/5b844b306aa72cea5f8b4567/DownloadableItem/5fb82a0d5fc138093dcc0e1c.

Ohta Y. (2012) Interview with Carol Goodden about food. SoHo Memory Project. https://sohomemory.org/interview-with-carol-goodden-about-food.

Picard L. and Wilke H. (1973) Hannah Wilke: sexy objects. *Interview*, January.

Piper A. (1996) *Out of Order, Out of Sight*, vol. 1. *Selected Writings in Meta-Art 1968–1992*. MIT Press, Cambridge, MA.

Piper A. (1996) Xenophobia and the indexical present II. In: *Out of Order, Out of Sight*, vol. 1, *Selected Writings in MetaArt 1968–1992*. MIT Press, Cambridge, MA, p. 261.

Platzker D. (2018) Adrian Piper: unities. In: Cherix C., Butler C. and Platzker D. (eds), *Adrian Piper: A Synthesis of Intuitions: 1965–2016*. Museum of Modern Art, New York, NY, pp. 31-49.

Pollock G. (2010) Hannah Wilke: elective affinities. *Art Monthly*, No. 339, pp. 34–35.

Princenthal N. (2010) *Hannah Wilke*. Prestel Publishing, New York, NY.

Public Art Fund (1982) Agnes Denes: wheatfields for Manhattan. Public Art Fund. https://www.publicartfund.org/exhibitions/view/wheatfields-for-manhattan.

Quabeck N. (2019) Intent in the making: the life of Zoe Leonard's "Strange Fruit". *Burlington Contemporary*, No. 1. https://contemporary.burlington.org.uk/journal/journal/intent-in-the-making-the-life-of-zoe-leonards-strange-fruit/pdf.

Rakowitz M. and friends (2019) *A House With a Date Palm Will Never Starve*. Art/Books, London.

Roberts J. (1996) Mad for it!, *Third Text* 10(35), pp. 29–42.

Rollins T. and Gonzalez-Torres F. (1993) Interview by Tim Rollins. In: Bartman B. (ed.). *Felix Gonzalez-Torres*. Art Resources Transfer, New York, pp. 5–31. https://www.felixgonzalez-torresfoundation.org/attachment/en/5b844b306aa72cea5f8b4567/DownloadableItem/639385f3fa829db6a90469fb.

Rooney K. (2014) A sonorous subtlety: Kara Walker with Kara Rooney. *The Brooklyn Rail*, May. https://brooklyn rail.org/2014/05/art/kara-walker-with-kara-rooney.

Rose S. (2009) Darwin, race and gender. *EMBO Reports* 10(4), pp. 297–298.

Rosenblum L., Scharlatt A. and Scharlatt M. (2019) *Hannah Wilke: Sculpture in the Landscape*. Tyler Contemporary, Tyler School of Art, Temple University, Philadelphia, PA.

Schenkenberg T. H. and Harnish, K. B. (2021) *Exhibition Guide Hannah Wilke: Art for Life's Sake*. Pulitzer Arts Foundation, St Louis, MO.

Schjeldahl P. (1991) Warhol and class content. In: Wilson M. (ed.), *The Hydrogen Jukebox*. University of California Press Berkeley, CA, pp. 44–52.

Schjeldahl P. (2011) Proto Soho. *The New Yorker*, 9 January, p. 2. https:// www.newyorker.com/magazine/2011/01/17/proto-soho.

Schneemann C. (1992) The obscene body/politic. *Art Journal* 50(4), pp. 28–35.

Schneemann C. (2014) Response to a reappropriation request. *PAJ: A Journal of Performance and Art* 36(1), pp. 7–9.

Schneemann C. and McPherson B. R. (eds) (1997) *More than* Meat Joy. McPherson, Kingston, NY.

Schulman S. and Leonard Z. (2010) Interview 106: Zoe Leonard, January 13, 2010. Act Up Oral History Project. https://www.actuporalhistory.org/numerical-interviews/106-zoe-leonard.

Shkuda A. (2016) *The Lofts of SoHo: Gentrification, Art, and Industry in New York, 1950–1980*. University of Chicago Press, Chicago, IL.

Shohat E. (2017) Culinar ghosting: a journey through a sweet and sour Iraq. *Crítica Cultural* 12(2), pp. 219–226.

Sholis B. (2007) Agnes Denes. *Artforum* 45(9), pp. 373–374.

Steel C. (2020) *Sitopia: How Food Can Save the World*. Chatto and Windus, London.

Stillman N. (2013) Agnes Denes. *Artforum* 51(5), pp. 203.

Sussman E. (2007) *Gordon Matta-Clark: "You Are the Measure."* Yale University Press, New Haven, CT.

Tavlin W. (2016) Public space is the place: art and politics in Battery Park City. *The Indy*, 29 April. https://www.theindy.org/892.

Temkin A. (1998) The conservation of 20th-century art: two case studies. *Conservation: The CGI Newsletter* 13(2), pp. 12–15.

Time (2014) Grain becomes a weapon. *Time*, 21 January. https://content.time.com/time/subscriber/article/0,33009,952534,00.html.

Valentine J. (2003) Contemporary art and the political value of culture. *Critical Quarterly* 41(1), pp. 9–19.

Velasco D. (2018) Reveries of a solitary dancer. *Artforum* 57(1).

Ward A. (2023) *Sensational: A New Story of our Senses*. Profile Books, London.

Warhol A. (1977) *The Philosophy of Andy Warhol (From A to B and Back Again)*. Harvest Books, New York, NY.

Waxman L. (2008) The banquet years: FOOD, a SoHo restaurant. *Gastronomica* 8(4), pp. 24–33.

White K. (2015) Meat System in Cologne. *Art Journal* 74(1), pp. 56–77.

Woods N. L. (2014) Taste economies: Alison Knowles, Gordon Matta Clark and the intersection of food, time and performance. *Performance Research* 19(3), pp. 157–161.

Wooster A.-S. (1975) Hannah Wilke. *Artforum* 14(4), pp. 74–75.

Yerxa D. A. (2013) The deepest sense: an interview with Constance Classen. *Historically Speaking* 14(3), pp. 27–28.

Zalman S. (2019) Eat, live, work. Tate. https://www.tate.org.uk/research/publications/in-focus/walls-paper/eat-live-work.

Zuber D. (2006) Flânerie at ground zero: aesthetic countermemories in Lower Manhattan. *American Quarterly* 58(2), pp. 269–299.

Image Credits

COVER
Hannah Wilke, *Gum in Cherry Tree* (detail), *California Series*, 1976. Archival pigment print, 2019. © 2024 Marsie, Emanuelle, Damon, and Andrew Scharlatt, Hannah Wilke Collection & Archive, Los Angeles / Licensed by Artists Rights Society (ARS), New York.

PAGE 6
Jan Davidsz. de Heem, *Still Life with a Lobster, Fruit and Blue and White "Kraak" Dishes*, c.1650.

PAGE 15
Sarah Lucas, *Two Fried Eggs and a Kebab*, 1992. © Sarah Lucas. Courtesy of Sadie Coles HQ, London.

PAGE 24
Sarah Lucas, *Eating a Banana*, 1990. © Sarah Lucas. Courtesy of Sadie Coles HQ, London.

PAGE 33
Louis-Léopold Boilly (French, 1761–1845), *The Five Senses,* illustration from the series *Recueil des Grimaces*, 1823. Purchased with the SmithKline Beckman Corporation Fund, 1978. © 2023 Philadelphia Museum of Art.

PAGE 47
Adrian Piper, *Catalysis III*, 1970. Documentation of the performance. Three silver gelatin prints (reprinted c.1998). Each photo 16.14 × 16.14 in. (41 × 41 cm). Documentation photo credit: Rosemary Mayer. Generali Foundation Collection—permanent loan to the Museum der Moderne Salzburg. © Generali Foundation and Adrian Piper Research Archive (APRA) Foundation Berlin.

PAGE 52–53
Adrian Piper, *Five Unrelated Time Pieces (Meat into Meat)*, 1968. Six pages. One typescript page and eight color photos mounted on black paper. 11 × 8.5 in. (27.9 × 21.6 cm). Collection of Paul McCarthy, Altadena. © Adrian Piper Research Archive (APRA) Foundation Berlin.

PAGE 58
Adrian Piper, *Catalysis III*, 1970. Documentation of the performance. Three silver gelatin prints (reprinted c.1998). Each photo 16.14 × 16.14 in. (41 × 41 cm). Documentation photo credit: Rosemary Mayer. Generali Foundation Collection—permanent loan to the Museum der Moderne Salzburg. © Generali Foundation and Adrian Piper Research Archive (APRA) Foundation Berlin.

PAGE 62
Carolee Schneemann, *Meat Joy*, 1964. Judson Dance Theater, Judson Memorial Church, New York. Photo: Al Giese. © 2023 Carolee Schneemann Foundation / Artists Rights Society (ARS), New York. Courtesy Galerie Lelong & Co., Hales Gallery, and P•P•O•W, New York.

PAGE 71
Carolee Schneemann, *Meat Joy*, 1964. View of actors on stage as they perform Carolee Schneemann's art piece in the Judson Memorial Church auditorium, New York, 16 November. Photo: Fred W. McDarrah / MUUS Collection via Getty Images. © 2023 Carolee Schneemann Foundation / Artists Rights Society (ARS), New York. Courtesy Galerie Lelong & Co., Hales Gallery, and P•P•O•W, New York.

PAGE 79
Hannah Wilke, *Gum with Grasshopper* (detail), *California Series*, 1976. Archival pigment print, 2019. © 2024 Marsie, Emanuelle, Damon, and Andrew Scharlatt, Hannah Wilke Collection & Archive, Los Angeles / Licensed by Artists Rights Society (ARS), New York.

PAGE 84
Hannah Wilke, *Super-t-Art*, 1974. Twenty gelatin silver prints framed together and signed "From a performance at the Kitchen, Nov. 1974". © 2024 Marsie, Emanuelle, Damon, and Andrew Scharlatt, Hannah Wilke Collection & Archive, Los Angeles / Licensed by Artists Rights Society (ARS), New York.

PAGE 91
Hannah Wilke, *S.O.S. Starification Object Series*, 1974. Black and white gelatin silver print. Performalist self-portrait with Les Wollam. © 2024 Marsie, Emanuelle, Damon, and Andrew Scharlatt, Hannah Wilke Collection & Archive, Los Angeles / Licensed by Artists Rights Society (ARS), New York.

PAGE 95
TOP Sarah Lucas, *Fucked*, 1995. © Sarah Lucas. Courtesy of Sadie Coles HQ, London.

PAGE 99
TOP Sarah Lucas, *Au Naturel*, 1994. © Sarah Lucas. Courtesy of Sadie Coles HQ, London. BOTTOM Sarah Lucas, *Bitch*, 1995. © Sarah Lucas. Courtesy Sadie Coles HQ, London.

PAGE 105
Sarah Lucas, *One Thousand Eggs: For Women*, 2018. Performance views, New Museum, New York, 26 September 2018 – 20 January 2019. © Sarah Lucas. Courtesy of Sadie Coles HQ, London.

PAGE 110
Alison Knowles, *Proposition (Make a Salad)*, 1962. Festival of Misfits, ICA, London, 24 October. Gelatin silver print, sheet: 10 × 8 in. (25.4 × 20.3 cm). The Gilbert and Lila Silverman Fluxus Collection Gift. © The Museum of Modern Art/Licensed by SCALA / Art Resource, New York.

PAGE 117
Alison Knowles, *Journal of the Identical Lunch* (detail), 1971. © Alison Knowles.

PAGE 123
FOOD, New York City, 1971–2. Photo: Cosmos Andrew Sarchiapone. © 2023 Estate of Gordon Matta-Clark / Artists Rights Society (ARS), New York.

PAGE 129
Tina Girouard, Carol Goodden, and Gordon Matta-Clark outside FOOD restaurant prior to its opening, 1971. Photo: Richard Landry. © The Estate of Gordon Matta-Clark / Artists Rights Society (ARS), New York. Courtesy of Richard Landry, The Estate of Gordon Matta-Clark, and David Zwirner

PAGE 136
FOOD, New York City, 1971–2. Photo: Cosmos Andrew Sarchiapone. © 2023 Estate of Gordon Matta-Clark / Artists Rights Society (ARS), New York.

PAGE 140
Andy Warhol eating cereal, *c.*1975. Source unconfirmed. All efforts were made to identify works with the artist's foundation.

PAGE 146–147
Andy Warhol, *66 Scenes from America*, 1982, directed by Jørgen Leth. © Jørgen Leth.

PAGE 152
Andy Warhol, *Eat*, 1964. 16mm film, black and white, silent, 39 minutes at 16 frames per second. © The Andy Warhol Museum, Pittsburgh, PA, a museum of Carnegie Institute. All rights reserved. Film still courtesy of The Andy Warhol Museum.

PAGE 161
Prospectus (Andy-Mat), 1977. The Andy Warhol Museum, Pittsburgh / Founding Collection, Contribution The Andy Warhol Foundation for the Visual Arts, Inc. TC161.245.1-TC161.245.3. © 2024 The Andy Warhol Foundation for the Visual Arts, Inc. / Artists Rights Society (ARS), New York.

PAGE 164
Agnes Denes, *Wheatfield: A Confrontation*, 1982. Battery Park Landfill, Downtown Manhattan. © Agnes Denes. Courtesy of Leslie Tonkonow Artworks + Projects.

PAGE 171
Agnes Denes, *Wheatfield: A Confrontation*, 1982. Battery Park Landfill, Downtown Manhattan—with the Statue of Liberty across the Hudson. © Agnes Denes. Courtesy of Leslie Tonkonow Artworks + Projects.

PAGE 189
View of Zoe Leonard's studio, New York, 1995. Photo: Jack Louth. © Zoe Leonard. Courtesy of the artist, Paula Cooper Gallery, and Hauser & Wirth.

PAGE 194–195
Zoe Leonard, *Strange Fruit*, 1992–7. Photo: Ron Amstutz. © Zoe Leonard, Philadelphia Museum of Art. Purchased with funds contributed by the Dietrich Foundation and with the partial gift of the artist and the Paula Cooper Gallery, 1998.

PAGE 200
Michael Rakowitz, *The Invisible Enemy Should Not Exist*, 2018. Trafalgar Square, London, UK. Photo: Gautier DeBlonde and Caroline Teo. Courtesy of the Mayor of London.

PAGE 205
Michael Rakowitz cooking at Refettorio Felix, 2018, London. Photo: Joe Woodhouse. Courtesy of Plinth (plinth.uk.com) and the artist.

PAGE 211
Kara Walker, *A Subtlety, or the* Marvelous Sugar Baby*, an Homage to the unpaid and overworked Artisans who have refined our Sweet tastes from the cane fields to the Kitchens of the New World on the Occasion of the demolition of the Domino Sugar Refining Plant*, 2014. Photo: Jason Wyche Artwork. © 2014 Kara Walker.

PAGE 215
TOP Cooking Sections, CLIMAVORE: On Tidal Zones, Isle of Skye, 2017. Photo: Cooking Sections. BOTTOM Cooking Sections, CLIMAVORE: On Tidal Zones, Isle of Skye, 2017. Photo: Colin Hattersley.

About the Author

Ellen Mara De Wachter is a writer based in London. She is the author of *Co-Art: Artists on Creative Collaboration* (Phaidon, 2017), which explores the phenomenon of collaboration in the visual arts and its potential in society at large, and a regular contributor to books and magazines about contemporary art and culture, including *Frieze*, *Art Monthly*, *Art Quarterly*, *Tate*, *Etc.*, and *The World of Interiors*.

Author Acknowledgements

Thank you to Rebecca Morrill and Harriet Moore, who helped shape early plans for this book. I am grateful to Kate Wiseman and Rachel De Wachter for comments on early drafts. Thank you to Naomi Annand for highlighting the importance of the senses in making sense of the world; and to Guy Robertson and Mahler & LeWitt Studios for hosting me on a residency in 2022. Thank you to the artists and their representatives and estates: Adrian Piper, the Generali Foundation, and the Adrian Piper Research Archive (APRA) Foundation Berlin; Carolee Schneemann and the Carolee Schneemann Estate; Hannah Wilke, and Marsie Scharlatt at the Hannah Wilke Collection & Archive, Los Angeles; Sarah Lucas, and Isla Macer Law at Sadie Coles HQ, London; Alison Knowles; Carol Goodden, Tina Girouard, Gordon Matta-Clark, and the Estate of Gordon Matta-Clark; Andy Warhol, and Patrick Seymore at The Andy Warhol Museum; Agnes Denes, and Leslie Tonkonow; Felix Gonzalez-Torres, and the Felix Gonzalez-Torres Foundation; Zoe Leonard, and Tiffany Wang at Hauser & Wirth; Michael Rakowitz, and Elise Seigenthaler at the Rhona Hoffman Gallery;

Kara Walker, and Monica Truong at Sikkema Jenkins & Co.; and Cooking Sections: Alon Schwabe and Daniel Fernández Pascual. Thank you to the British Library and Jennifer J. Snyder at the Archives of American Art at the Smithsonian Institution for facilitating my research; and to Ariana Martin for compiling the bibliography. Financial assistance from the Society of Authors and the Authors' Contingency Fund & Francis Head Bequest, and Nancy Roach and the Southshore Writers' Gift helped support my writing. A special thank you to the devoted team at Atelier Éditions, particularly Pascale Georgiev for her unfaltering confidence in this project, Lucy Kingett for shaping my manuscript so elegantly, and Ananda Pellerin for guiding questions and insights. Finally, thank you to Samuel Levack, for more than can be expressed in words.

A book by Ellen Mara De Wachter.

This book was typeset in Grotesque Display (Monotype), Ionic (Monotype) & Untitled Sans (Klim).

PUBLISHED BY
Atelier Éditions
1545 W Sunset Blvd
Los Angeles, 90026
www.atelier-editions.com

CO-PUBLISHED AND DISTRIBUTED BY
ARTBOOK | D.A.P.
75 Broad Street, Suite 630
New York, New York 10004
artbook.com

For Atelier Éditions
PUBLISHER Pascale Georgiev
EDITOR Lucy Kingett
MANAGING EDITOR Mindy Ramaker

COPY-EDITOR Melissa Larner
PROOFREADER Rich Cutler, Helius
INDEXER Annette Musker

DESIGNER Tegan Ella Hendel
PICTURE RESEARCHER Sarah Bell

First Edition of 3500.
This product is made of FSC ® –certified and other controlled material.

ISBN 9781954957046

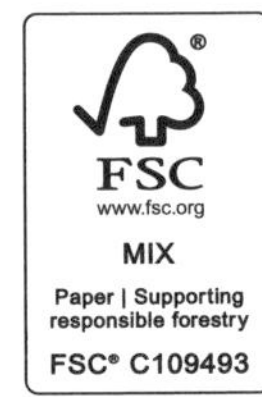